Write Out of the Classroom

Write Out of the Classroom is a ground-breaking, highly practical book which provides teachers and creative writing tutors with great ways of tapping into the huge inspirational and educational potential of the richly diverse world beyond the classroom walls.

Effective learning occurs when the process feels exciting, inspiring and 'real', and there is nothing more stimulating and 'real' than the real world itself. Working with groups in interesting and evocative settings can generate exceptional participant involvement. Well-led 'locational brainstorming' in such places increases vocabulary and produces an astonishing freshness of observation, ideas, language, plot and metaphor. Teachers commonly notice a quantum leap in writing quality arising from these sessions.

Based on the author's extensive experience in developing and leading out-of-classroom 'intelligent observation' and writing workshops, this unique book steers educators through the subtleties of guiding thoughtful data collection sessions in varied environments; selecting appropriate and motivational places and forms of writing, and running sessions linked to specific creative and factual writing tasks.

The book covers the following areas and techniques and how they relate to out-of-classroom work:

- planning outings and choosing locations;
- leading language and ideas brainstorm sessions;
- descriptive poetry inspired by outdoor settings;
- 'reflective haikus', cinquains and minimalist poetry;
- creating stunning plots and storylines;
- collective story writing;
- fictitious diary forms;
- descriptive travel writing;
- understanding poetry's mechanics and sound patterns;
- assisting students with editing.

This detailed, practical book also contains examples of remarkable student creative writing produced through these techniques, as well as photocopiable pages which include original examples of specific writing forms to model from, explanatory diagrams, helpful checklists and handy teachers' 'crib sheets'.

Write Out of the Classroom is the perfect 'insider's guide' to teaching and inspiring creative writing. It is an essential tool for classroom teachers in both Primary and Secondary schools, creative writing tutors, literacy co-ordinators and PGCE students, as well as leaders in residential centres and forest schools.

Write Out of the Classroom

How to use the 'real' world to inspire and create amazing writing

Colin Macfarlane

Routledge
Taylor & Francis Group

LONDON AND NEW YORK

First published 2014
by Routledge
2 Park Square, Milton Park, Abingdon, Oxon OX14 4RN

and by Routledge
711 Third Avenue, New York, NY 10017

Routledge is an imprint of the Taylor & Francis Group, an informa business

British Library Cataloguing in Publication Data
A catalogue record for this book is available from the British Library

Library of Congress Cataloging in Publication Data
A catalog record for this book has been requested

ISBN: 978-0-415-63528-8 (hbk)
ISBN: 978-0-415-63529-5 (pbk)
ISBN: 978-0-203-09385-6 (ebk)

Typeset in Celeste
by RefineCatch Limited, Bungay, Suffolk

MIX
Paper from
responsible sources
FSC
www.fsc.org   FSC® C013056

Printed and bound in Great Britain by
TJ International Ltd, Padstow, Cornwall

for my beloved elf
who shares the magic

Contents

Preface

This book is a practical guide to powerful, well-proven techniques for inspiring, teaching and developing exceptional creative writing based on the infinite, language-rich resources of the 'real' world outside the classroom. Many of the methods described have been designed to model thinking processes employed by professional poets and writers and to generate outstanding writing in schools and on residential courses.

The text explains in a clear, practical way how to employ these techniques and tips, and gives detailed suggestions and advice for specific writing challenges and forms.

Before the practicalities, we should first look at the rationale behind the development of these workshop practices. . .

Photo 1.1 Sharing ideas in a school nature area

Acknowledgements

The author would like to thank the following:

Highdown Junior School, Portishead for kind permission to reproduce photographs taken by their staff during workshop sessions led by the author.

Katie Wilkinson for creating the graphic diagrams illustrating the conducting method and x-point 'thinking trees'.

Ayesha Wyatt for kind permission to include her 'Diary of an African Elephant' as an example of an 'animal diary'.

Bea Hammond, Catherine Banks, Katie Wilkinson and Will Milner for kind permission to reproduce poems written by them during courses run by the author.

CHAPTER 1

Introduction and theory

Running discreetly structured writing workshops based on the boundless educational riches outside the classroom can dramatically improve young people's language, creative and factual writing, and the specific thinking skills that underpin good writing.

Here is some of what such workshops can do:

- Develop students' skills of 'thoughtful observation' through looking closely at the world while thinking intensely and originally about what they see.

- Help model how to question independently – another key skill for any creative thinker and writer, but one that young people find difficult to evolve on their own.

- Make novice writers' ideas and creative language more exciting, more original, sometimes stunning, and altogether less predictable or clichéd.

- Inspire participants to discover and use significantly richer language through an addictive hunt for the most accurate, original and subtle description of locations, environments, things, movements, situations, characters, happenings, thoughts and feelings.

- Ensure that students are not struggling to write in a 'creative vacuum'.

- Trigger positive creative and educational responses, not only from those individuals who normally excel in class but from those who perform less well.

- Engross and enthuse young writers so deeply that they absorb related 'hard' information about writing, form and structure more organically.

- Make specific forms of writing challenge feel 'real' by linking them directly to the real world.

- Build a safe, sharing environment in which participants feel free to take innovative risks with ideas and language.

- Entail joyous creative activity in which all participants feel involved and inspired.

Reproducing the thinking behind good writing

Writers don't just write. The actual act of writing is only the most obvious part of a complex process. A creative and original writer must also become a thoughtful observer of the world around as well as the world within; a watcher, a thinker and mental or physical note-taker; an experimenter with words and ideas; a dreamer and a schemer.

Creative writing cannot take place in a creative vacuum. We all know it helps to feel inspired if one wants to write well, and the techniques in this book are highly inspirational. However, we will also look at fundamental skills which prospective writers must develop in order to write to a standard that envelops their readers and carries them with them.

Through their carefully organised words, successful fiction writers and poets have to re-create, or create in others' imaginations, believable real-life or constructed worlds, characters and experiences, and somehow allow the reader to hold together and participate in this complicated and addictive construction of dream, 'reality', thought and emotion throughout the entire reading experience, no matter whether the piece is a short poem or a lengthy novel.

Any writer who can create such compulsive, 'real-seeming' dream worlds has learned not only to describe well, subtly, and in fresh ways, but also to be a thoughtful observer. To describe well you first need to 'see' well. Learning the latter is a skill that evolves. It requires time and effort, but there are ways of accelerating the process. Some of the most effective of these involve utilising the educational and inspirational wealth of the 'real' world beyond the classroom because it is so diverse and authentic.

Teachers have to make miracles happen

Frankly, we expect much from our young students when we sit them down in the schoolroom and ask them, within that insulated environment, to write an original poem or story which will transport the reader and fire the imagination. Quite apart from the young people's relative lack of writing skills and experience, they will hardly have begun the vital process of becoming 'thoughtful observers', they will have limited life experience and world knowledge to draw on, and sadly, in the case of too many children, they may have had little exposure to the multifarious worlds and language that can be found in well-written poems or story books. Some may lack breadth of 'creative imagination' as much has been spoon-fed to them through the mass media (television, video, internet, movies), pre-digested and packaged into 'finished' experiences requiring minimal imaginative input from the consumer.

Because of these inevitable shortcomings, most schoolchildren, when they are writing, can do little more than copy things they already know from their limited lives and the ubiquitous sphere of mass culture: the same sorts of (largely clichéd) descriptions, the same two-dimensional characters, nearly identical story plots, unoriginal poems, etc.

It doesn't help that teaching creative writing in schools is frequently a relatively time-poor activity which can end up teaching writing without much creativity. It can stifle potential originality in favour of easy clichés and results often seem dull and formulaic. Even when children have a relatively wide vocabulary and a reasonable grip on grammar, they may write competently for their age but their writing doesn't necessarily set the reader on fire.

However, once they start to develop a more creative 'writer's eye', everyone can see the difference. A young writer who is beginning to discover thoughtful observation will paint better imagination pictures, describe more convincingly, and select interesting and well-observed 'authenticating' details. Their language choices will grow richer and less predictable, and they will automatically search for and use fresher metaphors and similes.

Growing exceptional writers

Writing development in hypothetical children

If, heaven forbid, a child grew up permanently locked in a room without reading material or conversation, they would be incapable of speech and writing, even of describing the room, not to mention the unseen outside world. If allowed regular conversation with visitors they would be able to describe the room and a certain amount of the greater world outside, but the latter only through second-hand descriptions given to them. The youngster would, in effect, describe it largely in clichés because, due to a deficiency of personal experience of the outer world, their words would lack truly original, individual observations or descriptions.

Given a good library of well-written fact, fiction stories and poetry to read, the quality of the child's descriptions would no doubt improve considerably. He or she would widen vocabulary, improve phraseology and the use of metaphor and simile, develop more subtle ways of internally seeing and describing, and relate all this to the outer world to a certain extent. It would still be unlikely, however, that truly personal, original and affecting ways of describing the world outside, or new metaphors and similes for things in it, would arise naturally in this unfortunate child's language, due to their lack of direct experience.

He or she wouldn't *organically* know what running fingers through damp soil actually feels and smells like; that gorse flowers can be scented like toasted coconut or sugared almonds; how a mole might sneeze softly and twitch its mud-spattered whiskers as it appears from the ground; how cool, damp and exciting it can feel to be hidden among rank, early summer undergrowth during a game of hide and seek. Apart from metaphors or descriptions copied from others, the child might well never grow up to produce writing with that 'oh gosh, that's so true!' factor which can be found in a well-observed and thoughtful poem or novel.

Worse, if, like a great many actual children, the youngster had been provided with a diet of largely animated, mass-market television programming instead of well-written books, any increase in descriptive language quality would be minimal and would rely much more heavily on clichéd descriptions and ideas.

Let's say, however, that the child is suddenly freed from the confines of the room to explore the real world. Just imagine the brimming-over of excitement and enthusiasm which would occur. The youngster would no doubt be bursting with desire to ask about the amazing things encountered, and to 'name' many of these. Sadly, he or she might even then struggle to describe this greater world and their experience within it in original ways, partly because these experiences did not start occurring early enough in their development, and partly because they have not yet acquired the necessary skills of thoughtful, individual observation and questioning, or of putting those observations and ideas into subtle, sometimes figurative language.

To turn the whole thing on its head, just imagine the original writing potential of a child who has been continuously exposed to, and engaged in, rich adult conversation, has read and been read lots of good books, who has been taken into many interesting and varied environments and been given rich experiences by adults who have automatically questioned and described those environments and experiences, and engaged the child in the process.

There are glaringly obvious lessons to be drawn from the theoretical variations of experience of each of those hypothetical children and their outcomes in terms of their language skills, confidence and creativity.

Filling gaps in literacy development

Although, as educators, we strive to enrich children's literacy environments as much as possible in the classroom, we cannot miraculously give other peoples' children the same enviable levels of past and present 'natural literacy' experience as that of the latter child. We can supply books, help with reading, writing, listening, performance and a general celebration of language; but it will never be the same.

There are, however, techniques we can use which replicate the ways language-advantaged children develop questioning and thinking skills, breadth of vocabulary, a sense of grammar and general 'natural literacy'. Similarly, we can model some of the vital observational and thinking skills of excellent writers and poets. Those are some of the key things that this book and the techniques described in it attempt to achieve.

Basic determinants of language ability

Apart from any inborn talent, some of the things that determine the standard of a young person's language and writing are:

- the quality of language used in the family;
- the quality of the home literacy environment;
- the effects of teaching and school;
- a developing love of reading;
- a discovery of the enjoyment of writing;
- increasing confidence in reading;
- increasing confidence in writing;
- the effect of peer language quality;
- the effect of peer interest in language and literature; and
- the 'wash off' from language in television, film, computer 'action games', etc.

The effects of those media described in the final bullet point are thought to be considerably less valuable than the others at increasing a young person's literacy standards and confidence, partly because they are passive forms of experience which do not engage the child in active language response. As with the other points described, any positive effects derived increase in line with the quality of language provided and the amount, if any, of personal 'language-type processing' stimulated by the programme or game.

Vocabulary is the key to the door

At a fundamental level, vocabulary is the key to quality language development at any age. Words are the varied bricks and stones of the literacy builder, while grammar is the pliable mortar. Generally speaking, the wider the vocabulary a child gains, the greater the confidence he or she has to use it in speaking, reading and writing. Having a large vocabulary puts children into a 'positive learning loop' because they can read more advanced texts and understand more advanced conversation, and so learn more words that can then be reinforced by using them in greater variety in their speech and writing, eliciting more complex vocabulary and ideas in return.

A slow rate of progress in comprehension from age 8 and onwards in children from a lower income band, compared with their middle class peers, has been shown to be largely the result of a lack of vocabulary (Becker 1977). This, in turn, is generally caused, not by a lack of mental ability but by a lack of learning opportunities (Becker 1977, Biemiller 2003, Chall et al. 1990).

Just as children require a widening vocabulary to develop in reading, they also have to be able to read well before they can write well. Sadly, as all teachers know, many children begin their journey through the learning environment with low levels of vocabulary and are potentially locked into a negative loop because lack of understanding of words leads to lack of reading, which leads to less new vocabulary being taken on board, less confidence in both reading and writing, and so on.

In those cases, their exposure to items in the list of bullet points above is topsy-turvy. There may be limited literacy and language use in the home and peer environments; reading and writing is minimal; conversation is nominal, contains a restricted range of vocabulary and doesn't involve resourceful questioning; the goal of gaining a wide vocabulary may be uncelebrated, the language quality of media accessed low; and most activities relatively 'language passive'. For those children it is obvious that schools must strive to find ways of making up for such shortcomings, but, at the same time, they still need to find effective ways of raising the literacy standards of all their pupils, even the most language able.

Embedding new vocabulary

Reading is, of course, essential, but children also need experience in 'building, activating and applying their vocabulary' (Sanacore and Palumbo 2009). They must be actively involved during teaching and learning to fully absorb and use new words.

> Whether children are engaged in vocabulary activities or immersed in other literacy learning events, they benefit immensely from increased participation and interaction in the classroom. This instructional direction reduces passivity and improves academic engagement during reading and writing.
>
> (Sanacore and Palumbo in The Educational Forum, 2009).

The out-of-classroom 'guided brainstorm' sessions (which are described in most detail in Chapter 4) are highly effective in engaging participants and involve them not only in finding, sharing, discussing and reinforcing new words but in seeking out and using existing and fresh metaphors, similes and wordplay, experimenting with new forms of phraseology, and generating fresh ideas for writing. With careful guidance, they can even lead to increasing awareness of the 'magical qualities' of sound patterns in language, which all good poets know.

Discoveries, occurrences, ideas, facts and feelings shared on such intensive, involved and 'mind-alert' forages into the outside world also charge young batteries with useful personal experience and world knowledge. This concentrated 'experiential learning' can provide useful, almost visceral background material for writing and helps embed new language effectively.

I think of children as having (and not having) four main areas of vocabulary:

- the words and phrases they don't know;
- the words and phrases they know of but don't understand;
- the words and phrases they understand but don't use;
- the words and phrases they understand and use.

The fourth area of vocabulary listed above I call the young person's 'user dictionary' for obvious reasons. I refer to the third type (and the second to some extent) as their 'orbital vocabulary' because they know it or are aware of it but it's as if it whirls around outside their heads without being used inside them. Ironically, I believe that, in this world of mass media, mass education, vast specialist terminologies, etc., most children have more of this sort of orbital vocabulary than ever before, which can make it even more frustrating for teachers when their pupils don't or can't employ it.

In a well-led, out-of-classroom brainstorming session, large amounts of rich new language, both factual and figurative, are winkled out of the environment and the experience by group members, or occasionally by the leader or accompanying adults. It is shared, appreciated and discussed in context, written down, then later read thoughtfully by each student (sometimes several times) before possibly being chosen to be rewritten into their creative piece and later retyped into a 'neat' copy. Much of it may then be heard or spoken again in sharing sessions or presentations, or read from displays or a 'class book'.

This is a powerful way for group members to connect personally with a whole raft of wonderful new words, phrases, metaphors, similes, observations and writing ideas, and also a highly efficient vehicle for moving much of this new material up into at least the 'orbital vocabulary', and often into the 'user dictionary', of each participant.

It has been shown that a new word has to be used several times in different contexts before it becomes learnt or (better) 'owned' by a child, and this process is a superb way of achieving this goal effectively. Better still, these techniques can achieve this for a wide swathe of new vocabulary at the same time.

Copious amounts of rich new language can be joyously discovered in a directly relevant setting, a situation which makes learning it more effective for all types of mental 'processors'. This language is subsequently multiply re-encountered and used, then rapidly 'owned' by participants through these sorts of techniques. Vocabulary and speaking and writing confidence can grow rapidly if such sessions are a relatively regular part of schooling.

The value of varied experience

Even apart from the intensity of thinking and observation driven by guided brainstorming sessions, the organic experiencing of the world encountered by children on these occasions should not be discounted. I was once told by the respected headmistress of an infant school in Portsmouth, England, that they took all their pupils to the seaside for a full day every year just to play at the edge of the sea, collect shells, build sandcastles, poke around in rock pools, and talk about it all with their peers and accompanying adults.

She explained that, even though the town of Portsmouth is effectively an island, with the sea on three sides and a tidal channel separating it from the mainland, and despite the fact that the ocean could be seen gleaming not far from the windows of their tower block homes, many of the children at her school had never been to the seaside. She considered this sort of experience was important for the social and educational evolution of her charges. Many other teachers have told me they have found that similar kinds of early experiences in varied environments can help underpin a child's basic world knowledge, vocabulary growth, confidence and educational development in general.

I have led groups in sessions using guided brainstorming techniques in all types of environments, on literally thousands of occasions over many years, and have regularly seen teachers gasp in surprise at the quality of vocabulary and ideas elicited by them. More importantly, I have watched many regular residential course students of mine leap spectacularly ahead in writing accomplishment (frequently leading to notable all round educational achievement) after repeated involvement in such sessions and the various writing challenges based on them.

Wider personal experience and increasing awareness help youngsters write more convincingly

Common sense dictates the obvious here. If, from an early age, a youngster has been repeatedly taken to varied and interesting outdoor and indoor places and, along with a group of peers, led through joyous games that involve observing, questioning and describing the settings and experiences in the most accurate, interesting, fluent and creative ways possible, before using this material creatively within their writing, it is inevitable that the breadth, quality and control of their language is likely to race rapidly forwards.

Many of the basic outdoor-inspired learning exercises described in this book can enthuse and drive improvements at all ability levels. Adaptations have been employed effectively with groups of less literate students, 'average' mixed-ability groups in schools, groups of exceptionally language-able students on intensive residential courses, and adult writing enthusiasts.

The techniques can be used successfully with either selected or mixed-ability groups, although, inevitably of course, each of those options has its advantages and disadvantages. Generally speaking, working like this with a cluster of roughly similar-ability students is the most effective and confidence-building for those involved. All levels gain through those techniques, but of course those with the highest base level of literacy and vocabulary will find proportionately more complex ideas and language.

Out of the (classroom) box, thoughtful observation and 'naming' sessions help young people to become more immersed in an environment. This is vital because strong writers have experienced immersion in varied environments in order to immerse others in the virtual environments they build.

Used proficiently, these out-of-classroom-inspired techniques can drive more advanced observational skills in both the 'real' world and that of the imagination; can increase and reinforce vocabulary; stimulate and model language creativity; supply 'reasons for writing'; extend craftsmanship in various written forms, and develop writing quality and related thinking skills at all levels.

For students, such sessions often feel like an engrossing detective hunt for words and ideas. Participants become 'positively competitive', the activities seem more 'real' for many than desk-led exercises, and they are invariably voted by students as 'much more fun than normal classroom work'. That's great news because learning is most effective and permanent when it is enjoyable, active rather than passive, feels 'real', and is underpinned by creative, intellectual and emotional involvement.

Inspired by 'reality'

Examples of student poems

Working in the 'real world' can give participants a genuine 'reason for writing'. With careful guidance, such observing, thinking and creative writing exercises often produce huge leaps forward in the quality of writing and language produced and the depth of thought that goes into all stages of the process. But don't just take my word for it . . . read the following poems individually written by some of my students. They all result from group brainstorming in interesting locations.

I have ordered the poems by the ages of their writers so teachers can choose examples to read to students of similar peer groups.

The Rooks

The rooks are watchful eyes
looking down on the misty moors;
like kings and queens, they rule the skies,
sooty gods of the land.
Their penthouse nests are lodged
in the treetops like rubbish
but are works of art.

They spend busy weeks redecorating,
collecting and endlessly
re-arranging . . .
feathered twig,
straw and string.
Heralds of the night,
with their funeral coats
they bring the darkness on.

Amy Vowles
(aged 9 at time of writing)

Just two years older than the previous student, the following young writer was able to combine thoughtfully observed detail with strong rhythm and rhyme control:

Churchyard

Ivy crawls in cracks and corners,
wreathing every graveyard stone . . .
some are black as clothes of mourners,
others marble, grey as bone.

Sunlight filters through the leaves,
tracing patterns on the grass,
the yews are great guardian trees,
mindless of the ones who pass.

Cracked and crumbling stones are scattered
through the graveyard's solemn still
where the stones are lichen-spattered
on this ancient holy hill.

Katie Wilkinson
(aged 11 at time of writing)

The next poem was written by a student who had learned to observe carefully and thoughtfully on previous courses. During a group session she noticed a bird of prey and asked if she could break away to brainstorm that instead.

Kestrel

The kestrel hovers lightly,
glaring down through beady eyes,
hazel feathers ruffled . . .
deadly beauty of the skies.

Translucent fantail flutters,
hooked talons, gleaming black,
gently curved wings waver,
legs held stiffly back.

A rustle – something moves
then crouches rigid in the moss,
a panic-stricken mouse;
the deathly shadow drifts across.

Heart quivering with fear,
body flattened on the ground,
anticipation in the air . . .
kestrel circles round and round.

A harsh shriek of triumph,
tapered wings arched high,
taloned legs outstretched,
drops like a missile from the sky.

Death rushing down . . .
mouse feebly squeaks and cries
but talons tear through fur:
end arrives, mouse dies.

Clasping the tiny corpse,
wings flutter as it flies,
the limp body hanging-down . . .
deadly beauty of the skies.

Bea Hammond
(aged 12 at time of writing)

Complex language in the following poem mirrors the complex thoughts of the young writer. Despite that complexity the piece is solidly 'grounded' in authenticating description.

Fountains Abbey

From off the fractured tower's head
(rearing from the land alone
& witness to a dead king's whim)
is raining old and tired stone.

A winter's cloak for ageing rock
against the ache of time's cold gloom
is nature's mocking tapestry
where hands of ivy, grasp the room.

Standing tall, survivor walls
are stubborn to time's teasing ways,
dusted by the early dew
with cracks of silver in the greys.

The river still reflects the past,
nine hundred darkened years gone by.
The age-wise water sees it all,
every swallow soar and fly

above the dreams of long ago –
of man and God, of monk and king –
to nest among the fallen stone
and through the empty roof-holes, sing.

Catherine Banks
(aged 13 at time of writing)

The following piece is by a student already featured in this list. I have included this poem to demonstrate the development of increasingly subtle poetic thinking, including the ability to compose poetry with an underlying 'layer of meaning'. On reaching the final line, readers are surprised to discover that a descriptive poem apparently about beach-combing is really an extended metaphor for the process a poet goes through in gathering ideas and inspiration.

Shell collector

She scours the shore, ignoring the pebbles
and monotone scraps crushed into waste,
lower back aching, expectancy yearning
for a sun-glinting treasure to start off the chase.

But squinting down means forgetting your footprints
and slowly her thoughts tread on some of their own;
sitting back for a moment, she wanders through images,
subconsciously shifting the silence of stones.

Crinkled in newness, perfection leaps out,
translucent in suddenly realised light,
the shell hunter plunges to gather her gem
that gleams in the sun as her hand starts to write.

Katie Wilkinson
(aged 13 at time of writing)

Though brainstormed outside a nuclear power station, the writer of the following poem rose far beyond simply describing the location to create these potent verses looking at the two sides of nuclear power.

Nuclear family

Power clenched in leaden fists,
gripped in fiery fingers, milked
to hum like wasps through umbilical cords
and glow incandescent through television sets,
to sweat through your bathtubs and pule into lights,
to judder through trains and hide from the night,
to scrub out the shadows, the cold and the wild.
To burn for your family, to burn for your child.

And a fiery slap, aimed and precise,
ripping and tearing through brickwork and flesh
to roar like a freight train through screams in the streets,
to glow on horizons and flash across skylines,
to smash apart living rooms, kitchens and homes,
to scatter the seed of skin and bone,
to cast you as shadows, immortal, defiled.
To burn for your family, to burn for your child.

Will Milner
(aged 15 at time of writing)

References

Becker, W. C. (1977). 'Teaching reading and language to the disadvantaged: What we have learned from field research.' *Harvard Educational Review 47*, 518–543.

Biemiller, A. (2003) 'Vocabulary: Needed if more children are to read well' *Reading Psychology, 24*, 323–335

Chall, J. S., Jacobs, V. A., and Baldwin, L. E. (1990). *The reading crisis: Why poor children fall behind.* Cambridge, MA: Harvard University Press.

Sanacore, J and Palumbo, A, (2009) 'Understanding the Fourth-Grade slump: Our point of view' *The Educational Forum, 73*, 67–74.

CHAPTER 2

Choosing locations for interactive writing visits

First considerations

Depending on the age and number of students, the time available, and whether it is planned or spontaneous, taking a group out of the classroom to work on writing can involve anything from an informal brainstorming session by the pond at the end of the school field to a guided wander in a nearby wood; from a trip by coach for a working picnic at a site of antiquity to a tightly focused museum or art gallery visit; from standing under cover brainstorming a rainstorm with excited infants to inspiring a rich outdoor writing project for older students as part of a residential stay.

No matter which, the first decision you face is whether or not you need to hold your interactive brainstorming sessions in a specific place or type of setting. This will depend on whether or not the writing project linked to it requires a particular location or kind of environment to be examined and 'absorbed' by your group.

For sessions on which purely creative writing will be based, and particularly with poetry workshops, visits often don't need to be to very specific places, but settings need to be inspirational, complex and potentially packed with rich language and metaphorical possibilities. Further on, in this chapter and others, we will look more at what types of site can supply these qualities.

Factual writing, on the other hand, often calls for exploration of a particular locality or type of environment, as do creative projects that relate to specific course-work or subject areas. Examples of the former might be fact-finding or questioning visits to places such as post-industrial sites, ancient earthworks, themed museums, harbours, busy shopping centres or manufacturing plants, which are designed to link directly with a history, science or geography topic. If the site is evocative enough, the same location can also be chosen for an inspirational poetry or story brainstorming session that might or might not tie in with that topic.

Dual factual and creative sessions

There is no rule that says a fact-gathering visit for project work can't be combined with an intensive creative brainstorming session to 'feed' a poem, story or fictional diary. For your students this will creatively and emotionally extend the project, further embedding their educational experience with 'organic' understanding, and it should also produce a great piece of writing as legacy!

'Dual approach' projects like this are sometimes best separated into relatively distinct sessions with the factual section usually coming before the creative brainstorm. That way, when participants reach the more creative part they will already have a bank of ideas, background facts, anecdotes and links in their heads and hearts which can broaden their creative questioning beyond what would initially be obvious to them in that setting. If the factual input required is relatively short, these sessions can be connected together. However, it is important to remember that a good 'creative-questioning' session should be very intensive, which can be mentally tiring, especially for younger ones, so participants need to be alert throughout. With this in mind, if the initial factual segment is fairly demanding or takes up more than a short amount of time, it might be a good idea to have a short snack break, or even lunch before moving on to the creative one.

When a language brainstorming session involving in-depth, 'thoughtful obser-vation' is well led, most students will finish it feeling fired up and ready to get on with their creative writing, which is another reason why it's more effective to have the 'creative questioning' part after the factual one, to make use of this surge of creative energy. However that doesn't imply that students should start their writing straight away.

Inspiration is essential to good writing so it's certainly best for the actual writing process to follow the creative brainstorming session(s) without too much distraction. It's often necessary to start the writing itself on the following day, however, because students may be too mentally and creatively exhausted imme-diately after all their hard thinking during the visit, and there might simply not be enough usable time left that day in which to begin the lengthy process of writing.

If there is a time gap it's advisable to recap just before students start to write, and to deliver some input on writing forms and helpful tips to ease them back into the mood and generate a more immediate sense of the required form and task, as well as the 'feel' of the place visited. Later in the book we will look at something particularly helpful in this situation, which I call 'second stage brainstorming'; it not only brings back the atmosphere of a place and experience but, because it connects with semi-processed mental material, can drive and deepen inspiration in new ways.

Of course, the depth and number of all inputs, and the period and timings of sessions will also depend on the age and focus of the group, as well as the total length of the visit and on-site brainstorming. Group leaders need to assess all this beforehand and perhaps be prepared to adjust their planning on the day.

As long as the students are old enough and the duration of any on-location factual section is not too great, dual factual and inspirational sessions are often best experienced on the same day if possible, because returning to a site on a second day for the creative part can soften the creative 'shock of the new'. However, achieving all the on-location work on the same day or in the same session is not always possible or essential, especially if age, tiredness, focus, timings or available light require more than one visit.

Dual 'creative' sessions

Students can perform better on two separate inspirational visits to the same general location if they work in slightly different areas of it on another part of the same day or on a second day, or if an interesting change will have occurred at that location, such as the tide having gone out at a seashore, or a place that was earlier quiet having become thronged. Going to the same location twice can be both an advantage and a disadvantage during a poetry workshop because, generally speaking, you want to try and trap the atmosphere of a certain setting around a certain time; otherwise students' writing directions can become confused.

On the other hand, juxtapositions caused by significant differences between conditions at a particular location at different times can create interesting comparisons. For instance, a busy shopping centre, main commercial street or school before and after closing time; during and after an event such as a festival, a carnival, a building on fire; a town park at lunchtime on a warm sunny day as opposed to a bleak, rainy one.

The same holds true for visits to two different but interestingly related or comparative locations (e.g. an idyllic water meadow next to the metallic new industrial complex built on part of it) because, again, the juxtapositions observed can be excellent drivers for a poem too. As always, the best choice or variation of setting is dependent on age, ability and available timings. More able, older students will often pick up on such greater subtleties, but all groups can be led towards them.

Although children need to learn to focus, 'see' and question deeply during brainstorming activities in order to achieve the most from a site, it's also important to remember that it's possible to 'blunt' inspiration for a poetry visit through too much volume of input and preparation immediately before the writing stage It is worth bearing this in mind, especially with younger groups, or if running a sizeable factual session before a creative one.

For very different reasons, this 'over-cooking' can sometimes apply to more able, older groups. They will have deeper focus, greater endurance for inputs, larger vocabularies, potentially more complex mental links through their personal reading and world knowledge, and will both pick up and give much more, much faster in a session. Many of them will probably have had their inspiration triggered at some point during the brainstorm and may be itching to write before they have even left the site.

Timings of sessions

Timings required for sessions can vary due to how much aspiration and mental stamina your group have, how language rich the location is, how much distraction there is, the age of the students, etc. When working towards individual descriptive poems I usually allow around two hours of actual brainstorming time on location for most groups from about eight or nine years of age up to adult. With younger age groups it may be advisable to split the creative questioning session into two parts with a break in-between.

For most groups the minimum time required to achieve a nominal depth of thinking and variety of material is probably at least an hour and a half, but this is only if the group is highly responsive and the leader well-practised. Enthusiastic older groups aged from around thirteen years and upwards have often brainstormed with me in stages for most of a day and evening as part of projects involving the eventual production of longer pieces of descriptive-factual prose, such as travel writing, or several vaguely related pieces of individual poetry or prose required for a themed final performance.

Places for poetry brainstorming sessions

Principal considerations

The principal considerations for choosing a location in which to hold an interactive brainstorming session for poetry are:

- Is the site reasonably evocative, interesting or atmospheric?
- Is the location 'vocabulary rich'?
- Will the group have sufficient time at the location to achieve a good depth of thinking and collect a wide variety of material?
- Can parts of the location potentially generate interesting metaphors and similes?
- Can parts generate 'vibrant' verbs? (but see next entry)
- Will significant aspects of the location remain present long enough for the group's speed of thinking and rate of note-taking (especially if they are scribing for themselves)?
- Will this location create questioning and ideas that go beyond the purely descriptive and entail a deeper level of background and thoughtfulness?

- Are any 'cultural concepts' or history embedded in the site, or facts linked to it, within the comprehension of the group?
- Are there rich brainstorming sub-locations there where a whole group can see, and feel immersed in, both the wider setting and also the detailed near foreground and middle ground?
- Can all participants fit into these sub-locations and work tightly together?
- Will everyone be able to see the leader and what is being focused on at each sub-location?
- Can everyone hear each other's ideas and suggestions?
- Will the site be relatively free of distractions such as noise, risk, outsiders playing up to the group, etc?
- Are these brainstorming sub-location sites acceptably safe and accessible for everyone in the group?

Let's look at each of these in more detail.

Evocative sites

For poetry brainstorming and, to a slightly lesser extent, for story workshops, the best sites are evocative in some way because these trigger excitement, interest, ideas and emotions . . . key ingredients of inspiration. A stream tumbling excitedly through a woodland clearing would fit that bill, or the landscape on and far below a dramatic hilltop.

Of course, this evocative effect is often enhanced when sites contain elements of human history or culture, which in turn can increase the depth of a group's questioning and the amount and quality of descriptive data available from them. Locations such as this might be, for instance, a long-abandoned quarry, the site of a battle or a run-down urban graveyard. That stream in the clearing would be even more evocative if it tumbled through the mossy ruins of an ancient water-mill, and the hilltop would produce deeper questioning if it was scarred by the humps and bumps of an Iron Age hill fort settlement.

It can be even more helpful to the process if you can also add a certain amount of the 'shock of the new' by taking a group to a location or type of place which is not familiar to them, or at least not on an everyday basis. Of course this is not always easy or convenient because it will depend on time available, helpers, transport, and so on.

Going to more distant or unusual locations is not so important with younger groups, especially infant groups, because their life and language experiences are limited; so brainstorming nearby things like the school pond area in summer or autumn, or the view and life down the peaceful street from the school gates may challenge and supply enough new ideas, vocabulary, descriptions and metaphors.

These sorts of relatively everyday locations can also be 'flash focused' on by small groups of story writers looking for 'reality details', plot ideas and vocabulary with which to authenticate parts of their stories.

An evocative location can only live up to its potential if a brainstorm there is well led. When this is the case, all abilities benefit from the surge of ideas and inspiration it will produce, which in turn will generate more enthusiasm to find outstanding metaphors, descriptive words and poem or story ideas. For those in urban areas, a park on a hill on the centre of a town will do well enough because participants can see and think about the town spread below as well as the life of the park itself.

Language-rich sites

Generally speaking, however, for a relatively natural location, the wilder and less organised it is the more original vocabulary will come out of it. For instance, an unkempt churchyard provides more language, and more interesting language, than a neatly manicured one. The first reason for this is that an overgrown or even abandoned churchyard is clearly more evocative and moody than a tidy one, and that generates the enthusiasm to hunt deeper for interesting words. Another reason is that chaos brings more variation, and greater variation provides more 'naming' possibilities.

For example, some marble headstones will still look relatively clean and shiny, but older stones will have become 'tilted and tumbled', 'bruised and broken as old soldiers' or be 'softly warmed by jackets of moss'. The grass, shrubs and trees may have become overgrown and unruly, so scavenging jackdaws might 'bob about in Mexican waves of windblown grass', yew trees may stand 'like dark guardians' or 'loom, twisted and disfigured, bleeding deep pools of shadow'. I hope you are beginning to see what I mean and, yes, after a bit of careful guidance, many groups can come up with those kinds of original descriptions, spiced by alliteration, metaphor or simile.

Although most churchyards are fairly well-looked after they can still provide plenty of vocabulary, but more interesting word choice and figurative language arise where there's greater variety and detail to be seen and, of course, evocative locations breed evocative language!

'Language-poor' locations

I should also mention here the sort of location that is apparently language poor, or perhaps we should say 'new language poor' because it's the process of striking away from the limited language of the everyday that we want to activate. Apart from for very young pupils, a place they know well, such as the classroom they inhabit, might seem to be 'new language poor'.

Obviously, a cluttered primary school classroom will be more language rich than an anonymous, uncared for room, belonging to no particular teacher, in some large secondary school or college. The more sterile and empty it is, the less language can be found there, yet your students may still have difficulty finding many new words and metaphors in a classroom they are based in all the time because they are used to using everyday words for the things that are there every day. Generally only able, older groups (and professional poets!) will be able to extract exciting new language and ideas from that situation.

On very few occasions, a teacher who had heard that I would want to lead a group in brainstorming outdoors, has looked out their classroom window and decided on the first place they could see . . . the school playing fields. If students do not have exceptional ability, wide vocabulary, and cultural and world knowledge, an empty playing field can be one of the most uninspiring and 'language poor' settings possible! It is a deliberately reduced world: the grass is short and uniform, no weeds or swaying trees are allowed to exist there, and the only wildlife might be a few seagulls which have descended in the hope of scavenging fragments of break-time snacks.

Most children brainstorming there, especially younger ones, would struggle to come up with original words and ideas because there is so little detail, so little variation. If a leader is stuck with such an unfortunate decision, or there is absolutely no other location available, they will have to work with the subtler points of what is there in order to rise above the mundane. Working intensely on metaphor would be one of the best ideas and the regularity might well become the focus itself. So, for instance, the short lawns might become 'crew-cut grass' or 'exact as Astroturf, or 'an emerald desert'. Any variations or intrusions, such as the behaviour of scavenging seagulls might drive descriptive and metaphorical ideas.

I was once given the challenging task of brainstorming on a massive, empty expanse of playing fields with a group of 15-year-olds, but I was lucky on two fronts because, first, I realised we would see an interesting sight if we walked into the centre of this vastness of grass and, secondly, the group were all enthusiastic and fairly able.

The school was in Glastonbury in the UK, and, from the centre of the playing fields we could see the famous and evocative, tower-topped hill of Glastonbury Tor, featured as if on centre stage in a gap between wide 'curtains' of poplar trees. Even better, it was illuminated dramatically by a rare patch of sunlight. This produced several extended metaphors and complex ideas about drama performance, performance in life, belief systems, history, and monarchs on emerald thrones.

Turning the group towards the school from that distance made them think about it in a different way and, deciding the buildings looked industrial, they began to develop extended metaphors around the idea of the school being a 'factory for learning', that they themselves were 'products' being manufactured to fit into society and others' expectations. These philosophical and metaphorical ideas were combined with relevant collected 'authenticating details' from the location which enriched their poetry.

Most empty spaces or over-manicured sites such as playing fields won't produce enough strong ideas like this and are lacking in rich detail, so it is obviously best to avoid them if possible.

Good sites for generating original metaphorical language

As we've seen, the sorts of site that are most effective in spawning original metaphorical language are mostly those which are rich in variety and somewhat separate from the everyday. For instance, the seashore can, unsurprisingly, generate more metaphorical quantity and originality than school grounds, partly because there is more variety there, partly because of the constantly changing qualities of the sea and shore, and partly because a less mundane environment is more interesting, so participants put more effort into thinking.

Commonly encountered places, things and situations are more mentally pre-linked to clichéd metaphors and similes so even a relatively commonly encountered setting such as a sandy beach can bring its own holiday brochure clichés (e.g. 'golden sand' or 'waves like white horses') and observation of it can be limited to the obvious because many children have a concept of seaside that makes them view it through what I call 'ice-cream and candyfloss glasses'.

On the other hand, ragged coastline comprising areas of rock, cliff, pebbles or acres of mud is less commonly encountered or appreciated, and so less liable to throw up clichéd metaphors. It also contains more variety than a neat sandy beach and can generate wonderful texture and mood metaphors. For instance, the mud might be described as 'crinkled grey leather', the way the rocks jab out of it as like 'the fossilised backbones of dinosaurs', high, banded rock faces become 'layer-cake cliffs', or 'dark headlands frowning down / on diminutive figures below'.

Places rich in 'vibrant verbs'

Poets and writers of rich prose love lively verbs and we will discuss why this is in the chapter on brainstorming for poetry. Verbs are abundant in places where there is movement and some of the easiest settings in which to find interesting and varied movement are those containing water, trees or other vegetation. Water is a poetry workshop leader's star player when it comes to the hunt for exciting verbs because it rarely stays still and has several different main forms of movement: the directional movement of a body of water in sea, streams, rivers, waterfalls, mills, etc.; the movement of the surface on lakes, ponds, bays and flooded places, and the multifaceted movements of light, shade, gleam and reflection on its surface, caused by the latter.

Water also makes an infinite variety of sounds, such as dripping, sploshing, washing, gurgling, burbling, pittering and pattering, as well as a great variety of

Photo 2.1 Winter inspiration

subtle and complex sounds which often require very specific verbs, or even the invention of new words, such as 'glooping', 'plooping', 'shushing' or 'cymbal-crashing' to describe them. One able group I worked with spent ten minutes trying to find a word to describe the sound of a small streamlet dropping into a wide hole with a tiny pool at the bottom. They finally came up with total agreement on 'plottering water', which perfectly described the sound better than any existing words. The phrase also had the added advantage of an assonance and consonance echoing the 'awt' sound on the stressed beat of each word, which accentuated the key parts of the sound.

Weather also generates an amazing variety of interesting movements, the questioning of which can guide groups towards flocks of vibrant verbs. We can't always plan to hold a workshop session in certain weather, but we can sometimes make or alter our plans in order to brainstorm in locations which take advantage of these movements. For instance, working in a wooded area or beside fields of tall crops during a windy period, watching thunderous waves and windblown gulls from a transparent seafront beach shelter during a storm, finding a spot under cover to observe rain pelting into puddles and pools, or organising to be on the opposite side of a lake or river from a low sun in order to catch the infinite movements of rippled and splintered golden light.

People-watching

People-watching, as part of a poetry or story brainstorming session can be another productive area in which to tease out interesting doing and movement words as well as new metaphors, but observing and describing humans is harder to execute effectively than observing more static environments. One reason for this is that individual people often do something, or move past, too quickly for inexperienced groups to have time to dig out appropriate verbs and descriptive words. It's generally easier to trap and describe the movements and intentions of a mass of people, such as a large demonstration, or a parade, or the flow of rush-hour crowds.

When student poets observe individuals, even if they do think of relatively subtle movement verbs, they often can't reach as much depth in their wider ideas and metaphors in that situation. Successfully watching and describing people and their activities in busy streets is relatively difficult, but doing the same activity where movements are slow, repetitive or fixed within a visible area can be language and idea productive for students. That's why observing people such as gardeners in allotments, factory workers, park keepers, market stall holders, crafts people, shore fishermen, grave diggers or a farmer ploughing a field can be fruitful, especially if the environment around them is rich or evocative so that descriptions and metaphors of both can be entwined together.

Inevitably, groups which can benefit most from people-watching are generally those whose members are older, more able, fast thinking and hold reasonably wide vocabularies. Despite that, simplified forms of the activity can be used successfully down to small groups of young infants, especially if the activities don't pass too quickly and if someone scribes their words and ideas on their behalf. This is where the use of a portable computer such as a net-book or laptop comes in very handy, but it's safer to carry two of them or one with a spare battery, or a clipboard, paper and pencil for backup!

Moving beyond the purely descriptive

With younger or less able groups you might already be happy at the surprising quality and variety of nouns, adjectives, vibrant verbs, metaphors, similes and 'sound echo' words your students find and, as long as the session also gives them a good sense of the atmosphere, setting and any activity within it, your charges will have increased their orbital and user vocabularies and will still be able to produce a rich enough poem. However, just as the employment of original and apt metaphor gives descriptive writing that extra 'wow factor', helping a group move on to adding a dash of relevant 'philosophy', emotion, humanity and a touch of personal 'voice' can lift writing onto a higher plane. Some ways of doing this are:

- to guide your young poets into seeking and imagining any human, cultural or historical elements 'embedded' in a site;
- to lead them in the hunt for interesting mental links;
- to imagine past times there in richly sensory language;
- to help them move beyond the purely descriptive by spicing the writing mix with aesthetic, emotional or thoughtful language and connections.

We will look at this further in the chapter on leading a poetry 'data collection' session, but these possibilities are important to bear in mind when choosing locations for groups of appropriate age and ability.

Examples of places that lend themselves to deeper questioning might be a ruined abbey; an old churchyard; an overgrown quarry; a military barracks or training ground; bleak post-industrial landscapes; a railway station, bus station or airport; an abandoned harbour; a former battlefield; an exhibition of powerful art; places with dramatic views.

Sites that speak of change, progress, regression, tragedy, timelessness, meeting and parting, and those that trigger a sense of the sublime and a soaring of the spirit are perfect places in which to activate this more personal questioning. For older, more able students and adults, it is, after all, the ability to combine unique personal viewpoint and experience with originally observed and described 'authenticating detail' which can create outstanding poetry that is at once original and universal, makes the ordinary glow with the light of the new, and embraces the reader with a sense of empathy and the 'presence' of place and poet.

For some sites to generate the necessary depth of questioning, your students must be capable of understanding the context, history or purpose of the setting, something that has to be borne in mind with younger groups.

Practicalities of working areas

Spaces in which to brainstorm

During brainstorming sessions, participants must be able to fit into each sub-location tightly but comfortably, either standing or sitting. They also need to be near enough to the leader and each other in order to hear and share ideas and language. Students will require a little more space when sitting down, especially if they are scribing individually on clipboards because an adult isn't typing or scribing the group's language on their behalf. It pays to keep everyone close together because focus will be tight if the group is tight.

The most effective group size is usually around 10–16 students, but I frequently brainstorm with entire classes. If you need to take more students than that to a particular location, it can be best to split them into classes or smaller groups with different leaders for each. They might do similar work with different leaders or one group can do background work while the other does creative brainstorming, before switching roles and possibly leaders.

Although students often concentrate better and fidget less when seated, limited space, weather, ground conditions and time don't always allow this. Some sub-locations seem more like links to others in that they contain some additional language and inspiration, but don't justify the time required to get everyone seated comfortably.

Sitting on damp, cold or uneven ground outdoors is problematic and is not in any way essential, although there are methods of dealing with these discomforts. The first is to ask all the students to bring a plastic carrier bag to sit on, but I have been in a few well-organised schools which provide their pupils with cheap offcuts of waterproof sponge or carpet underlay, referred to in one school as 'sit-upons'. On a series of visits each pupil carried their own 'sit-upon' as we walked to and moved around the location, which meant that all their mixed-ability classes gave me over two hours of exceptional, in-depth focus while working on stony seashores, muddy headland grass, soaking forest floors, etc.

It's helpful when scouting a location to check for suitable brainstorming sub-locations, bearing in mind these practicalities, and working out where the best places for leaders to place themselves might be. These will generally be immediately in front and to one side of the group without blocking much of potentially interesting views and subjects, towards which the group will be aimed. Like this, leaders can also be strategically stationed between the group and any possible hazards such as water or steep slopes. If an adult is typing or scribing for the group, they can sit on a folding stool where they won't block anyone's view but are within easy earshot of both leader and participants.

Safety and other considerations

Off-site locations will need to be risk assessed in advance, but this does not have to be a daunting procedure. While doing this, it might pay to consider whether each potential brainstorming spot is accessible for everyone in the group, including helpers. Sometimes it might be necessary to work out a way of bringing a participant with mobility issues by car and moving them between sub-locations on more accessible routes.

In a few places, one of the biggest distractions can be noise. For instance, although brainstorming in the vicinity of heavy machinery, in a busy city centre, in a noisy factory, or on a seashore during a storm, can produce great language and ideas, the leader and scriber may struggle to hear all of the student's answers and the 'fizz' of the session might slip. If this is likely, you may have to do a little contingency planning such as checking out sheltered areas or finding sub-locations where everyone can see the action without being deafened by it.

On the other hand, being aware of the different types of sensory stimuli available in an area can be important in deciding which sub-locations will be inspiring and produce more varied language and ideas for rich 'authenticating detail'. For instance, I have run both poetry and travel-writing brainstorming sessions on station platforms and inside the carriages of moving steam trains on several occasions over the years, and the noises and rhythms of the train often become significant within the writing produced. This is especially obvious with poetry as the changing but repetitive sounds of trains help generate strong poetic rhythms.

It is important that, in most sub-locations, participants can see not only, say, a dramatic view but also details close at hand. For instance, a leader might want to guide a brainstorming session in a small clearing beside a lake, but a certain sub-location there might not be very practical because the group can only see the far shoreline due to a nearby wall or hedge between them and the water. That will cut out much of the site's language potential because an enormous amount of it can come from foreground and middle-ground details, such as the magical movement and light of rippled reflections, how droplets on a duck's back resemble pearls, or the soft swish of rush and reed.

Timing it best

Although your choices will often be dictated by school or other timings, many locations are at their best at certain times of the day or year. For instance, there is vastly more activity, plant and animal life, scent and sound to be seen and discussed in a rural location during late spring, summer and autumn than in winter. However, although this equates to a significant difference in the amount of available 'naming' language, a bleak winter's morning or evening can make up for this deficit in detail in other ways because it can be so moody and evocative.

The time of day also affects how atmospheric a site feels. Evening is often one of the most evocative times because, not only does the yellowing light keep changing and repainting the land in deepening tones but features are dramatically highlighted by light and lengthening shadows, the sky can explode in a show of changing hues, and observers' spirits can be lifted and ideas sharpened.

On night brainstorms, although darkness obscures most colour and detail, new language, metaphors and inspiration can be found in the drama of a star-pricked sky, a moon-bow illuminating fissures in cloud, a lake shimmering with metallic light or a distant coastline strung with the golden tinsel of streetlights. Even when sky is obscured by cloud, I have run highly successful workshops on canal towpaths and in sleepy village centres, with students describing the houses, shadows, sounds and smells, lights reflecting on water, the creep and flit of night creatures, and the ritual drawing down of the human day. These types of brainstorming activities can open young eyes, produce rich and original writing, and make a residential stay even more memorable.

Weather can make a considerable difference to the atmosphere of a location. Although a blissful summer's day may ensure a group can focus comfortably for an extended period and possibly also work on part of the writing stage on-site, students often produce deeper and more atmospheric writing when it's grey and gloomy, when passing shower-clouds are splitting sunrays on hillsides or rooftops, or waterfalls are frozen into curtains of ice and branches are laden with snow.

Brainstorming on a shore can be more productive when the tide is low or at the half-way stage, rather than when it's fully in, because there is so much to be seen in the littoral zone: shimmering rock pools, empty expanses, scavenging gulls, beachcombers, mopheads of seaweed, crawling crabs and piles of polished pebbles.

If brainstorming at a railway station you may need to consider whether you want the group to be there when there are plenty of trains and vibrant crowds of people to watch, or whether it will be easier for the group to cope with the slower pace of things outside busy rush-hour times. You may have to think about the advantages of observing the hectic atmosphere filled with rushing travellers, pressured body language, and emotional partings and meetings, yet balance that with the possible difficulties of keeping a group tightly together and being able to hear each other over the background din. It's usually possible to find suitable spots in most locations, even busy ones, and a little forward scouting can help make things run more efficiently on the day.

Comfort is essential for deep concentration

The secret in all conditions is to make participants feel enveloped by their environment while keeping them as comfortable as possible at all times. In cold weather and in exposed conditions it is essential to ensure that students are dressed in exceptionally warm and waterproof clothing. This usually entails wearing at least three times as much as they want to, and even carrying spare jumpers or jackets tied around their waists or in rucksacks.

When running outdoor brainstorming workshops in hills, countryside or on coasts during colder months I insist that participants wear either two pairs of trousers or a layer of thermal underwear or tights, or both; two pair of thick socks; either wellingtons or walking boots; multiple layers of warm fleece or wool on their top halves; and a thick waterproof jacket plus a warm hat, gloves and waterproof overtrousers if available.

In summer weather participants still need to take jumpers as well as sunhats because they may have to work in shade for part of the time. This is especially true if they are writing outside as well as brainstorming when the sun is high. There can be much to gain from writing in situ as some students will pick up and develop additional ideas and observations themselves, but their brains and their writing can turn to mush if they are out in direct sun for long.

Brainstorming story ideas on location

Although poetry brainstorming is usually best achieved in one general type of setting so as not to confuse students' writing directions and to imbue participants with the atmosphere of a place, story brainstorming can often be more effective when groups are taken to more than one place or where there is plenty of variety to be observed in one area. Individuals can imagine and develop different 'plot triggers' out of this variety, and selected, well-observed details from different locations can help them create more convincing 'worlds' and be the basis for different 'scenes' in their stories. This is essential if you want each story to be different and original, and especially if students are employing the powerful 'x-points' system of story plot creation described in Chapter 12.

I have often walked a group to various sub-locations, or driven them around in a mini bus, stopping in a few very different settings to observe and describe and to brainstorm x-point plot ideas. Before we get back to base to write, many students are usually bursting with original story ideas, and some are often scribbling down ideas on the way. The descriptive brainstorming parts of these sessions can effectively combine what is observed in the real world with descriptions linked to what is imagined through the x-point ideas.

Sessions on observing and 'naming' the real world as part of story preparation don't have to be as lengthy or in-depth as for a poetry brainstorm because your trainee writers are not trying to be so specific about one location, many of the words and ideas brought up won't be used by some people, and most of the settings will be imaginatively varied to fit individual plot ideas and scenes.

Collective story writing sites

I have also found *collective*, location-based story writing to be extremely valuable, particularly with groups of students from 7-year-olds up to 11- or 12-year-olds. This is often best achieved by brainstorming plot ideas in parts of one interesting and perhaps evocative setting, or in various settings, and we will look at this in more depth in Chapter 13. I usually combine plot brainstorming 'in situ' with some observational and descriptive brainstorming, so outdoor story sessions might involve some poetry-like observation combined with imagining interesting or peculiar occurrences, objects or characters coming into, being in, or interacting with, parts of that environment.

Because stories are so fluid and multifaceted, and involve brainstorming plot, character, setting and action ideas, story triggering sessions can involve imagining x-points in all sorts of locations, even fairly mundane ones, such as the corner of a street, in a transport café, at the upper window of a pub or in a rainy field of wheat, as well as in more evocative ones such as a wooded ravine, inside a church tower's belfry, on huge boulders within a thunderous mountain river, in the deep mud of an estuary, on the windswept roof of a skyscraper, and so on.

Almost anywhere can be used effectively for story inspiration, especially if you include some places that are fascinating or evocative.

Location-based writing linked with coursework

Creative and factual writing projects that relate to coursework or current topics can be based on relevant locations. This kind of work can make a topic come alive and deepen the subject in more personal, more experiential ways.

Imagine the effect of taking a group studying the Romans to a genuine Roman site, such as a camp, villa, or amphitheatre, helping students to see how aspects of their learning fits there, and brainstorming both the current place and also participants' imaginations of descriptions and individual experiences that might have occurred in ancient times. 'Live brainstorming' and writing creatively, evocatively and emotively on aspects of a subject are excellent ways of embedding and widening knowledge about it. The learning becomes real to the writer in a personal way.

Before the visit, it would be useful to learn about the lives and livelihoods of Roman citizens in varying social positions so that students at that location can then be led to brainstorm what might have occurred there. They can then write poetry or diaries of, or about, imaginary Roman characters who may have lived there, or evocative poetry about the remaining edifices, with echoes of what might have been done or felt there in the past, or they can compare their modern lives, clothes, school with the colour and hardships of the past. The possibilities are legion if you'll excuse the pun.

Similar projects can equally effectively be based on studies of native American, Canadian or Australasian peoples; on industrialism and post-industrial sites such as derelict mines, railway yards, closed-down car plants or iron smelters; on subsistence farming and the Dust Bowl, or on whatever topic that you can find evidence of in your local landscape or local museum.

'Real' sites are generally better locations than museums for this type of brain-storming because they are 'raw' and contain valuable sensory discoveries. These primary sources have certain visceral and descriptive qualities for students to question and seek out themselves, rather that the predigested and professionally presented data in a museum. The exception is where a museum is based on an authentic site, especially where students can feel wrapped up in its atmosphere. Examples of this would be an old coal mine where student groups can actually be taken into the machine rooms and the pit itself, a railway museum with working engines or a museum of the sea in a genuine harbour setting.

Those studying Norman, Medieval, Scottish or Welsh history, or Shakespeare's historical tragedies such as *Macbeth, Hamlet, Henry IV* or *King Lear*, might be able to visit a suitable local castle or abbey in which to brainstorm the sights, sounds, smells and atmosphere of the place, and write a creative piece blending this language with hints of deeds, decisions or outcomes discovered in those topics. The important thing is to make dry facts become 'atmospheric and alive', first in the students' psyches and then in their writing. Anyway, descriptive poetry is not really about repeating facts, it is about thoughts and feelings, humanity, individual 'voice' and other 'voices', grounded by authenticating details from the real world which give it atmosphere and imbue it with a visceral sense of reality.

Primary groups working on natural science or geography projects can extend these by adding creative aspects based on suitable locations. This might involve, for instance, poetry based on a river, related to a topic about river systems or river ecology. Those studying the water cycle could write individual or collective poems on each part of the cycle after groups of them have brainstormed on visits to watch mist, clouds and rain; or have observed and described hills and springs. They may have brainstormed the water, vegetation, movement and light at higher and lower parts of a river, and where it flows into the ocean. This might all be put together into a booklet or website, or woven into a performance in school, possibly for parents, some of whom may have helped with transport and other logistics.

For many years I ran a highly successful 4–5 day residential course for able secondary students entitled Life Cycles, which wove performance of original location-based poetry, movement, music and song, word collage and dance into a wonderfully evocative show that never failed to astonish parents by its qualities of detailed observation and blissful creativity. As it was loosely based on the water cycle we visited and brainstormed all those types of locations described above, usually starting by climbing to the top of the highest hills in the area. With the right questioning, the brainstorming detail morphed into much more than just descriptive poetry and included subtle and sometimes emotional aspects of life and death, war, drought, the power of Nature and human destruction of natural habitat.

More practicalities

Whether brainstorming rich words and ideas for poetry, stories, travel writing, animal or historical 'diary' projects, or simply absorbing information for factual writing sessions, leaders inevitably need to take into account school or centre timings, the physical needs of their charges, return travel, walking, food and toilet breaks, plus a little contingency time. I find a poetry brainstorming session requires at least two hours' actual working time at a site with most groups. For more able, older groups, this working time can be extended but, if running longer intensive sessions, all groups will need to take little breaks and change sub-locations, otherwise ideas will dry up and brains become tired.

If weather or venue allow for it, it's often practical for a group to take along snacks and packed lunches to give you flexibility and so that you can take short or long breaks whenever you decide it's suitable. With any age band it is helpful to play games or allow students a run-around within set boundaries after a concentrated session, then move them on to a new location or sub-location for another session or to begin actual writing. On longer workshops I sometimes carry a Frisbee or a ball, or have my assistant organise a relatively physical game as a way of warming up cold students and switching off brains for a short while. It's helpful to think about these aspects when viewing a location so that you can plan for them and include them in your risk assessment.

Weather permitting, I also sometimes intersperse intensive inputs and long writing sessions with short physical activities because they are both team and enthusiasm building, benefit both mind and body, and the improved writing results justify the time allotted to them.

Out-of-classroom sessions: preparations and practicalities

Although we have already looked at practicalities linked to locations in the previous chapter, this chapter discusses more possible preparation requirements and supplies checklists to help busy leaders get organised quickly.

Clothing and equipment

Taking groups offsite to work might seem a little daunting to some but it needn't be; after all, many teachers and leaders move groups of children around offsite on a regular basis. It just needs a small amount of preparation and an alert focus on

Photo 3.1 Thoughtful observation at the docks

safety before and during the visit, especially while walking beside and crossing roads, or near to hazards such as steep drops or deep water.

I've already mentioned the need for participants to wear many more layers of clothing than normal while outside in anything but the warmest weather. This is crucial to their ability to concentrate, achieve and enjoy the experience. I have come across the occasional teacher who has remarked that a few of their pupils have left their jackets at home but they will go on the outdoor session anyway.

As an experienced outdoor group leader, I can never accept this if the weather is even slightly cool or shows any possibility of rain, especially if we will be working in remote or exposed places. Not only can it be a risk in such situations but, when one or a few group members become too physically uncomfortable, they cease to participate or start to complain, which affects the entire group's morale, enthusiasm and focus. Everyone must be appropriately dressed and comfortable for a brainstorming session to work well, even if this involves carrying extra layers. I transport bags of spare outdoor clothing in my car for this type of contingency.

Teachers may even need to bring extra clothing from home, raid the school's lost property or ask under-equipped students to borrow items from friends or relatives in school. If your group is going to be visiting an outdoor centre they may have stores of spare outdoor clothing and equipment such as coveralls, jackets, boots, gloves, torches and group shelters, so it is worth checking this in advance.

Watching the weather

It is essential to keep checking the weather forecast until almost the time of departure and adapt workshop timings, sub-locations and clothing as necessary, especially when leading groups any distance off-road. As long as group members stay reasonably comfortable, stronger ideas and more inspired writing often derive from visits where the location is evocative and the weather is atmospheric, sparkling, moody or dramatic. Due to careful preparation I have never had to cancel a brainstorming session because of the weather. My assistants and I always make contingency arrangements for extreme weather ahead of extended sessions in remoter areas and this has paid off on all the instances they were required.

On one occasion where we were working on exposed hilltops, despite wearing many layers of clothing we also carried a roll of large black plastic bin bags. When a gale-driven rainstorm approached, we tore arm and head holes in the bags and had our students pull them over their heads so that their jackets and trousers were covered until the storm subsided. As always, once we were in a more sheltered area, the students wrote with short pencils onto clipboards inside clear plastic 'freezer' bags and the morale of the group actually grew hugely during the long walk despite the rain.

I have occasionally had to alter sub-location quickly due to changes in the weather and once, during a torrential downpour on a forested mountain, I had to adapt and lead the input stage inside a mini-bus. Ex-students still tell me they fondly recall the exceptional depth and originality of ideas that flowed from that tightly focused session and the incredibly creative outdoor brainstorming session which followed once the rain had passed. To me this illustrates the unique creative power deriving from the blending of situation, mood, atmosphere and joyous team work which would be impossible to replicate in a classroom setting.

Recording of ideas

To scribe or not to scribe?

The question of whether students should scribe for themselves or not during brainstorm sessions does not have a simple answer. It can certainly be good practice for students to scribe on clipboards for themselves as long as it doesn't detract from their ability to keep up with the fizz of the brainstorm, think in real depth and contribute well. By scribing themselves they learn to write fast while thinking fast, they have more ownership of the words, metaphors and notes they jot down, and the process helps them discover, use and embed lots of new language effectively.

On the other hand, younger children and those who struggle with scribing at speed can miss out on deep involvement in the brainstorming session and might become slightly dispirited. If a child has an obvious special need there may well be an adult scribing just for them, but that doesn't prevent others in the group from missing out. Some of these less confident writers may, if freed from the tension of scribing, be the sorts of students who astonish their teachers, and sometimes themselves, by discovering they can contribute vibrant verbal language and truly original metaphors.

I have sometimes found this to be the case with dyslexic or borderline dyslexic students, or those with other unspecified learning and writing difficulties, and I love to see teachers become happily surprised at the poetic quality of language that some unlikely candidates produce verbally. I have watched a few regular residential course students like this progress from requiring 'special needs scribers' in mid-primary school to becoming some of the most exceptionally creative and gifted secondary students. A surprising percentage of self-made entrepreneurs and 'creatives' are dyslexic, which surely shows that there is something interesting about the creative thinking processes going on inside certain young heads.

The advantages of having a typist or scriber

For many years I have nearly always employed able assistants to type or scribe for groups as there are many advantages to this. Mostly they are ex-students of mine. These keen and literate young helpers can scribe or type every word, idea, phrase and metaphor produced by a group, no matter how fast the brainstorm fizzes; they occasionally contribute lovely ideas to the brainstorm and even add the odd interesting word to the brainstorm sheets as they go. If you struggle to find assistants, you might be able to ask a nearby college to lend you a fast-typing teaching student, or persuade a parent governor or late teenage relation to help. They must be able to spell well and be fast at thinking and typing, or able to scribe quickly and clearly.

I much prefer if my helpers type everything on a laptop or net-book computer because, that way, we can instantly print off all the group's words and ideas for the students to draw from while writing. Type is readable by everyone, can have more words to a page yet still be spacious and clear, and avoids having the challenge of multiply photocopying many handwritten sheets, some of which may be creased and have faint, water-blurred writing on them.

One important thing we have learned repeatedly is to keep a memory stick in the computer during typing and save both to that and the computer as continuously as possible. We learned this the hard way when one education centre's laptops turned out to be programmed to wipe everything new when switched off, and when a hard drive died on us in the middle of a session!

Back-up typing or scribing

With almost any age group, even when students are self-scribing, I prefer to have a helper type as we go because it means that slower writers don't have to worry they are getting behind as we will have a full record to copy from for those who might need all or part of it. This is especially useful when brainstorming for collective work because the words and ideas can later be displayed through a digital projector as we are writing together.

Having an adult type or scribe for a group is especially useful in wintry conditions because then all students need to do is think and share ideas and language, so the brainstorm moves further faster, and fingers can stay warm in gloves instead of clutching pencils and clipboards, which reduces circulation and makes them even colder.

One handy innovation has been to carry a small folding 'fisherman's stool' with us so that the typist can type quickly on his or her lap. Another is to carry a pair of warm fingerless gloves for the typist in winter (preferably the sort with a finger cover flap), and yet another is, on wet days, to carry a lightweight plastic sheet or 'mini tarpaulin' to drape over the seated typist like a loose tent during rain showers. It may look odd to passers-by but it keeps both typist and computer warm and dry!

For the reasons already discussed, if you run out-of-classroom brainstorming sessions on a regular basis, it might be best to use 'backed-up self-scribing' on some occasions and arrange to have a helper type for the group on others.

Why not type or scribe yourself while you lead?

The simple answer is that, for a brainstorming session to function well you need focused involvement with your group, and typing or scribing yourself makes this difficult. You must be in a position to view and think about the environment and possible language deriving from it in depth, to decide how best to lead and when, and how to adjust the direction of your questioning. You must also, of course, be sharply aware of your students' ideas and words, who is answering well, who needs to be pulled into the action, general group focus, safety, etc.

It is challenging enough to keep a brainstorm fizzing successfully while doing all these things simultaneously. Concentrating on typing or scribing as well makes this harder and will reduce the depth and originality of ideas and language, dull the dynamism of being an inspiring leader, and slow the workshop's pace below the optimum.

Those rare occasions when I do scribe while leading are when I am working with small groups of 5- to 7-year-olds, because I can keep up with their simpler ideas, language and slower pace of thinking, while also working out what my next questions may be. Even then, this only occurs on the odd occasion when a school has been unable to supply a scriber to assist me.

Pre-visit inputs

If you are going on a substantial out-of-classroom visit you will, of course, need to explain something about its aims and processes to the group, and possibly to parents. Depending on the setting or venue, you may wish to feed the group some factual data about the location, such as relevant history or background. This can save time at the site (sensible in inclement weather) and prepare the students mentally for the occasion.

On the other hand, it may be worth saving some of this input until the group are on location if you think it will help set the atmosphere better or if you are worried about pre-preparing them so much it takes away some of the visit's feeling of spontaneity and 'shock of the new'.

Depending on the location, you may want to explain in an enthusiastic way how you are all going to work; the special quality and 'treat' of being on location, hunting for ideas and language in a 'real' setting; how the process is designed to model the way professional writers research and think; and how you want wholehearted participation and teamwork from your students in the brainstorming sessions in order to find more original words and reach deeper levels of thinking.

The checklists that follow may seem a little fussy but are simply there to make things easier for you. You can copy them, then score out anything irrelevant for that occasion. If, for example, you decide to pop out into the school grounds to brainstorm some background or additional poetry or story ideas with a group for an hour on a mild, sunny day, you might not need to worry about the clothing suggestions or making new risk assessments.

Checklist for brainstorming sessions within school sites:

- ☐ Risk assessment if required

- ☐ First aid kit if site is large

- ☐ List of any required clothing and equipment (in advance) for students to bring

- ☐ Assistant to type or scribe if required

- ☐ Clipboard for each student and

- ☐ Plenty of plain A4 paper (about 4–9 sheets each depending on age, ability and duration of session) plus plenty of spare, and

- ☐ Sharp pencils (or stubby pencils if using clipboard cover-bags) and spares *or*

- ☐ One or two portable computers, fully charged in advance (*or* one computer plus spare battery) for group typist

- ☐ Memory stick for typist

- ☐ Small folding stool or chair for typist *or*

- ☐ Clipboard and lots of A4 plain paper for group scriber

- ☐ Clear, larger-than-clipboard sized freezer bags to cover boards, paper, hand and pencil in the likelihood of rain or snow

- ☐ Multiple layers of very warm and waterproof clothing for participants *or*

- ☐ Sun cream, sunhats, spare jumper in summer

- ☐ Cushions or plastic bags if available (optional)

Checklist for brainstorming visits to offsite locations:

- ☐ Risk assessment (in advance)
- ☐ Transport arrangements in advance (if required)
- ☐ Arrangements with venues or sites in advance (if required)
- ☐ Permission letter from parents
- ☐ List of required clothing and equipment (in advance) for students to bring
- ☐ Assistant to type or scribe (if required)
- ☐ Adult helpers for safety and 'crowd control' (check minimum adult–child ratios for the age group)
- ☐ First aid kit
- ☐ Fluorescent safety vests or jackets for adults (and possibly for some or all students), especially if walking on narrow or busy roads
- ☐ Mobile phones, fully charged
- ☐ Inhalers or medicines as required
- ☐ Snacks or packed lunches (if required)
- ☐ Filled water bottles (if required)
- ☐ Clipboard for each student unless an adult is scribing on their behalf
- ☐ Plenty of plain A4 paper (about 6–12 sheets each depending on age, ability and duration of session) plus plenty of spare
- ☐ Sharp pencils (or stubby pencils if using clipboard cover-bags) and spares *or*
- ☐ Two portable computers (laptop, net-book, etc.), fully charged in advance, *or* one plus spare battery, for group typist
- ☐ Memory stick for typist
- ☐ Small folding stool for typist (optional) and possibly plastic sheet to protect typist and computer in rain *or*
- ☐ Clipboard, pencil, cover-bag and lots of A4 plain paper for group scriber
- ☐ Clear food bags, each large enough to loosely cover a clipboard, paper, hand and pencil in the likelihood of rain or snow
- ☐ Multiple layers of very warm and waterproof clothing for all participants
- ☐ Suitable footwear such as walking boots or wellington boots if moving around on damp or rough ground
- ☐ Rucksacks if necessary
- ☐ Sun cream, sunhats, spare jumper, spare water in summer
- ☐ Foam, cushions, jackets or plastic bags to sit on (optional)
- ☐ Games or distractions if taking breaks on location (optional)
- ☐ Large torch and individual torches if working or walking in the dark
- ☐ Specific safety equipment (e.g. rucksack with map, compass, head-torch, survival bag, group shelter, throw-line for deep water) and possibly relevant leadership training if leading groups onto hills, along exposed coasts, etc.
- ☐ Briefing to students on safety, risks, boundaries, being involved, etc.

 © 2014, Write Out of the Classroom, Colin Macfarlane, Routledge

CHAPTER 4

Leading a descriptive poetry brainstorm session

Aims and fundamentals

Two ingredients are fundamental to leading a successful poetry brainstorming session outside the classroom. The first is an ability to guide your students into closely observing, questioning and interestingly describing everything relevant around them. The second is to lead with demonstrative enthusiasm!

If you are slightly apprehensive about doing this well, please don't be. Most literate and communicative people with a reasonably wide vocabulary can lead a basic session in this way for children even though it is a skill that can be developed. As a teacher, you already have many of the required skills, such as the ability to communicate, hold focus and be alert to the needs and involvement levels of your group.

On top of these skills, however, accomplished poetry brainstorm leaders will have developed a sense of how a poet or other strong creative writer observes and questions the world around them and its reflections within themselves. Leaders should strive to achieve new levels of 'thoughtful observation' of the environment so that they can sense how to generate and encourage this 'poetic heightened awareness' in their students.

The process seems simple, but doing it well involves a fairly complex blend of looking, sensing, feeling, questioning, thinking and describing. As a creative language facilitator you will want to encourage your students to challenge their easy perceptions of the world, and to learn to test, change and evolve the language that flows from this increasingly detailed and imaginative awareness.

For a writer it is not enough simply to see the world in interesting and sometimes novel ways, it is also essential to describe these observations and discoveries in ways that are interesting, uncommon and original, otherwise clichéd language will make them stale. It is impossible to separate the nature of the description from the nature of the described. Like all good writers, your students must learn 'to make the everyday special' in order to show it afresh to their readers. After all, that's what poets do . . . pass on their own 'heightened awareness' to readers by creating a sort of multimedia experience (through language, sound patterns, emotions, intellect, visual and other sensory descriptions) of happenings, people, places, relationships, experiences and unique moments.

Leading and listening

A descriptive poetry brainstorming session is a dynamic event. The quality of the words, ideas and metaphors 'discovered' by a group is, to a great extent, dependent on the quality of the leader's own observational, questioning and descriptive skills, as well as on the strength and quality of feedback from participants. An able leader will, of course, acknowledge and praise individuals' verbal suggestions but they will also learn to sense when to ask students to continue varying or building on a particular idea, when to widen discussion to related areas of language, metaphor or concept, and when to move the group on to looking at new things.

The process is a 'positive feedback loop', with the leader supplying the direction and keeping the creative energy flowing. When well executed it entails classic inspirational teaching and learning. Given a little skill and practice, an enthusiastic group and an inspirational setting, the experience can be enormously enlivening for all concerned. When a creative brainstorming session is running particularly well on location, leaders and students often share a palpable sense of being 'in the zone', perhaps an English teacher's equivalent to the way a professional athlete feels when everything flows perfectly, creating winning results.

Photo 4.1 'Poetry brainstorm in a walled garden'

Through a location-based poetry brainstorm we aim to:

- Guide students to observe the world in more detailed, thoughtful and interesting ways, including through multisensory information gathering.
- Allow participants to discover or rediscover that fresh, interesting and convincing writing depends on well-observed, interesting and convincing descriptions of the world and experiences in it.
- Show young writers that originality in the choice and description of 'authenticating details' ('reality effects') can wake up a reader's creative imagination and emotions, and allow the synthesised worlds of poems or stories to appear more vivid, engaging, believable and real.
- Broaden students' vocabularies and increase their enthusiasm to learn new words.
- Encourage participants to create and develop fresh metaphors, similes and potent descriptions in a situation where they can actually see, hear, feel and smell the things they are describing. This is important and inspiring for all participants and often especially valuable for types of learners who may not achieve their potential in a classroom setting.
- Use the 'vital presence' of the setting to encourage students to experiment with refining and extending metaphors based on aspects of it.
- Demonstrate the precision and strength of vibrant verbs by searching out the most accurate to describe subtle movement, actual happenings, etc.
- Help young writers escape from the clichés (of ideas, conceptual models, descriptions and metaphors) that teaching creative writing in the sensory vacuum of the classroom tends to reinforce.
- Introduce awareness of, and experimentation with, powerful but largely unnoticed 'sound echoes' in language.
- Allow participants to experiment with adjusting fragments of language 'found on location' so that these start to fall into poetic rhythmic patterns.
- Model how to follow through and deepen ideas and language.
- Encourage students to start taking on the questioning and thoughtful observation processes personally and show them how location work can teach them that, even when writing while remote from a physical setting they are describing, they can still use similar processes to find more original 'authenticating details' from within their own memories and imaginations.
- Celebrate together the enchantment of language and the 'thrill of the hunt' while seeking out more precise descriptions and more evocative metaphors.

'Thoughtful observation' models natural literacy learning

What I call 'thoughtful observation' techniques employed in locational brain-storming sessions can be thought of as intensified forms of processes that occur naturally within literate and communicative families and, to an extent, in creative schools. The fundamentals of looking, questioning, sharing, discussing, varying, improving, testing and learning are similar in both cases.

Perhaps the main differences are that, in a collective brainstorming situation, the practice is usually more intensive, more coherently planned and led, always includes the goal of widening and improving language use, and is usually targeted towards the final purpose of writing to a specific or general form.

In some ways the process is similar to scientific observation in that participants attempt to 'name' (describe accurately) and make sense of aspects of the world around us. In this, however, there is often not a 'right' answer, unlike in science or maths, but only *better* ideas and words. These can take the form of the most 'accurate' words, phrases or metaphors to describe something, but can also be the most original, or most 'musically', aesthetically or emotionally pleasing. Writing deals with all aspects of being human in a more encompassing and 'human' way than science. It seeks, for instance, not only to observe and describe emotions and images but also to recreate these in its readers.

Building on the natural process

Some sort of thoughtful observation process is essential to the development of language and literacy. We are only aware of our worlds through our senses working in conjunction with our brains, yet this awareness is hugely coloured or dimmed by familiarity, culture, conceptual models, clichés, lack of really looking, lack of thinking, and lack of time to do these.

Children who read deeply and often mostly reach higher literacy standards and consequently gain superior scholastic achievement compared to those who don't. Similarly, children whose parents and peers habitually involve them in observing and questioning all aspects of the world (from the physical and aesthetic to the social, emotional and intellectual) also grow wider vocabularies and reach higher levels in literacy and academic achievement. These two learning routes are of course strongly linked.

As teachers, even though we do as much as we can to develop students' reading and involve them in constructive discussion, we often can't make them desire to read keenly and intelligently in their own time. Nor can we be with them in the world outside school to ensure they share communication with relatives and friends in the way that those in aspiringly literate families will do.

Through their richness and intensity, location-based brainstorming techniques can, if employed relatively regularly, be a way of partially levelling the playing field for many children as well as being an excellent tool for inspiring the more literate to higher levels of challenge and achievement.

I often describe a well-run observational brainstorm as a 'cream on top' exercise. The richest material rises to the surface from individuals within the group, enabling everyone to know it, share it, consider it and perhaps use it. First, the more accurate, original and pleasing ideas, words and metaphors are discovered and praised. They are discussed, refined, written down, then later read and re-read, constructed into poems or stories and, later again, may also be read out and heard in presentations. In this way, not only does interesting, more powerful and more nuanced language keep rising to the top and become progressively more embedded in young minds, but effective usage of the *process* itself is repeatedly modelled and reinforced.

Working up your own ideas in advance

If, like most teachers, you are new to running locational brainstorming sessions like this, it can be a good idea to practice a little thoughtful observation at any relatively evocative location or at the site itself. You can, of course, do this yourself but it is usually more effective and enjoyable to share the process with family, friends or colleagues because this creates a partial group 'fizz', will produce more varied ideas and language than you can on your own and, if you lead the process you will get a better feel for the real thing.

Although not essential, if you can manage to brainstorm a little in advance like this at the planned location you should have more starter ideas and additional productive directions in which to lead your group's questioning on the day. The only slight drawback is that conditions may be different when you take the group there, so some of the descriptions and metaphors you've already thought of won't apply.

It is also important for leaders not to allow ideas already in their heads to prevent them from taking in, and leading the development of, other ideas supplied by the group. Obviously participants must feel valued and involved – otherwise, interesting, off-the-wall ideas and language will dry up.

Starting a session

First essentials

Before you begin to lead thoughtful questioning you need to ensure everyone is as comfortable as possible, sitting or standing within easy hearing and 'focusing' distance, and aiming in the right general direction, which is probably facing you and the interesting part of the sub-location behind you.

Students, if they are writing the words down themselves, or assistants who are scribing for them, should be asked to use only one side of each sheet and to write down mostly key and descriptive words or occasional short phrases, scattering these widely apart on each sheet so that there is plenty of white space showing between them. This is creatively helpful because, while students are writing their poems later, new words, metaphors and ideas will lift off the pages unconsciously and blend more richly and less predictably with words and ideas already in their heads.

Participants may need to be reassured at this point that they will be able to write and answer at the same time and that they mustn't worry about neatness, getting spellings correct or missing out words at this stage, especially if you have a back-up scriber.

If it looks like it is going to rain, you can hand out large, clear plastic food bags that are quite a bit bigger than clipboards, then demonstrate how to pull them over the top of the boards so that participants can keep the paper dry but still put their hands and pencils inside them. At this point I always remind younger groups of the suffocating hazard of placing bags over faces.

Some younger students hold clipboards in a way that makes it tiring and difficult to write, so it's a good idea to show them how to grip the boards with their non-writing hands so that they rest comfortably upon that wrist and forearm.

Introducing the session

This brings us to the question of how to prologue a session. For observational brainstorming to function especially well, a leader has to be enthusiastic and inspiring, and participants need to feel involved and 'competitive in a co-operative way'.

Students should be made to feel they are contributing to a team effort and valued for this, but they must also feel inspired and 'safe' to take risks in order to find fresh concepts and words. For these reasons I like to set an informal and positive tone which makes students feel less nervous about taking chances with ideas.

As this is a creative exercise, with few right or wrong answers, you need them to feel confident to put forward ideas that they may not be entirely sure about to begin with. After all, some of the most original ideas in poetry can seem ephemeral or odd to start with and would be disregarded by many before they were thought out properly. Poets learn to be sensitised to catch and consider these because sometimes they constitute the formings of ideas or metaphors which are most treasured.

That is why one of the first things I do is to explain some basic reasons for the way we are working, and try to make everyone feel comfortable about participating, and part of a team. I might explain that, through nothing but words, writers have to create realistic or invented worlds inside readers' heads, or recreate aspects of the real world or happenings they have personally experienced.

On some occasions I ask participants if they have ever read a book which made them feel that at times they were almost more in the world of the book than in the actual world. I might discuss how amazing it is that, through only a few scribbled marks on a piece of paper based on patterns of sounds from the mouth, readers anywhere can be transported to more or less the same 'world' (or at least a similar one) that was in the writer's mind or imagination.

Illustrating the purposes of the session

Sometimes I talk about how a reader will only feel truly wrapped up in that synthesised 'dream world' if the writer can make it both interesting and vivid enough to trigger the reader's imagination strongly. I might ask younger groups what kinds of words can have that effect and, inevitably, some will say descriptive or describing words. This might lead to the following question:

Imagine you have had the same wallpaper or the same poster on your bedroom wall for many years. You would hardly even notice it most of the time. However, if the wallpaper or the poster has just been changed and you walk into your room after school looking for a lost pen, what's the first thing you will notice in the room?

Inevitably voices in the group will call out "the new wallpaper or poster". I then explain that, to me, that new wallpaper or poster is like a fresh and interesting description or a surprising metaphor:

A boring or clichéd description you've heard many times is like wallpaper or a too-familiar poster you've had for years. A reader hardly sees it in his mind.

Just as the new poster seems to scream 'I'm new and exciting . . . look at me!', fresh and interesting descriptions or surprising and well-fitting metaphors awaken the reader's own interest and imagination. They cause readers to be creative in their heads and form more vivid pictures. And these pictures also have feelings attached.

Escaping from limiting mental models

If there is enough time available I may discuss how we see the world through 'models' in our minds. We hardly need to think about walking along a pavement because our brains have modelled everyday walking so we do it largely unconsciously, mostly while thinking about other things, until we encounter something slightly unusual, such as having to step over a fallen tree, or pause at the edge of a road.

Some models are passed down to us or absorbed from our cultural viewpoint. For instance, when we are toddlers drawing our first pictures we are usually handed the brown crayon to colour the trunks of trees, and the blue one to colour in a river. Except for trees such as pines and redwoods, most tree bark is actually grey, mottled, or even sometimes green-tinged, and rivers are commonly grey, brown or dark, greenish or khaki, or whatever colour they reflect, but they are seldom blue except when all they reflect is blue sky.

To show how strongly these concepts affect our views of things I sometimes tell groups about the intelligent fifteen-year-old boy who, while group brainstorming about a metre in front of an ancient willow tree, kept insisting the bark was brown. Others in the group suddenly realised it wasn't and called out 'no it isn't, it's actually grey!' The boy still argued that it was brown and the group started laughing. I noticed the poor lad jolt as if he had just switched on a new pair of eyes, and then he muttered in an embarrassed way: 'I mean, yes, of course it's grey!'

The point is that he had clearly 'seen' the bark as brown until he was forced to start looking afresh, uncoloured by the default models of tree trunks he had in his head. We all see the world through models and concepts but, although they make life easier and more efficient for our conscious brains, they are also the writer's enemy because they can lead to clichéd descriptions.

Explaining the need for 'reality details'

I often explain to students that the sorts of descriptions which tend to come into most people's heads first are those they have known for a long time, have heard or read several times before, or have encountered recently, so a writer has to learn to look and think hard to find fresher descriptions and sometimes less obvious aspects to describe. I might continue by saying something like this:

> That's why we have come to this special place: so that we can observe what is actually here, try to escape from those boring descriptions we already all know, discover new details to describe, and find fresh and accurate ways to paint pictures in the reader's head.
>
> Writers sometimes call these 'authenticating details' or 'reality effects' because they make a scene in a reader's imagination more vivid, more interesting, more exciting, more 'authentic' . . . more 'real'. These details can be of places, things, characters, happenings, action. As writers we use what we need of these depending on what we are writing. All good writers do this, both in poetry and in stories.

Selecting reality details

If there is enough time and the students are old enough to utilise the information, I normally try to emphasise the importance of quality over quantity in the use of description. We have all read stories in school, sometimes written by quite able students, where the reader has to wade through sleep-inducing amounts of mediocre description before anything interesting gets under way. I sometimes mention this (diplomatically) to a brainstorming group and expand on it in something like the following words:

One can also over-describe, though, and bore a reader senseless, especially in a story where too much unimportant description can hold back action for too long. The trick is to select details carefully, choosing some which really evoke the place, thing, character, action or situation, and then describe those details interestingly and creatively. Write that a tramp 'was all dirty and ragged, and sat on the pavement at the side of a busy road begging' and few, if any, will be particularly fascinated or form anything more than a vague visual image of him.

See if you think your reader would visualise a stronger image of him and feel more involved if you wrote this about the tramp instead: 'A catastrophe of tattered tweed, baler twine and shredded polythene bags, he lounged on the mud at the edge of a vast puddle, picking his nose with the rounded end of a broken plastic spoon, twisting it slowly and carefully as if it were a bizarre form of meditation'.

Okay, the second one is a bit longer and contains more detail, but the observations and descriptions of the tramp's clothing, his surroundings and his actions are much more unusual and curious, yet potentially fitting for an eccentric tramp. Despite being more unusual, they make him more real, more believable and more interesting. We all know tramps might sit on the ground, but isn't the verb 'lounged' more interesting than 'sat'? It seems to tell us something about his mood or attitude as well as showing us that he was on the ground.

Many of the other words in the second version also form slightly uncommon ways of describing the situation and the character that should hopefully awaken a reader's lazy imagination, such as 'on the mud at the edge of a vast puddle', 'a catastrophe of . . .' and that list of evocative 'authenticating details' which make up this 'catastrophe': '. . . tattered tweed, baler twine and shredded polythene bags' . . . not to mention the oddly distinctive description of how he picked his nose!

Similarly, isn't what the tramp is doing in that second version much more attention-grabbing and image-creating than simply 'begging' as he was in the first? To beg is an obvious 'base verb' for a tramp. It's what we expect. However, even if we need to make him beg for some reason in the story plot, perhaps we might put it something like this:

'The man-creature unexpectedly raised his dishevelled head and fixed me with pallid, watery eyes. Extending a calloused palm, his furrowed face broke into a desolate smile that seemed to mirror years of deep despair'.

Or perhaps even more curiously like this: 'the untamed human rolled slightly into the puddle, seemingly unaware of the filthy water seeping into his bound-up mess of clothing. He looked up sharply, almost as if recognising me, then barked in a gravelly voice: 'Give me some money now if you want to survive another month!'

The difference between the first version and the more interesting ones that followed is that the first one is basically just **telling** us about the tramp and his situation, but the others are **showing** us those things . . . and hopefully also intriguing us so we want to read more. Learning to 'show' mostly, rather than 'tell', is essential in writing poetry.

Stories mainly need to be mostly 'show' as well, only using 'tell' sections to take the reader quickly through less dramatic or less interesting happenings, connecting scenes, or to mention things we need to know but that aren't happening to those characters at that time. Strong story writers may use 'tell' to fill in necessary but duller parts of the plot in fewer words, or to mention some relevant background history to the story without producing too many pages. In effect, many authors mostly use dry 'tell' to link the juicier bits of 'show'.

The funny thing is that through learning to look at the real world in fresh ways as we are doing in this brainstorm session, and through discovering interesting or new descriptions for those things we see, we can also begin to be better at finding and describing interesting details inside our own imaginations and from our own memories, even while we are sitting writing in a room away from the sort of setting we are describing. After all, those short pieces about the tramp were written in a small room with the curtains closed, and with no roads or beggars in sight.

Discuss 'show not tell' early in a session

It is helpful to discuss and illustrate this concept of 'show not tell' in the early part of a poetry brainstorming session, then build on this in various ways through the rest of it. Taking on board not only the basic show not tell concept but the realisation that there can frequently be better quality 'show' is an essential of good poetry and also, of course, a fundamental of success in 'thoughtful observation'.

Giving students some illustrations, such as the lines about the tramp, helps model the concept and sets high expectations at an early stage. This unvaryingly drives participants towards looking and thinking harder and producing superior responses, as long as the leader also remembers the essential three P's of 'pace, patience and praise' throughout the session.

Working towards enhanced ideas and language

With all groups, and especially when dealing with younger or less able students, I am happy for participants to give reasonably accurate but still fairly predictable descriptions in the early stages of the brainstorm, even though I'm secretly waiting for them to start finding fabulous, 'jewels in the crown' ideas and metaphors.

Often a group must cover some relatively mundane language and ideas first in order to be guided towards bringing to light more exciting words and richer phrases. Sharing a number of moderately interesting words can start the 'fizz', gets the group off to a confident start, can help increase everyone's base vocabulary, will trigger more thoughtful directions and supply basic 'scaffolding' language on which to hang more exotic material.

I am always honest about this and tell participants at the start that we are searching for really exciting new observations, descriptions, metaphors, similes and vibrant verbs, but no-one should worry if some of the first words that come to mind are fairly basic. I might say something like "it's normal that our brains need to build a platform to work from if they are going to reach to higher language ideas. What matters is that everyone enjoys joining in, tries their best and doesn't worry that their ideas might not be exactly right, because there is no right and wrong in creative writing ideas . . . only better."

Guiding the brainstorming session

First questions

Obviously many questions you ask will depend on the location chosen, the age and ability of the group, and the ultimate writing form, but I find the best way to begin is usually with something general, such as describing the sky, the type of day or the weather. This often produces a flow of words which, to start with, may be a little basic and only loosely related to the topic, but the practice builds patience and, most importantly, starts a slide towards a kind of overriding mood for that situation, scene, day or place. Discovering 'mood' can quickly edge the brainstorm into more interesting ideas and language territory.

I might, for instance, spend quite a little while getting students to describe the sky because it's helpful to look at something apparently easy to begin with in order to show how difficult it is to be exact (and original). I'll need everyone to realise eventually that, although I appreciate all contributions, nod and smile, often ask questions based on the answers I receive and get excited by interesting answers, I also keep asking more questions to lead them into more detailed, different and interesting ways of looking at a particular aspect.

Students soon discover that I'm cheerfully dogged about hunting for better, fresher, more accurate, apt or evocative words, metaphors or fragments of language to describe each aspect we look at. On a descriptive poetry brainstorm I will also add questions aimed at making participants more aware of the magical effects of sound patterns and 'sound echoes' in the language. Searching for 'echoing' words can also be a surprisingly effective way of triggering new descriptive words and helping build more evocative phrases.

An example beginning

Starting a 'thoughtful observation' session with a group on a cloudy, greyish day at the seaside, the first answer to my question about describing the sky might obviously be 'grey'. The imaginary sky I have chosen here is complicated because there is cloud of different thickness all over it, it is moving very slowly across and within itself, has light and dark variations, and several small wispy parts hang in front of the background cloud, some light grey and some very dark.

A questioning sequence might go like this (My questions are in italics, students' possible answers follow, sometimes in abbreviated form):

Okay, is the grey stuff clouds or cloud?

Cloud because it's all over.

Yes. *Some people have said 'grey' but what kind of grey is it?*

Dark. Dull. Pale. Dark and pale in places.

Discovering appropriate words with sound repetitions

'Dark' and 'dull' have similar letter sounds at the beginning; what's that effect called when they are placed near each other?

Alliteration.

Yes, that's right. Can you give me some more 'd' alliterations for the sky today? For instance 'dark and . . .?'

Dark and dingy. Dark and dismal . . .

And some others, not using 'dark'?

Dull and dreary. A drab, dingy, dismal day.

Oh good, we're really getting a 'mood' into the ideas now! Any more?

A dull and desolate sky. A drab and dreary day. A dismal, disappointing day.

Bringing mood and emotion into description takes it to a deeper, more interesting level. Seeking alliteration pairs can help kick start this.

Good. People said 'grey' to start with, so can you use alliterations with 'g' words to trigger new word combinations that fit the setting?

Grey and grizzly. Gloomy grey. Grey and glum. Grim and grey.

Any new 'g' combinations without the word 'grey'?

Glum, gappy cloud. Grungy, ghostly cloud.

Improving accuracy

These are very good. 'Gappy' is interesting and I like 'ghostly' but I'm not sure the cloud is all ghostly. Which parts might fit that description best?

The wispy bits.

So, can you describe that idea of ghostliness but only for those parts?

Grey ghosts float overhead.

Hmm . . . good, but there's just one potential drawback because, if I were a reader, who of course hadn't been here at the time, I might think this was going to be a horror poem and that there were real ghosts flying around!

Making a metaphor 'available'

Avoiding this problem is what I call giving the reader 'a door into the metaphor'. When young writers create their own metaphors they often forget to give the reader a clue to what they are relating them to in the 'real', non-metaphorical world. It can be better when a reader has to work a little at understanding a metaphorical or figurative connection because that can give them a greater sense of personal ownership of and connection with the work, which can seem to add more depth to it. However, it's hopeless if the reader is misled and forms a totally wrong idea of what the writer is describing!

Forgetting to give readers even a pointer to the subject of the metaphor is a common oversight when more able students are trying to build depth and 'riddle quality' into their poetry. I always try to cover this potential pitfall in brainstorm sessions for appropriate groups and usually mention my 'giving the reader a door into the metaphor' term as a memory tool.

Improving metaphorical precision

By changing the words around can we somehow explain or give a clue to what these 'ghosts' actually are?

Ghosts of cloud. Grey ghosts of clouds. Cloud ghosts.

These are excellent and less confusing than 'grey ghosts float overhead' although it sounds like they might be the ghostly remains of real clouds. Is that what you want? Also, perhaps we need to show they are small and wispy?

They might actually be the ghosts of bigger clouds. Or perhaps we could say 'ghostly wisps of cloud'? Or 'wispy ghosts of cloud'? Ghost wisps of cloud. Frail ghosts of cloud.

Yes, those solve the problem, and I like that last one, it is unusual and has a poetic quality about it. Now, can you add some more words so as to describe what they do and maybe where they are in relation to other things?

Ghost wisps of cloud ... move against a glum, grey sky.

Finding more precise and 'vibrant' verbs

Okay, but I'll bet we can find a more interesting verb (or 'doing word') than 'move'? 'Move' is what I call a 'base verb', a verb that does the minimum. For instance, all rivers run or flow, but sometimes they might trickle, rush, gallop, glide, meander, chatter or dance. Birds fly but some might also flutter, hover, dive, slice the sky, skim a hillside, surf the wind or tremble on the breeze. Do these more closely observed verbs make clearer and more vivid pictures in your imaginations?

Murmurs of agreement.

Reinforcing 'show not tell'

Using more precise or vibrant verbs is a part of 'show not tell', which, as you'll remember, means that, to paint vivid images in a reader's head, we need to create a strong or clear picture of an aspect of a place, thing or happening, rather than just tell the reader about it. For instance, saying 'it's a nice day at the seaside' is weak description. 'Nice' is a painfully vague adjective. It's overused, a bit non-committal, and as unnoticeable as that wallpaper you've lived with for too long because it doesn't trigger creative excitement in the reader's imagination.

However, writing 'it's a beautiful day' isn't much better. Well, it's a teensy bit better, because it's a little more precise in that it means you are talking about the weather, whereas 'nice' might also mean that the subject in the poem was having a relatively good time. 'Beautiful' is a little more emphatic and has more attractive associations, but it still doesn't show why it's a beautiful day, it just tells that.

*It will have a much stronger effect on readers' imaginations and emotions if we **show** them why it's a beautiful day. For instance, something like:*

'Glittering ripples skip over polished pebbles
where tiny toddlers squeal with joy . . .'

By showing how lovely the day is, does that make a more vivid and emotional impact on your imagination than just being told 'it's a nice day'?

Nods of agreement.

Searching for better 'show'

*What poets are mostly looking for is a fresh and more precise 'show'. And that's why they love 'vibrant', precise verbs. Like the verb 'skip' in the line I just said. That verb has appropriate movement but also echoes the mood of playful happiness of the children, making the day seem more beautiful. It helps **show** readers that.*

Can you find a more interesting verb for those lines we had: 'Ghost wisps of cloud / move against a glum, grey sky'?

Float. Drift. Glide . . . except the last one might seem a bit fast because they're hardly moving.

Excellent words for these. Are any of these also suitable for 'ghosts' or can we find even more appropriate or spooky verbs that still have that slow-moving quality?

'Float' is not bad, or 'drift'. How about 'creep'? Hang. Haunt.

Triggering greater complexity in descriptive fragments

I decide this might be a suitable moment to model some longer phrases using the language fragments they've found so far. The forward slash is to indicate a pause that would fall on a natural caesura or a line break if these were fragments of a poem. Pausing in those places is a way of helping familiarise the students with poetic rhythm patterns because they are often only conscious of the mostly random patterns of prose.

> *Wow, these are even better! So now we might build a line or two like 'frail ghosts of cloud / float across a glum, grey sky',*
>
> *or 'ghost wisps of cloud / haunt a dim and desolate sky'*
>
> *Who likes those lines?*
>
> (Nods of approval)
>
> *Can you think of any other words for ghosts?*
>
> Phantoms. Gremlins. Spirits.
>
> *Okay, which of these are best suited to the wispy clouds?*
>
> Phantoms. And maybe spirits.
>
> *Let's play around with either of these. How about*
>
> *'Cloud wisps drift like misty phantoms'? Can you vary that or use 'spirits' instead?*
>
> Wispy phantoms of cloud.
>
> *Yes, and can you keep the line going and say what they do?*
>
> Wispy phantoms of cloud / haunt a grey and gloomy sky.
>
> *Brilliant! Some more?*

Helping to develop complex descriptions

I might help the students build a few more of these sorts of phrases verbally and even start off other beginnings with words already found, or with a few new ones. Once they have a start to a line I sometimes persuade them to swing their arms softly in time with their beginnings as they think out the next part. This helps continue the rhythmic flow as they build the rest, and they are beginning to feel a sense of making poetry while hardly thinking about it.

> Wispy spirits of cloud / possess a dim and dreary sky.
>
> Will o' the wisp clouds / drift across the gloomy grey.
>
> Ghostly wisps of cloud / hang in a lifeless sky .
>
> *Wow again! Lots of lovely sound echoes in these too! Who thinks the ideas and words are getting better and more interesting than the first ones we found?*
>
> All hands rise.

Broadening observation to another aspect

Let's look at the background cloud. Is the overall cloudiness regular or irregular?

Patchy

Any other words for that?

Irregular. Messy. Blotchy.

Yes, I see what you mean. Any others?

Stained. Mottled.

Oh, these are super words!

It's quite scrappy. It's untidy. Yes, and the messy cloud has those little raggedy, wispy bits we were talking about, sort of hanging from it.

Widening and working up metaphorical ideas

I feel this is a good time to start introducing more metaphorical elements to the brainstorming process. It's always handy to ask what something might be made of, or remind them of, if it's not the same physical material as the subject.

What does that background cloud remind you of? Let's make some metaphors for it. Can you think of something resembling it which isn't cloud or ghosts?

Torn paper. Torn dirty paper. Smudged and crumpled paper. Scruffy fabric. Tatty tie-dye. It's like sponging with paint. A grey-sponged sky.

Great! Any more?

Over-worked water colour. Painted in tones of grey. A blotchy watercolour. Dull stone. Grey marble. Raggedy clothes. Dirty rags.

Super! Try putting some of these words together in different ways

The sky's ragged clothes.

Yes! Any more?

A sky of gloomy marble. Cloud like murky marble.

A blotchy painting in shades of grey.

Really great . . . and with lots of 'ay' sounds there! Any more?

Scruffy rags of cloud.

That sounds interesting, but wouldn't readers think there are only little bits of cloud but no general cloud? Can you make it sound like both, perhaps by building a longer phrase?

Torn fragments . . . trail from dirty grey cloud.

Great, but do you need to say grey if you've said 'dirty'? Doesn't 'dirty' suggest grey rather than white?

Torn fragments hang from dirty cloud.

Extending metaphors

I decide to push the boat out and work a little on extending the students' metaphors. I help as necessary by restarting phrases or reminding them of words they could use to help complete lines.

If we are using the word 'ragged' it sounds like tatty material, so . . . can we build some long lines by extending the metaphor so it's all to do with tattered fabric or something like that?

Tatty fragments hang / from torn and tattered cloud.

Ragged little scraps dangle / from dirty, tattered cloud.

Wonderful! Not long ago you found the lovely phrase 'the sky's ragged clothes'. There's a mood in that description. Decide on the mood and see if you can you add a word or words to contribute to that mood.

The sad sky's ragged clothes.

The sky's ragged clothes of cloud / are dismal and grey

We can also try changing the words a little. Let's start with 'the gloomy sky . . .'

The gloomy sky / wears tattered clothes of cloud today.

The gloomy sky is sad with cloud.

Encouraging students to take on the questioning process

These are excellent, well done!

To find a new description for something it's sometimes a good idea to ask the question 'why might it be like this?' If, for instance, the sky was a person, what would have made it 'sad'?

It's lonely. It's lost. Someone or something was horrible to it.

Okay, now you can start trying to develop slightly more detailed questions yourselves. Try the 'five w's and h'. . . who, where, what, why, when and how. Come on, let's have some possible questions!

Why is it lonely? Why is it lost? Who does it miss? What horrible thing happened to it? Where has it been that made it sad?

Good! Now try and find any answers to those questions that also fit the look, mood and state of the sky!

The sky is sad, it has lost its friend, the sun.

The sky has lost itself in cloudy thoughts.

You could maybe tighten that line to make it even more effective:

'The sky is lost in cloudy thoughts'.

Any more?

The sky is sad because the sea is too ... or the other way around.

The sky is beaten and bruised.

By what?

The sky is beaten and bruised by cloud.

The sad sky is bruised by cloud.

What sort of colour or tone are bruises? Where do you get bruises if you are hit repeatedly? Use these sorts of questions to try and find ways to alter and improve your lines.

Dark cloud has bruised the face of the sky.

The solemn sky is bruised by cloud.

If the cloud is horrible, think what its character might be then add that to the line.

Selfish cloud ... has bruised the skin of the sky.

The sky is bullied and bruised by jealous cloud.

Mean cloud has beaten up the sky.

*Great! Now you're getting the idea of asking different questions to trigger interesting and unusual language ideas. And you've managed to drop 'sound echoes' into all of them too . . .' **sk**in of the **sk**y', '**b**ullied and **b**ruised', and '**mean**' and '**bea**ten'. Well done!*

Let's go back to those lovely metaphor ideas we had about the sky being like dirty fabric with ragged bits on it. What were they?

I, my scriber, or the students read out some of the words and phrases we had before.

Can you build longer lines using these fabric metaphor ideas? I'll give you a minute or two to write some longer versions down on your clipboards and then we'll pick a few. Perhaps you could think about what might have made them dirty or tattered.

I might help a little, but I want the students to take on as much as they can for their age and ability.

Wispy bits trail, / torn from the tattered fabric of cloud.

Tangled threads of cloud hang, / tatty scraps on the tattered clothes of sky.

Oil-stained rags of cloud / hang from the filthy fabric of sky.

Absolutely fantastic! Any more?

Ragged remnants dangle / from a filthy blanket of cloud

Who thinks these are really good? (lots of hands go up)

Increasing awareness of sounds within and between words

*Which **sound** better together, 'torn fragments' or 'ragged fragments'?*

Ragged fragments

I agree. Can you say why it sounds slightly better?

Because ragged is a better word.

Yes, I suppose it might be. It seems a little more specific and it certainly sounds more raggedy than 'torn'. After all, it has two syllables and having two makes it sound more raggedy than one. Ra-gged. Torn.

(I check to see they are with me, then move on to explain and expand upon this.)

Lot of interesting effects are caused by the sounds of words, the sounds of certain words acting together, and even sounds within words. For instance, 'sl' often sounds slippy . . . slip, slide, slither . . . but which of these words 'slip', 'slide', 'slither' show something moving in a straight line and which show a more zigzag movement?

Slither sounds more zigzaggy

Yes. That's because it has two syllables.

I demonstrate going from side to side with my hand in time with the syllables 'sli – ther'.

Similarly, 'walk' sounds relatively straight compared to 'wander' which seems to 'wan-der' about more. It's to do with the sounds and rhythms within each word. 'Wo-bble' seems to wobble, like a jelly-ish movement, partly because of its two syllables. 'Ob' sounds seem heavy or 'fat' and the '. . . ble' ending is rather like the way a wobble can jiggle uncertainly to a stop. Also, compare the made up words 'ib' and 'ob'. Can you see which one sounds fatter, heavier, possibly slower?

(Nods of understanding.) Yes, 'ob' sounds heavier.

You're right. Also, to think about some other word sounds, 'stomp' is quite sudden and sounds a bit like the noise of each foot hitting the ground, in a determined or grumpy way. English is full of wonderful onomatopoeias in words, not just the obvious ones like 'moo' or 'hiss'. 'The horses were swishing their tails', for example. 'Swish' is like the soft sound of their tails of long, fine hair sweeping through the air. 'S' is a wet sound or a hissy sound, 'sh' softens that tone, so 'whoosh', 'rush', are soft and sound like what they represent.

'Whisper' seems like the soft, hissy noise of secret talking and has two syllables so it's more continuous, just like whispering is. 'Whisp' wouldn't do as well for people whispering, it stops on the 'sp' so it's not continuous.

The real word 'wisp' sounds fine and small, like a wisp of cloud or a wisp of hair, so 'whisper' covers small, fine sounds that continue. There are subtle and complex effects

*caused by the sounds of language, so, when you are writing, as well as thinking about
how accurate the meaning of your word choice is, it's a good idea to test the sounds of
a word or phrase to decide which feels right for that subject. This is especially true of
poetry where all sorts of sounds and sound patterns can be part of the underlying
structure and feel of the work.*

I always take an opportunity to expand the students' awareness of sounds and
sound echoes in poetic language. How detailed this is will depend on the age of
the group and the time available. When I talk about letter sounds to them I use
the actual sound of the letter, letters or syllable as it is heard in those words. For
example, the 'i' as in 'lid' as opposed to the 'I' as in 'eye' or 'mine', or the 'a' as in
'fragment' as opposed to the hard sound of the letter 'A' in 'day'.

Introducing assonance and consonance

*By the way, there's a sound that repeats in that phrase 'ragged fragments'. Can you tell
what it is?*

It's the 'A' sound.

*Yes, although I call it the 'ah' sound here. Poets think about letter sounds the way they
are actually heard.*

*It's called assonance when words have the same vowel sound echoing in them. Like
'driving quietly', 'softly washing', 'gloomy yews' or 'ticking swiftly'.*

I ask them to identify the pairs of assonance in each.

*The vowel sounds don't have to be spelt exactly the same way, just sound the same, or
similar, as in 'gloomy yews', 'I spy' or 'first and trust'.*

*By the way, there's another letter sound echoing in 'ragged fragments'. Can you hear
it? Ragg-ed frag-ments.*

It's the 'gi . . .' sound.

*You're right. And when consonant letters (all letters of the alphabet except vowels)
echo somewhere in the words it's called 'consonance' such as 'silly' and 'fall', or 'the
slow motion of a summer hammock'. What causes that effect here?*

The 'm' sounds.

*Yes, the consonance is caused by the repeating 'm' sounds. And, out of interest, you'll
notice another letter sound repeating in that phrase. Can you hear it?*

It's the 'oh' sound in 'slow' and 'motion'.

*That's right, it's an assonance on the 'oh' sounds. Although, motion is a bit general, so
'the slow sway of a summer hammock' might be better 'show'. It's still got the 'mm'*

sound twice but, although it loses the echo of the 'oh' sounds in 'slow' and 'motion', it has gained an 's' sound three times in 'slow', 'sway' and 'summer', and I think you might feel that the new line seems to 'sway' more as it swings from 'slow' to 'sway'. I demonstrate by softly swinging my arm in time as I say the line again.

We've discovered that, together, those words 'ragged fragments' have an assonance (the 'ah' sounds) and also a consonance (the 'gi' sounds), which together form a sort of inner rhyme 'ag'. If the words actually stopped on the 'ag' sound they would be actual rhymes, as in 'rag' and 'bag'. Rhyme is when the later parts of words echo and it is rather like the opposite of alliteration where the first letter sounds echo.

*And now, to sort of take us back where we started, you've probably realised that when consonance appears at the beginning of words it's a special sort of consonance called alliteration, as in 'a **f**eather **f**loats **f**ree' or 'the **s**low **s**huffle of **t**owering **t**rees'.*

You can have full or partial alliteration too. 'Slip' alliterates fully with 'slide', but only partially with 'side'. That's because alliteration is heard on the first consonant or group of consonants in the word.

*Another special case of consonance is called 'sibilance'. That's when the repeating consonant sound is an 's' sound, as in 'a **s**nake **s**lither**s** acro**ss** the wi**s**py gra**ss**'. The word 'sibilance' itself has a sibilance in it, and one of the 's' sounds there is actually created by the letters 'ce'. So it just shows that it's the sounds, not really the spellings that make it work.*

Developing an ear for varied 'sound echoes'

Fairly early on in a poetic brainstorming session I like to tell students that I call these repeating identical or similar letter (or letter group) sounds 'sound echoes'. I explain that they are common in poetry and their inclusion can make a relatively ordinary line seem more magical.

Talking about this, modelling examples and flagging up instances that appear throughout the brainstorm can be a surprisingly effective way of helping students begin to hear more 'musicality' in language. For youngsters who are trying to write poetry that actually sounds like poetry, learning to use sound echoes well can be an important part of the process, along with learning about rhythm, where to break lines, and how to control rhymes if used.

Given enough modelling of sound echoes early on, leaders will normally find that, as the brainstorm progresses, many students will start building phrases and lines which, almost automatically, include assonance, consonance, alliteration, sibilance, and imperfect or 'slant' rhymes within their structure. More able students will quickly start to vary word choice and order to bring these effects into play.

Lines seem much more evocative, apt or powerful with several of these sound echo effects woven through them. However, care must be taken to prevent irritating or ludicrous overuse of one particular type of sound echo, such as alliteration, so it can be worth modelling good and bad usages of this. Just as with bad control of rhyme, younger and weaker students who have discovered alliteration have a tendency to place too many identical alliteration repetitions close to each other, sometimes creating nonsensical writing.

> *Where repeating letter sounds, or similar sounds occur relatively near each to other in a line I call them 'sound echoes'. These could be alliteration, assonance, consonance, 'not-quite-rhyme', and so on.*
>
> *Do you remember those little lines I made up to explain how to 'show' readers it's a beautiful day, rather than tell them? Can you find some 'sound echoes' in those?*
>
> *'Glittering ripples skip onto polished pebbles*
>
> *where tiny toddlers squeal with joy . . .'*

Students will slowly unravel the various sound echoes woven into a piece like this, usually hearing the alliterations first, then any assonance, then either slant rhyme or consonance. I have marked the various 'echoes' here:

> 'Glittering ripples skip over polished pebbles
>
> where tiny toddlers squeal with joy ...'

There is also an internal 'slant rhyme' building from 'glit . . .' to 'rip . . . to skip'. The sequence builds to drop onto the final p of skip, which in turn makes the following alliteration on the p's in that line even stronger. You may notice all the sound echoes land on the stressed parts of words (on every one of the nine stressed syllables in this case). There's also an echo between 'ripples' and 'pebbles', partly because 'p' and 'b' make similar sounds, being formed in a similar way by releasing small bursts of air through the lips.

> *If you write a line of descriptive poetry in two different ways, one with sounds echoes and one without, listeners will prefer the line with the echoes in it, even if the rhythm and meaning are nearly identical and the words just as strong. For instance, which sounds slightly better, 'gleaming ripples' or 'glittering ripples'?*
>
> Glittering ripples.
>
> *Yes, because of the 'i' echo. And which sounds better here: 'I listened to the nervous words of the breeze' or 'I listened to the worried words of the wind'?*
>
> '... the worried words of the wind' because of the 'w' sounds.
>
> *The interesting thing is that people usually think a line which has sound echoes in it is better because it has stronger words or meaning. They are mostly unaware of the sound echoes and the fact that they can make lines more powerful, pleasing and magical.*

Sound echoes are effective if used carefully, but the pleasure of that effect can be overturned by employing the same sound echo too many times. For instance, placing the same alliteration sounds in close proximity more than about three times can become a little irritating for the reader.

Do all these suggestions seem a lot to cope with?

By now you may be feeling slightly sidetracked and flustered by all these ideas and information that I attempt to put into the early parts of a session, but remember it's not essential to force it all into your first brainstorming session and you probably don't want to try and shoehorn it all in as quickly as in my illustration.

However, it is important to become progressively more aware of sound patterns and echoes in language because that helps in creating effective poetry. You will find that students get enthused by finding sound echoes themselves, and the hunt for them will also lead them towards uncovering new language and more original connections.

You may also be thinking that, in this illustration 'beginning for a poetry brainstorm', we have so far only managed to discuss the clouds yet there are a million other things at the seaside still to look at! There are two reasons for this. The first is that I want to illustrate to teachers as many of these 'poetry brainstorm leaders' pointers' as possible within a relatively short example. They will, of course, be used and reinforced throughout the rest of the session, in a recapping session back at school and in future creative writing work.

The second reason is that, if I feel a group is capable of processing it all, I try as soon as possible to give students as much familiarity as I can with sound echoes and building original and complex descriptions without them losing focus. Some of this can be done in class beforehand but, given acceptable weather conditions, enough time and a stimulating location, most groups enjoy these aspects, take them on board quickly, and improve their language, observations, confidence and enjoyment through using them.

Expectation is crucial

I believe intensely in cheerfully setting the highest possible expectations for each group early in the process because I know from my experience of running many thousands of such sessions that it will bring the best results.

To put it simply, exceptional quality results follow from:

- a high level of enthusiasm and expectation from the leader and assistants;
- skill and inspiration in guiding the session;
- brainstorming an interesting and 'language rich' location;
- the insertion of relevant, high quality information inputs;

- keeping the session fast-paced and highly interactive;
- ensuring a tight, focused and self-disciplined group;
- boosting confidence of all and building a joyous 'winning team spirit';
- staying relatively comfortable no matter what the weather is like.

Coincidentally, while writing this, I have just received a phone call from the head teacher of a school where I ran intensive location-based poetry sessions in the previous academic year for all their 11-year-olds. He told me that staff had been amazed at the quality of language those classes had produced during and following my visits and he was calling to ask if I would take on a writing 'residency' in which I would work with all the classes, teachers and LSEs in his school because he would like me to raise the entire school's expectations of what is possible in language and writing. He asked that the entire process begin with intensive brainstorming and writing workshops for all the teachers and assistants a few weeks before working with their classes. "Make the staff 'writers'" he said, "then you can show them how to make writers of the children."

This is an excellent school with wonderful staff dedication, students who read regularly and are part of aspiring families, and a happy, productive atmosphere. However, although his students read relatively well and regularly, they had been 'coasting' in English because language expectation was lower than it might be, something I had noted at the time and which had since been underlined by a government inspection.

This is a type of call I receive periodically from head teachers and heads of English, and I mention it here to help illustrate that, as I said in a previous chapter, in order to lift literacy standards beyond a certain level, reading and access to books isn't enough on its own. It is necessary to draw from, and build on, the examples of naturally questioning, literate and creative families who produce questioning, literate and original young writers. Location based writing, combined with the highest possible language expectation, is one of the most effective ways of doing this that I know.

Moving the brainstorm on to other aspects

At what moment a leader should move a group's attention to another aspect of a location is hard to define precisely because it varies with each place, the age, ability and focus of the group, what occurs in the location, and so on. Each decision must be taken at the time.

You may sense that ideas are running out on one area of a subject, that group members are losing focus as they want to move on to something new, or there might be an occurrence such as a spectacular sunset suddenly bleeding dramatically over the sea, a dolphin leaping across the scene, a black stallion galloping through the shallows or an eccentric old person wandering past picking up pebbles, that causes you or your students to realise that it is too interesting and 'poetic' a moment to miss. Like a professional poet, no leader should ignore such moments as they may create the stirrings of a particularly powerful poem.

You will also need to achieve a balance between: (1) covering the very wide variety of observations and inspirations required for the construction of rich and varied individual poems and, (2), exercises based around one aspect (as in my examples on clouds) which demonstrate to students how to dig much deeper in observing, questioning, describing originally and employing pleasing or effective sound patterns.

Choosing and treating aspects

Questioning well involves much more than simply saying 'describe those rocks over there'. It may be a perfectly effective question but, to create deeper thinking, you will also need to find more subtle questions to ask based both on your own ideas and on the language and ideas that students produce. You will have noticed in my illustration brainstorm beginning that I purposefully introduced many different types of questions about the clouds.

To boost the confidence of weaker or more reticent students in the group, leaders should start with basic description questions, such as those suggested in the first point on the list mentioned below, but progressively use a variety of other types of question in whatever sequences seem most effective and logical at the time.

For a detailed list of the types of questions that will help you lead groups during brainstorming sessions, please read the photocopiable pages at the end of this chapter entitled: Questioning pointers for poetic brainstorming on location.

Further notes on questioning

Hunting for increasing accuracy drives language improvement

Asking a group to seek out a range of alternative words and phrases for things in the environment can increase each individual's available vocabulary. Most participants will learn new words and many words will move into their 'user dictionaries'. One advantage of guiding this process in the 'real' world is that the subject matter is almost infinitely varied. Another is that the students can all engage with the vital challenge of finding the most accurate word, phrase, simile or metaphor because everyone present is observing the same, often subtle aspect of something. A great many of these observed aspects would not be thought of in the classroom, might appear in some new way during the out-of-classroom session, or are things which participants have not noticed or noted in the past.

Becoming deeply involved in this essential process of automatically searching for ever greater precision in language helps young minds become more disciplined and determined and, if the process is reinforced by similar location and classroom work, it will significantly and permanently improve the quality of students' language and writing.

Adding to this the elements of observing the world 'through an artist's eye' and the creation and extension of original similes and metaphors produces a potent combination of diligence and creativity in language and thought. There are numerous teachers and parents of children who have worked with me on location who agree with me on this.

Adult contributions to the brainstorm

Sometimes leading also involves teaching participants the correct name or term for something, such as the name of a wild flower, animal, material, fashion, artefact, craft or procedure. It might require a mention of common usage names or technical terms for things such as 'keys' for bunches of ash tree seeds, or terms such as 'reeling in' for a fly fisherman or 'spring tides' at the coast, local words such as 'rhynes' (in Somerset, UK, pronounced 'reens') for drainage channels, or relevant historical or military terminology.

There is no brainstorming rule which says that the leader or other assistants can't introduce personal knowledge or put forward their own ideas for words or metaphors. How this is done is what matters. It's crucial that participants should be given a clear head start in order to build their confidence until all are participating thanks to the excitement of the hunt and the leader's gentle coaxing where necessary. Even once all students are contributing, it is best if helpers or others present wait to give their contributions until the group appears to have almost exhausted the possibilities on any particular aspect observed.

It's valuable that participants can see everyone present is enthusiastic about the hunt for ideas and words, but essential that their confidence is not dented. It should also become obvious early on that they need to try as hard as possible to find better ideas and language themselves! A session works most effectively if students build up a good rapport with the leader and the leader is left to lead. He or she must be the hub of the whole process and it is detrimental to the depth of focus if adults or students discuss ideas between themselves while the leader is trying to concentrate eyes and minds on something while attempting to guide participants towards a particular goal.

Questioning through the senses

Language that involves the non-visual senses is particularly redolent. Poets and strongly descriptive authors depict through more than just the visual so as to produce a higher order of 'reality effect' for the reader. Our vision may involve a massive amount of the sense processing parts of our brains, but mentioning a particular smell, sound or taste can take us back through time. You only need to think of the smell of damp uniforms or wet trainers on the school bus, the taste of a sweet peach on a hot day, the sound of screeching tyres followed by the sickening smash of metal and glass, or the mixed scents of fresh coffee, croissants and perfume wafting from a foreign street café to see what I mean.

If there is a non-visual side to specific aspects on location I ask the group to try and describe it effectively. This is often not as easy as describing something visual because we don't seem to have anything like as many words for non-visual stimuli compared to visual. Participants may need to move on to forming metaphors or similes to trap the description in an original way.

Describing smells can be problematic too because our noses quickly become immune to them, so it can be best to brainstorm those as soon as you arrive at a new sub-location, before they fade from awareness.

Listening thoughtfully

Sounds need to be separated and considered before a group can find accurate or interesting descriptions for them. Switching off the visual part of the brain helps participants hear and separate sounds, so I ask my students to close their eyes and listen carefully for at least a minute. I suggest they choose a maximum of two sounds they can hear and don't simply name them when I ask, but describe each in two or more words. I do this because otherwise they forget to describe and simply say the sound, such as 'a dog is barking'.

We are looking for more than that. 'A dog is barking in the distance' would be a little better but 'a distant dog's bark echoes among the trunks' would be better, and 'a dog's sharp bark reverberates like gunshots off the canyon walls' would, of course, be even more exciting.

In a sonic equivalent to those internal models of 'brown' tree trunks are certain default descriptions that children always seem to come up with, even though they are patently incorrect at the time. The wind, for instance is often apparently 'whistling' or 'howling', although it rarely does either, except around building corners and through narrow spaces such as badly sealed doors or windows … or in clichéd, scary stories! It might however be 'breathing softly as a sleeping baby', 'whispering mischievously' or, on a very windy day, 'rumbling on eardrums' or 'roaring like a jet engine over the treetops'.

Some words are 'hybrids' in that they suggest being aware of what they refer to through more than one sense. I've already mentioned how 'sli-ther' is more zig-zaggy than 'slide' because of the swing between the two syllables (as is the case in 'zigzag' itself, of course) but there are often aspects to the sound of a word which makes it more specific than young people first think. For instance, they might refer to a car 'roaring past' on a rainy day when it's actually 'swishing', 'hissing' or even 'whishing past' on wet tar. Children say that a bird flying quickly is 'zooming' across the sky, but I would point out that a 'zoom' sound seems more like an engine, of a speeding, medium-sized motorbike, for example. A fat bumblebee might 'zoom' across a lawn in its hurry to reach the flowerbed however.

A jet plane could 'slice the sky' with its vapour trail, but leading well here might cause bright sparks to declare that it is 'ripping the fabric of the sky', 'splitting the pale blue silk of sky' or 'tearing across a tracing paper sky' because its noise might be similar to tearing paper or thin fabric. As a side note, each of the sky descriptions will vary according to the day, so, for instance, the tracing paper one would be a whiter, hazier one than the 'blue silk' sky. It is for leaders to try and guide groups towards these sorts of discoveries without giving answers themselves until other good answers have come in.

You may have noticed that thinking about descriptions for specific sounds can generate metaphor ideas and vice versa. It is useful to ask if participants can find metaphors or similes that fit non-visual stimuli or include non-visual elements as well as the visual; for example: 'the passing train unwound its tail of sound', or 'insatiable wavelets lick the broken shore', where you can almost hear the sound of licking both in the metaphor and in the sound echoes within the words.

Describing something's 'character' unearths further rich language

As in the previous two examples, personifying or giving an animal's character to a non-animal thing can be a useful way to throw up fresh metaphors and words. For instance, if a group was brainstorming a weir or waterfall on a river, after they had searched for descriptive words I might ask them what animal it reminds them of most. This could produce answers such as: deer, leopard, lion, dolphin, eel, frog. If you think about each one carefully, you should be able to get a feel for the types of fall in each case. A lion might represent a very loud and aggressive fall, a deer, a thin and sprightly leap of water, a dolphin for water bounding smoothly over a weir, an eel for a dark and wriggly rapid, a frog for a sequence of tiny falls that 'hop' downhill. You can then ask students to search for verbs or other words that relate to both the animal and that fall, and suddenly you will find they are not only coming up with fresh words but also with more metaphorical ideas.

You can change to asking what character or mood the fall, or part of the fall has (e.g. aggressive, angry, chaotic, mad, ravenous, rampaging, suicidal, foolhardy, blissful, playful, scatter-brained, joyful, mischievous) or what material parts of it might be made of that isn't water (ice, steel, glass, diamonds, fizzing beer, party streamers, shimmering silver, billowing silk, champagne bubbles, Guinness, foamy espresso coffee) then extend some of these until you get something like 'the weir's teeming streams sway and swing / like a glass bead curtain's jiggling strings'. Locational brainstorms have produced all those descriptions (and a vast number I've forgotten) from students aged between ten and adult.

Gender as part of 'character'

Despite the risk of being accused of political incorrectness by someone, I will mention that discussing gender and age as parts of the character of something can also be useful ways of throwing up new language or extended metaphors. For example, if I ask whether a young weeping willow is masculine or feminine, I always get the answer 'feminine'; whereas, if I ask the same question of an ancient oak tree, I always receive the opposite answer.

When students reply that the willow is feminine I will then ask them to give me words which suit something feminine as well as that particular tree (e.g. elegant, slender, supple, swaying gracefully, youthful grace). I might then ask what kind of feminine person it reminds them of (girl, dancer, gymnast, nervous girl) and whether any part of her person or clothing fits it best (dangling hair, swinging tresses, a fine green gown, a flouncy dress of leaves, wearing a leafy veil, etc.) before possibly connecting some of the basics of these ideas together on their clipboards if they are old enough. I might then ask what 'she' is doing beside the lake (trailing her hair in the water, tickling the water's smooth skin, lightly dancing upon the bank).

The oak will inevitably 'stand strong and proud', have 'muscular limbs', 'rough and wrinkled skin', be a 'king of trees on his velvet throne of grass', 'stare with a serious furrowed face', but what can be more challenging is to ask the same question of an old weeping willow tree. Some might initially describe it as masculine but most would say feminine, and soon the majority would probably decide it is like an old woman so, after further questioning, you might end up with 'a wrinkled old willow woman, stoops sadly on the bank', or similar, and you may even be able to lead some students into slowly building a couple of lines in extended metaphor such as 'the willow bends at the water's edge, an old washerwoman, scrubbing the stones with her windswept branches', or find another character appropriate to the metaphor, the location or its history.

Tightening descriptive phrases as they are put forward

Although that phrase about the washerwoman is fairly long, you'll notice it breaks naturally into poetic sounding parts where the commas are positioned, so all or some of these could be places where line breaks occur (i.e. where lines of a poem finish and start). In general, however, poetry is a tighter and more economic form of writing than prose, so having single words or shorter language fragments to work with from a brainstorm makes it easier for students to manipulate them to fit into the rhythmic flow of a poem in construction.

For this reason it is worth listening out for any descriptive phrases or fragments of lines suggested by students which can be tightened by removing redundancy, unnecessary articles or connectives, compressing the form of a verb, or shortening a fragment by turning it around and hyphenating it.

Leaders should be careful not to apply this tightening process too rigorously to lines with evident poetic rhythm in them, which students have carefully supplied, as rhythmic lines in the brainstorm can often trigger rhythmic flow in the poems they write. Teaching participants to sense and employ some form of rhythmic flow when writing is one of the most fundamental challenges in a poetry workshop for young people because most swim through life in a sea of prose at home and in school, so the vast majority of youngsters are unfamiliar with the sounds of poetry.

We certainly want to give participants confidence to extend descriptions and metaphors, and we need them to start sensing language order that sounds and feels poetic, so it's well worth asking them to extend some descriptions and metaphors, and to ask for and suggest ways of changing these longer fragments during, or after, the brainstorming session so they can see what sorts of things work and sound best.

In order to help participants move onto the writing stage with a collection of 'adaptable' descriptive building blocks which they can model into poetry containing meaning, feeling, sound echoes and rhythmic flow, it's important to ask students or scribers to record mostly key descriptive words, short phrases, metaphors or similes on the brainstorm collection sheets rather than less descriptive articles, connectives, pronouns, and so on.

Presenting 'found' raw data largely as longer phrases and sentences makes it harder for students to avoid writing prose instead of poetry because the prosaic sound of the material will carry on in their heads. It will also tempt them to be lazy and throw many ready-made, juicy-sounding chunks of language into their 'poem', which will then have no rhythmic integrity and of which they can claim little ownership. Even if students do not follow that lazy route, it is much harder to write tightly and 'poetically' when chunks of language need to be continuously deconstructed and re-formed into lines that fit the intrinsic sound patterning of the growing poem.

Let's take a line or two that a student might have built up for you in the brainstorm, or perhaps later while working on the poem: 'Lots of busy raindrops scurry quickly down the black, slanted slates of roofs'. First, 'lots of' is weak language. One could try exchanging 'lots of' for something like 'countless', which is more interesting and could be included, although the words 'raindrops' and 'scurry' seem to suggest there are lots of raindrops anyway.

There is redundancy here too, so 'quickly' is unnecessary if 'scurry' is left in, and the latter is a much better word. 'Slanted slates' strongly suggests roofs, so 'roofs' might be edited out as well. The definite article is frequently unnecessary and can be discarded here, as is usually the case in parts of most children's poetry drafts. Writing 'the' or sometimes 'a' all through a poem draft is another product of being brought up in a prose rich world.

As the raindrops are 'scurrying', it's redundant to say they are busy, so now the line might be: 'raindrops scurry down slanted slates' which contains the fundamentals of the description, is not diluted by redundant, weaker or unnecessary words, has strong sound echoes, is rhythmically more pleasing and can be fitted into the flow of a poem more easily with little or no alteration. It also allows readers to use their brains a tiny bit more in working out that the slanted slates are almost inevitably on roofs, making them feel slightly more actively involved in the poem. If people successfully spend effort on, or involve themselves in something they assume they like it more.

Looking at alternatives to the verb, students might come up with 'race' and then discover the sound echoes in other variations such as: 'raindrops race down slanted slates' or even 'raindrops race down slanted roofs'. The first one has more complex and pleasing sound echoes, and contains 'slanted slates' which suggests roofs. This is a type of sub-metaphor called synecdoche where an aspect of something stands for the whole thing. It is a useful figure of speech to explain to writing students, even if they are too young to remember its name.

You could become poetically playful with the language and ask students to try cutting even more words or parts of words, such as dropping the weakest word left ('down'), leaving 'raindrops scurry slanted slates'; or changing 'raindrops' to 'racedrops' to produce 'racedrops scurry down slanted slates'; or doing both: 'racedrops scurry slanted slates'.

Some effects of hyphenating

As it's a made up word, you might experiment by changing the first one in that last line to 'race-drops' but you will probably notice that it doesn't sound so suitably fast because the hyphen slightly slows the way it's read. If a writer wanted certain drops to 'feel' slower to the reader, he wouldn't put 'slowdrops' because that reads quickly. The hyphenated version 'slow-drops' is slower, but he would probably choose 'slow drops' as two separate words because the space between them causes an even bigger pause, slowing it further.

Used sparingly, hyphens can be helpful tightening aids in poetry and their use often throws up new-feeling combinations. If, for instance, a participant came up with a descriptive fragment such as 'dry leaves are spinning as they are dropping to the ground' you could ask the group to tighten it and you might get 'dry leaves spin as they drop to the ground' which is more pleasing because it doesn't involve the (double) use of the weak 'ing' syllable, and the unnecessary and weak 'they' has also been excised.

If you ask them to try tightening it further by using a hyphen they, or you, might come up with 'dry leaves drop-spin to ground' which is tighter, more original, has lost a 'dead' definite article, has an appropriately lilting rhythm and, in this case, also features a 'd' alliteration which highlights the most interesting syllables.

It is worth listening out during a session for fragments whose parts might be hyphenated by group members. For instance, someone might say 'the seagulls are bobbing where the waves are washing the rocks'. Simply removing one, two or all definite articles would be tighter and less irritatingly repetitive (e.g. 'seagulls are bobbing where waves are washing the rocks') but, through hyphenating, it could be further reduced to 'seagulls bob through wave-washed rocks', 'seagulls bob on wash-rock waves', or the even tighter 'gulls bob through wave-washed rock'. These are all more poetically interesting than the original line and, as an extra point of interest, the latter sounds slower than the previous two, which would suit a slower rate of bobbing.

Making up words

Playing and experimenting with language is essential both to poets and to students, who must become more creative and confident in their writing; which brings us to why it's good to encourage participants to attempt the creation of new words. The more aware a young writer is of the 'sound families' of words and parts of words, and the effects of sound patterning within and across words, the more sophisticated their writing will become, and especially their poetry. Trying to invent accurate and appropriate words for things helps aid this awareness.

Not all words exist, so poets make some up from time to time, just like we've done with 'racedrops'. Poets also do this because the 'shock of the new' of a previously un-encountered, but right-sounding word can cause an awakening 'reality effect'. I have included invented words in several of my own poems and three in one particular poem because I felt they worked better than any of the nearest equivalents. One referred to a tatty old pine plantation growing on a steep slope that I passed one summer evening. I described it as a 'tipple-tapple wood' and when I have read that small fragment to groups of students, many say that they see it as a wood with fairly straight trees but where quite a lot are leaning on each other. Some suggest that little patches of sunlight are scattered through it, and they are correct on both fronts. In fact, a following section: 'drunk on dusky bird-song / and its own garlicky peace' illustrates that their idea of the trees leaning drunkenly on each other is right.

In the same poem I wrote about 'the depths of a grously hedge' which most students visualise correctly as dark, tangled and thorny. That one made up word seems to cover several aspects at once, so I felt it was more evocative and economic than typical alternatives.

A group of 13- and 14-year-olds I worked with on a still night, near where a minute stream dropped erratically into a pool within a naturally hollowed out section of hillside, spent over ten minutes trying to describe the water's sound accurately. They tried all the usual things like 'dripping, dropping, spattering, splattering, etc., then decided to make something up that had the deeper 'awp' or 'awt' sound, but also had two, or even better, three syllables because the sound kept going, but in a slightly broken way. Eventually they worked their way to 'plot-tering water', which everyone agreed was a perfect description, even though the word isn't in the dictionary.

They had also created an effective sound echo with the 'awt' sounds in both words which made the most important aspect of the water's sound more prominent. You can imagine how they got there as some may have unconsciously sensed a sequence such as 'splitter ... splatter ... splotter' in which the tone is moving progressively deeper.

Accurately describing the sound of a particular church bell can be problematic too. If you say these possibilities all ending in 'ng' out loud you will start to hear marked differences: Ting! Ding! Dong! Bong! Clang! Dang! Tang! Clong! Blong! Plong! Plang! Blung! I've heard all these bell sounds at some time or another while working with groups in English churchyards! If your students start noticing differences as subtle as these, they are certainly beginning to observe closely and to become aware of the subtleties of sound in language.

Additional subtleties for more able groups

You may be puzzled about how to use the questioning ideas at the end of the photocopiable list covering synaesthetic words, oxymorons, 'split associations' and connections with random words, which are mostly too subtle to work on with younger or weaker groups who are still struggling to find more basic ideas and language. However, these are productive areas for creating original language combinations and I have used all of them successfully with more able groups, and even 'random word insertion' with relatively young groups.

The brains of people with synaesthesia overlap or switch incoming sensory information, so they might enjoy the 'taste' of large blue road signs they drive past, or 'hear' sparkles of sunlight as tiny tinkling sounds. It is sometimes said that we all have aspects of this, and trying to describe something through other senses can sometimes create a fresh and pleasing effect.

For instance, 'his words stank of rage' would be an effective synaesthetic phrase. If you wrote 'sunlit sparkles tinkle across the woodland lake' most people would understand. If you want it to seem more logical, you could alter the line to 'sunlit sparkles tinkle silently / across the woodland lake' and you still have an attractive idea. Ironically, you will also have added the logical impossibility of something making a noise silently, a figure of speech known as an oxymoron. 'The sweet pain of love' is an oxymoron, and that sort of idea could be transferred to describing a physical location with a phrase such as 'a sweet ache of lonely shore' suggesting a beautiful but desolate section of coastline.

'You could smell the green of the meadow's edge' appears synaesthetic but is perhaps more an association between the green colour of rank vegetation and an area of smell associated with those plants we might not know the names of. Hunting for associative words is another interesting way of finding fresh descriptions or building metaphorical ideas. Splitting and reconnecting these associations can create new cross-breeds of words and ideas.

For instance, a student might say that a particular full moon is round like a coin, someone else that it gleams like a new coin, others might think it is yellowish, the colour of banana, like candle wax, that it should have a witch flying across it, a wolf howling in front of it, that it looks cold, huge, and so on. None of these ideas on their own are particularly original or strong, but once group members have come up with a number of ideas, you can then ask them to take a key word from one and test it next to a key word from another until they find a combination they feel is interesting and plausible. They can change any words to similar ones of course.

Obviously a 'silver banana' or a 'banana coin' will fail to describe logically that, or any other full moon, but the group should find considerably more original and interesting fragments such as: 'a full, wolf-bay moon', 'a cool, witch-wax moon', 'a yellow, sliced banana moon', 'a huge, howling moon', 'a wolf-cool moon', 'a wide, icy, wizard's moon', and so on. Give your students the confidence to be brave and have a go!

Mixing in random words to trigger exciting new descriptions

The final suggestion in my questioning list is to call out random but interesting words and see if group members can find ways of applying these to anything at the brainstorming site. I usually only do this once the group has been answering well for a long time, or in a later session in class. Being an inspirational device, participants don't always have to apply the words in the exact form supplied, so 'skidding' could be used as 'skid', 'skids', 'skiddy', etc.

I carry several pages of relatively 'interesting' words which I previously extracted from dictionaries, thesauruses or my head. They are from all subject areas and comprise interesting verbs, adjectives, nouns, and sometimes abstract nouns. Very occasionally I place more than one word together to make a relatively ordinary word more interesting (such as 'flutter-moths' or 'smashed bones') or because they normally appear as two or three linked words, such as 'flotsam and jetsam' or 'vanishing point'. I have one version of the list for older students and another for younger students with slightly less unusual or challenging words in it.

By way of example, here are some words from a random section of one column: *mournful, drivel, scamper, baffled/baffling, seductive, jack-in-the box, heedless, cradle, balm, breakneck, bruising/bruises/bruised, wholesome, old trouper, flotsam and jetsam, sliver(s), shuffle, playmate/s, prey on, stutter, breathy, dilapidated.* If you try and mix any of these in with words or ideas which might emerge from that imaginary brainstorm session at a rain-battered bay, I think you will find that all of them can create interesting descriptions and sometimes new ideas or metaphors. I re-read through the list when I re-typed the fragment above and several strong ideas bounced into my head for each one of them.

Random mixing makes fresher connections

This is one of several surrealist-style techniques I employ on poetry sessions in an attempt to propel the brains of participants off the easy track of throwing out safe, mundane and often stale descriptions. Well-explained and well-employed, 'random words' stimuli usually impress students with how heavily we rely on undemanding word associations and descriptions we have heard or used often or recently (the 'availability effect' in psychology). With a little explanation, students may also begin to see how our brains can connect almost anything together in some way. The availability effect helps us make fast connections but it also tends to steer us into making common ones, producing clichéd ideas and language.

Throwing random words into the mix, and trying to link them with other things or words to which we had not initially thought of linking them, means that, if they do form some kind of logical connection, the resulting language fragment is often much fresher and triggers imaginations with a little 'shock of the new'. Ask your students to discount any obvious, very commonly used links, such as 'raging' with 'storm'.

I recall an occasion when 14–16-year-old students were asked to mix the word 'schizophrenic' into the context of a heavy rainstorm across a bay. Some examples produced were 'schizophrenic raindrops rebound from the ground' and 'schizophrenic ripples spin between stones'.

When asked to bring along some interesting random words to a workshop, one student chose to bring a short list of interesting words beginning with the letter 'e'. The unusual word 'enlaced' was mixed into the scene and the pretty lines 'ripples enlace a rocky spur' and 'a shore enlaced by foamy waves' came into being.

Picking two selections at random from my random words list I find 'heroic' and 'dark butterflies'. Mixing either into that heavy-rain-on-a-seaside-bay brainstorm we might come up with 'heroic seagulls battle the storm', 'a heroic beachcomber / bends against wind-driven rain', or 'dark butterflies of shadow / flutter in rain-pelted pools' (describing the shadows of raindrop-created ripples that waver across the bottoms of rock pools).

If you make your own list of random words, try to use ad hoc selections from it with your groups while avoiding any which obviously make everyday connections with the scene or are beyond the comprehension of your group. However, aspiration is important, so there is no reason why one or two of the words might not be known by most of the participants, as long as their meanings are clearly explained to them.

Photo 4.2 'Brainstorming military training on Dartmoor'

Questioning pointers for leading poetic brainstorming on location: 1

- **Find varied and interesting words** for an observed object, place, thing, setting, movement, happening, sound, observed character, human action, etc.

- Ask participants to describe these through **using different senses** as much as possible.

- Ask everyone to **close their eyes, to listen hard,** to choose two sounds they can hear then make accurate descriptions of those. 'Telling' the group each sound is not enough, they have to describe it as perfectly or interestingly as possible.

- Try **using 'sound echoes' to throw up new words and language fragments.** Start with alliteration but then add assonance, consonance and slant rhymes as well.

- Ask participants to describe in various ways **where something is or how it relates to its surroundings** (e.g. 'the full moon gleams through a short tunnel of cloud, tinting its innards with rainbow haze').

- Find **emotional or 'mood' words** for the subject or its context. (e.g. 'sad little wavelets struggle to shore', confused ripples trip each other up', or 'lanky, wind-blown grass / dances and whirls with crazy elation').

- Find words that suit **its 'character' or 'personality'** (e.g. 'dreamy sea', 'furious waves', patient cliffs').

- **Make similes** for what it looks like, for what it does or for how it seems in relation to other things present or not present.

- **Make similes for aspects** of it, such as 'grey as …', 'rough like …', 'soggy as …', lonely as …', 'empty as …', 'quiet as an abandoned playground', etc.

- **Make metaphors** for it, for what it does or does not do, for what happens or does not happen to it, or for how it relates to its context.

Questioning pointers for poetic brainstorming on location: 2

- Listen to all those answers and lead students to find ways of **extending the metaphors and similes or ways of adapting them to fit the subject more accurately.**

- Ask what **collective words** might apply to things observed or fit their metaphorical descriptions (e.g.: 'shoals of silvery ripples', 'a mad scrabble of ripples', 'gangs of seedy nettles lurk', 'scattered flocks of cloudlets').

- Try to describe things as if they were made of **appropriate different materials**, such as fabric, metal, stone, ash, water, blood, fire.

- Once there are enough single words on an aspect, ask contributors to **build on some descriptions.**

- Ask if there is anything they could **cut out of these descriptions** because it is unnecessary, weak or redundant.

- Try **hyphenating to reduce unnecessary words**.

- Ask if there are any words participants could change in these more complex descriptions in order to **make them more original, evocative or more 'musical'** through the inclusion of 'sound echoes'

- Ask them to describe **things as characters or characters as things, things as animals, or people as animals**, then work on ways of **extending those personifications and metaphors**.

- Enquire whether something seems masculine or feminine, then ask for **relevant 'masculine' or 'feminine' related words or phrases** which could also describe that thing, or aspects of it.

- Try asking for **age-related words** to describe things, for example 'rough-skinned oaks are grey with age' or 'newborn wildflowers, bright with life'.

- **Ask participants how something makes them feel or how they would feel if they were that thing.** For instance 'spirits lift on this windy hilltop' or, extended: 'on this wilderness hill / my spirit soars with the breeze-blown buzzards'.

- Ask participants to **invent words** which sound like the thing/sound/ movement,/... they are observing.

Questioning pointers for poetic brainstorming on location: 3

- **Imagine what might have occurred in the past** in that location or sub-location, using a sequence of questions such as 'describe what you might have heard at that time', 'what you might have seen', 'what you might have smelt', etc. Don't allow students to give only one or two word answers; they need to 'describe' each thing, then try to change it to be more original, try to make metaphors for it, add sound echoes, build on the idea, and so on.

- Ask what participants might observe here **in the future,** if you think it might be interesting or relevant.

- **Describe what is not there that you might expect at other times.** What you can't see, hear, smell, feel. For example, on a rainy day at the park, you or they might come up with something like 'sad swings hang their heads today / where happy toddlers often play'.

- Deliberately leave a key area or certain aspects of the location unquestioned, then **ask participants to take time and form their own questions** to ask the group about them. They can work up a few questions on their own clipboards before you allow some to put them to the group. This is one way of beginning to transfer thoughtful questioning over to each student themselves. To become strong writers they will need to take on responsibility for this process in their own heads.

- Try **synaesthetic descriptions.** This is best with older, more able groups but can sometimes produce spectacular results. Describe something through another sense (a 'loud shirt' is a classic one).

- Try to **find fitting oxymorons** (again with older, able groups). An example might be 'mice were making little noiseless noises in the hedgerow'.

- **Hunt for associations and 'split associations'** to create new word combinations.

- **Introduce interesting random words** and see if participants can fit them to aspects of the location.

CHAPTER 5

Possible pre-writing inputs on poetry's layouts, sounds, language, meaning and form

It is recommended that poetry workshop leaders read this chapter as some future chapters refer to its content.

Students enjoy uncovering secrets of rhythmic patterning and learning to control poetry effectively. Teachers must decide whether to share all or part of the material with particular groups, much of which can be delivered ahead of the writing session and then key items recapped.

Introduction to sounds and stresses

Acclimatising students to the sound of poetry

The most valuable thing teachers can do before poetry writing workshops is to give participants a sense of how poetry sounds and what makes it sound like that. We live in a language world that's brimming with prose and most young people's exposure to poetry is minimal, so many have difficulty making their writing *sound* like poetry without preparation.

It's important to read and show varied poems to students in the run up to a workshop and to ask individuals to read some out loud to themselves and to groups. This will help make the 'music of poetry' ring inside their heads.

Leaders should draw on age-suitable texts but add in more 'mature' poems too. The principal thing at this point is that students keep *hearing* poetry and don't only read it silently off the page.

Defining poetry and explaining the importance of sound

In order to write strong poems young people need to have a good sense of what poetry is. Despite anomalies caused by the relatively recent introduction of 'visual poetry', foreign styles such as haiku, etc., the fundamental difference between English poetry and prose has always been that poetry is much more obviously sound patterned. The simplest definition I can give young people is that 'it's probably poetry if it sounds like poetry'.

I explain that, although poetry is written down nowadays even if it's to be performed, it started being developed as a spoken art during the earliest stages of language. It was made and carried inside human heads long before people, or the majority of them, could read or write.

Evolving as a spoken 'sound art', it was embellished with sound patterning and 'sound effects' to make it attractive and mesmerising, to help listeners follow the meaning and form key images in their imaginations, and to help traditional performers remember not just the gist of the narrative, as in a prose story, but its precise sequence in words.

When students are asked what makes poetry *sound* like poetry they come up with 'it might rhyme' or 'it has a beat', and some may remember to mention 'sound echoes'. Occasionally a student will say that 'it sounds different because of the way it's written down', and what they are referring to is the layout of a poem on the page.

Exploring the relationship between the sound of a poem and its layout

How language sounds when broken up into lines on a page is central to writing poetry. This awareness is particularly important in 'free verse' because writers must continuously 'hear' and select from many line-breaking possibilities.

I explain that poets set their poetry on the page to reflect how they hear it so that readers will hear it that way too. To write poems successfully, students must realise that the layout of a poem partially controls its sound patterning through the use of different lengths of pauses.

Readers of any line of text hear small pauses, mostly where there are commas or full stops. At the end of each line their eyes disengage, tack left, drop down and re-engage, also creating a pause. A comma at the end of a line causes a slightly bigger pause, and a full stop creates an even longer one. Well-chosen 'line breaking' is a key part of the rhythmic structure of the poem.

I have encountered thousands of children who have been told that a comma must be placed at the end of every line of poetry. This is of course ridiculous because lines end with relevant commas, full stops, semi-colons, dashes and frequently no punctuation at all.

Blank spaces between verses, stanzas or sections also create pauses and these are slightly lengthened where increasing numbers of blank line spaces separate text.

Differing line lengths and layouts cause effects which slow or alter rhythmic flow. Returning one's eyes to the left margin from the end of a long line takes longer than from the end of a short line, creating a slightly longer pause. If an offset line starts immediately below or slightly to the right of the end of the line above, it causes a minutely briefer pause than if readers had to swing their eyes back to the left margin, and so on.

These outcomes are used to particular effect in free verse and semi-formal verse, which involve breaking and laying-down lines or parts of lines in varying positions on the page.

Identifying a key aspect of sound patterning

After reminding students of those things which make poetry *sound* like poetry (rhyme, rhythm, sound echoes, layout, etc.) I usually ask which of these is essential if the poem is still going to sound like poetry.

Someone usually replies correctly that it must have rhythm. Apart from those visual and introduced forms mentioned earlier, English poetry, including free verse, always has underlying rhythm.

Separating stressed from unstressed syllables

I invariably discuss stressed and unstressed beats in poetry if there's time. It's an important area for teachers and students to learn about if they are going to understand and compose it successfully.

One way to begin is by picking someone's two-syllable first name then asking which syllable is naturally stressed within that name. I explain beforehand that **a stressed syllable, or 'stressed beat'**

- stands out more and has more 'push' on it than on an unstressed syllable;

- makes one's voice pitch rise slightly on it when the word is said aloud;

- causes one's mouth to open wider on that syllable when the word is spoken.

Students should say how many syllables the name contains then decide silently which is stressed *when the name is said normally*. I speak the name once or twice, e.g. 'Co-lin', or 'Ju-lie', giving them time to think.

Asking them to close their eyes so as not to be affected by others, I invite those who think the stressed beat falls on the 'Co' part of the word to raise their hands. Next I ask the others to raise their hands if they think the stress lands on the 'lin' part of the word. Success ratios vary greatly at this point.

In most two-syllable English first names, the stressed beat lands on the first syllable, as in '**Co**-lin' or '**Ju**-lie'. A single syllable name such as **Kim** or **John** is always stressed.

The three-syllable name 'Re-**be**-cca' is an easy one to try next because the stress clearly falls on the second syllable. Longer names, as with any longer words, often have more than one stressed syllable, such as the two in '**Pol**-y-**ann**-a' or '**Hen**-ri-**e**-tta'.

It's not always immediately clear where stressed beats will fall on individual words in a line of poetry, however, because some naturally stressed beats may become unstressed and some unstressed ones become stressed within the greater rhythmic context.

Natural stresses can sometimes alter within a poetic line

For example, Elizabeth is normally E-**liz**-a-beth but the stress on part of it can change depending on the rhythm context into which it is dropped, so it would be the former in:

> *When E-liz-a-beth went for a walk in the park*
> *she returned to her house as the sky be-came dark*

but it would have two stresses in:

> *E-liz-a-beth was rather nice*
> *and brought me half a sack of rice*

Natural stresses commonly shift within lines of poetry where there are two or three unstressed syllables between the stressed ones.

Students will notice that the first version above (*when E-liz-a-beth went for a walk in the park*) has the busy (anapaestic) rhythm of 'ti-ti-**TUM**-ti-ti-**TUM**-ti-ti-**TUM**-ti-ti-**TUM**', with two unstressed beats between stressed ones, so the last syllable of the name stays unstressed to fit the pattern. The second version has a calmer (iambic) rhythm of 'ti-**TUM**-ti-**TUM**-ti-**TUM**-ti-**TUM**', so the final syllable of 'E**liz**a**beth**' has become stressed here to fit the surrounding pattern.

Students should be asked to place a flattened hand beneath their chins to feel their mouths widen on the stressed syllables, and reminded that these beats have 'raised pitch and push'.

It is essential *not* to clap hands to locate stressed beats. Teachers use hand clapping to help infants locate syllables but clapping tends to make them sound equally significant or make unstressed ones appear more stressed than those which are. For instance, anyone clapping my name 'Co-lin' as they say it slowly might be forgiven for thinking the 'lin' part was more stressed than the 'Co' part.

Putting this into practice

At this point it's useful to read a few lines of poetry from the whiteboard, initially choosing some with a relatively regular rhythm pattern. I ask participants to raise their hands when they think they know which the stressed syllables are. I frequently use a verse from a highly rhythmic children's poem of mine entitled *The train journey*. Here's how it begins:

"Is it going to be late?"
"No they're closing the gate!"
"The train now leaving from Platform Eight . . ."

Often the first stressed beat students identify is 'late' at the end of the first line, but there's also one before that on 'going'.

> The word 'going' has a diphthong where two vowels are semi-connected and so, within different lines, it can either have two syllables as in:
>
> When **go**-ing **down** the **road** one **day**
> I **saw** a **sway**-ing **load** of **hay**
>
> or one syllable in:
>
> if **folk** hesi**tate**
> they're **going** to be **late**

One by one, students identify all the stressed beats and I mark each one they find in red above the relevant syllables with a rising / mark. I then ask them to call out the unstressed beats and mark those with a red dot. There are many different marks used for signifying stressed or unstressed beats but I prefer a solidus for a stressed beat because that suggests its bolder 'push' and rising pitch and I use a dot for an unstressed beat to imply its lack of sonic strength, giving us:

```
  .  .   /   .  .   /
"Is it going to be late?"
  .   .    /   .   .   /
"No they're closing the gate!"
  .  /   .  /  .  .   /   .    /
"The train now leaving from Platform Eight. . ."
```

The fastest way to locate stressed beats in poetry

Many years ago I invented a way for students to locate stressed beats within poetry quickly and accurately. It also allows writers to check possible lines for rhythmic flow before committing to them.

The system, which has been adopted by many teachers and young poets, simply involves swinging one's writing arm in a horizontal figure of eight in time with the words.

To use this effectively, each person should make space between themselves and their neighbours in the group, particularly the person in front. This space should be more than the length of their arms; otherwise they make stiff, jerky movements if approaching others' personal space.

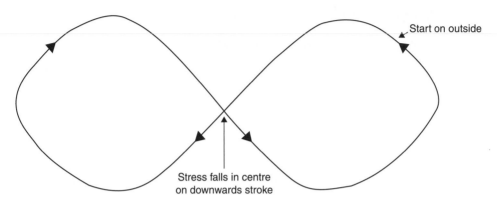

Diagram 5.1 Conducting for stressed beats

Participants should first practise *swinging their entire writing arms in a relaxed and fluid way, starting from the outer edge of the horizontal figure of eight and moving inwards and downwards across the centre.* They can begin on either side of the figure but never the middle, and should form wide, relaxed movements as if conducting an orchestra.

Next, ask them to hold their 'writing arms' up to one side, ready to 'conduct' as you read out the lines of the verse together. Holding your arm up and to the side for them to copy, count to three to start everyone simultaneously speaking and 'conducting' the lines.

Sometimes a participant begins too late or attempts to 'force' the rhythm awkwardly with a stiff arm rather than 'wafting' it fluidly and you might need to re-model the action.

Once everyone has it right, you can ask them what occurs whenever their hands swing down across the middle of the figure of eight. Often hands are already raised because some have realised their arms always cross the centre on a stressed beat.

Conducting properly gives true results

After minimal practice this 'conducting method' is fast and accurate, but participants must use the entire arm in a fluid movement to obtain a true result.

Unlike clapping, 'conducting' makes all stressed beats stand out clearly and allows for poetic variations in the number of unstressed beats between them, because these fall within the curved portions of the figure. If any students write a section of a poem in which the rhythm breaks down they will discover this through conducting because their arms will not keep wafting smoothly.

Discovering more about stressed beats

First identify the rhythm in a different extract

To demonstrate further aspects related to stressed beats, show participants the following extract:

> *The tiny stream comes tinkling down*
> *through rushes, reeds and boggy ground,*

and ask them first to read it aloud together while conducting to find the stressed beats.

They should identify them quickly as you run through it a second time and mark them in red.

Then invite them to call out the unstressed syllables and mark those too until it looks like this:

```
   .  /  .  /     .  /  .   /
The ti-ny stream comes tink-ling down
     .      /  .  /  .  /  .  /
 through rushes, reeds and boggy ground
```

They will clearly see that these lines have the regular iambic rhythm of

ti-**TUM** ti-**TUM** ti-**TUM** ti-**TUM**

Stressed beats and 'sound echoes'

Ask your students to find any 'sound echoes' in that text and then underline and link their discoveries in blue. You may need to remind them that sound echoes are not always made up of the same letters: what matters is the *sound* of them and *whether you can hear the effect* of the echo.

Students should discover alliterations on *tiny* and *tinkling*, and *rushes* and *reeds,* and the slightly slanted rhyme of *down* and *ground.* If you tell them there are more, some may also find the assonance between *stream* and *reeds,* and the consonance on *boggy* and *ground.*

If any students think there is also a 'th' alliteration between the definite article at the beginning and the word *through,* you can ask them if the 'th' part sounds the same in each case, which of course it doesn't as the first is a hard 'th' and the one on *through* is a soft 'thr' sound.

By now the text on your board will be plastered with red beat marking and blue linkages between similar sounding parts of words, so it's time to ask students if the sound echoes land on stressed or unstressed syllables. Most will notice that they always (or nearly always) land on the stressed syllables. In fact, sound echoes reinforce the stress on those syllables and, conversely, these sound echoes stand out more because they ride on stressed beats.

If a second or third occurrence of the same sound echo lands on an unstressed syllable it can make it sound stressed and confuse the rhythm pattern. Another reason why the somewhat different 'th' sounds at the beginning of each line don't seem to echo is because neither land on stressed beats.

Stressed beats mostly fall on 'the best bits'

When you ask participants if stressed or unstressed beats appear on 'the better or the boring words' (or bits of them), they will notice that stressed syllables mostly land on roots of words, the key parts of descriptive words, and you can ring these in green.

It seems that the roots of complex words have evolved with more weight on them as they carry most of their meaning or descriptiveness. Less interesting bits of language, such as articles, connectives, pronouns and endings, are generally likely to be unstressed as they are, largely, part of the mortar of grammar rather than being the actual bricks of core description and meaning.

How does all this link together?

We might ask why English poetry developed like this. I believe stressed beats act like tiny spotlights continuously illuminating important words or parts of words. Sound echoes make them stand out even more and add to the magical musicality of the rhythmic patterning. In effect, listeners are continuously 'tapped on the shoulder' by the stressed beats at each significant little part so they don't drift off or lose track. This was especially important in the oral societies of the past where poetry developed and where people were all listeners.

I referred to rhythm as 'magical' because it also helps us relax and set aside our primitive 'alert guard' mode, enabling us to be absorbed into the 'dream world' of the poem.

Poetry's sound patterning has always helped its creators and performers too. People can remember the gist of a story well enough to tell it, although rarely perfectly or in the same word order. A special quality of poetry is that, after gaining familiarity with a piece, one can remember it well enough to recite it from beginning to end, word for word. Its rhythm and sound echoes carry the performer along the lines while stressed beats continuously flag up new meanings, imagery and approaching words. At the completion of each line any end-rhyming used also helps alert the mind to what is coming next.

Poetic meter

More ways in which meaning, description and rhythm are linked in poetry will become clear when we discover what basic building blocks of rhythmic patterns are possible.

Traditionally, regular rhythmic patterns in English poetry are referred to as 'meter'. This is made up of units known as 'feet', which come in different types, nearly all of which contain one stressed beat and at least one unstressed one. The sound patterns they create work alongside effects caused by having specific numbers of 'feet' per line, or sometimes patterns in which the numbers of feet differ in equivalent lines in each stanza.

We won't delve deeply into variations of meter as this book is not about the finer details of prosody, but information is available online under search titles such as 'meter in English poetry' and 'rhythm, meter and scansion'.

The points raised below are designed to help students control poetry creation and can aid in solving problems as they write. Teachers must decide how much of this information to supply, depending on the age and ability of their groups.

How many stressed beats to a line?

I normally ask students what they guess might be the minimum and maximum numbers of stressed beats in a line of poetry. The actual answer is from one stressed beat up to about seven or eight, but the practical answer is usually between two and five (or six) per line in metrical poetry and from about one up to about six in free verse.

To make things simpler from this point, when I simply mention 'beats' I will be referring to stressed beats rather than syllables.

Because many words naturally contain two or more stressed beats, trying to write a poem with only one per line would create an impractical column of single or fractured words. So in poetry where each line contains the same number of beats, the minimum per line is usually two. Two-beat lines have an inbuilt 'swing' due to the proximity of the line breaks and the pauses these create. We'll look at ways to use these, and also three-beat lines, in the chapter on 'minimalist poetry'.

Regular three-beat lines tend to have a cheery skip to them and are often used in children's poetry; regular four-beat lines can seem to straddle the gap between being 'bouncy' and 'serious', and are practical for poets writing about complex issues or richly descriptive scenes, because more and longer words can be fitted into them than in shorter lines.

Using regular five-beat lines (pentameters) seems to add 'gravitas' to poetry. They can sound more 'stately' than shorter or longer lines and each line provides room for complicated ideas, language and description. Regular six beat lines lose some of the musicality found in shorter lengths of line and can sometimes sound a little more like narrative language.

It's important to remember, however, that effects created by certain line lengths will also be affected by the choice of 'feet' placed within them and by any sound echoes or lack of them.

Seven beat lines often involve a form of ballad rhythm. One variable type of ballad rhythm called common meter often has 4, 3, 4, 3 stressed beats per line. If they are unrhymed at the end of each four-beat line and the following three-beat line is joined to that, you end up with seven-beat lines.

None of the section above applies to free verse, which has varied numbers of stressed beats per line.

What works in meter generally?

Let's look at a shortcut way to show students what does and doesn't work within the meter of any type of cadenced poem, including free verse.

Between two stressed beats anywhere in a poem can you have one unstressed one?
  Yes, we've seen that in both the stream poem and the train one, for example:

  . / . /   .   / . /
  the **tiny stream** comes **tinkling down**

Can there be two unstressed beats between stressed ones?
  Again, yes, and we've seen that in the train poem:

  .   .   / . . /
  No they're **closing** the **gate**

Can you have three unstressed beats between two stressed ones?
  Mostly not, unless there are lots of unstressed beats between stressed ones in the surrounding rhythmic context. If this isn't the case, it will either sound like an ungainly mouthful (because the reader suddenly has to try and cram in all three before the next stressed beat's metronomic tick) or else one of those unstressed beats will 'jump up' and become stressed to match the surrounding rhythm.

It's impossible to have four unstressed beats between stressed ones because a speaker couldn't squeeze them all in quickly enough without causing the poetic 'metronome' to pause its regular ticking. One of the middle two will always 'jump up' and become a stressed beat.

Demonstrating three unstressed beats in a row

You can demonstrate some of these effects by adding in or changing words in the texts already looked at. We know that less significant words and parts of words have naturally unstressed beats on them. If you add one of these, such as 'the' to the third line of the train poem, you will get a slightly senseless line but it will now have three unstressed beats in a row. Ask students to listen to what happens to your voice as you conduct while reading through it:

> *"Is it **going** to be **late**?"*
> *"No they're **clos**ing the **gate**!"*
>   .   /   .   /   .   .   .   /   .   /
> *"The **train** now **leaving** from the **Platform Eight**..."*

It can still be conducted in time (just) but your voice suddenly has to speed up to squeeze in all three unstressed beats after only having one between stressed beats earlier in that line. It's possible to say, but clumsy.

Stressed beats together?

Can there be two stressed beats beside each other with no unstressed beats between?

The answer is sometimes yes, sometimes no, and sometimes it's ungainly or confusing. Whether it will work well or not depends on the metrical context at that point.

The incorrect placement of two stressed beats together in an unsuitable place is one of the most common reasons for apprentice poets losing control of the rhythmic flow and sometimes dropping into prose from that point onwards.

When stressed beats 'bump' together

Let's say we cut out a separating unstressed beat on the last line then try reading and conducting this:

> *"Is it **going** to be **late**?"*
> *"No they're **clos**ing the **gate**!"*
> *"The **train leaving** from **Platform Eight**..."*

Your students will notice that the two stressed beats on 'train' and 'leav' now knock against each other like bumper cars. That's because the rhythmic flow until then mostly had two unstressed beats between stressed ones but now suddenly has none.

It is too big a change and a writer's 'conducting arm' will either leap madly while trying to whip back quickly enough to fit the next stressed beat in, or will slow and waver vaguely as the stressed beat on 'leav' and following unstressed ones muddle together. Either way, the metronome of the poem will stop ticking regularly, as will the conducting.

This is a typical problem students encounter when trying to keep to a poetic rhythm. It's easily solved by adding an insignificant word such as a connective or preposition to separate the stressed beats (e.g. *the **train** now **leav**. . .)* or by changing the first stressed beat word to a two-syllable 'falling' word ending in an unstressed beat (e.g. *the **engine leav**ing', 'the **carriage leav**ing').*

When can two or more stressed beats in a row work?

After you have shown this, display the stream poem again and ask participants to say a one-syllable word of similar meaning to replace the two-syllable word 'tiny' near the beginning. Inevitably someone will come up with 'small'. When you ask your students if they think 'small' is normally a stressed or unstressed beat word they should decide correctly that it's the former (it's descriptive and now has a sound echo on it due to its 's' sibilance with 'stream').

Once you point out that this part of the line will now have two stressed beats in a row you can ask your students if they think those two beats will 'bump' against each other when the line is conducted and said out loud. Here is the amended line:

.　/　/　.　/　.　/
*The **small stream** comes **tink**-ling **down**
through **rush**-es, **reeds** and **bogg**-y **ground,***

Many will be surprised to discover that it does work, even though the rest of the line is in unbroken ti-**TUM** iambs. It works here partly because it's the very start of the poem and so there is no rhythmic context yet.

Now ask participants to conduct the new version as they say it again, then describe what happens to their voices where the two stressed beats are. Hopefully, some will realise that placing the two stressed beats of 'small' and 'stream' together cause the reader's voice to slow momentarily.

What we learn from all this is that changing a metrical 'foot' can alter the speed and mood of the poem at that point. The more unstressed beats there are between stressed ones, the busier, faster, more excited the poem or that section of it sounds.

Conversely, having only one or no unstressed beats between stressed ones makes a poem, or that part of it, slower, more peaceful, more thoughtful sounding, or sometimes a little sadder.

Three stressed beats together?

Though infrequent, it's possible to place three stressed beats in a row in parts of a poem, as long as they fit within its contextual rhythmic patterning. The poem (or sometimes the section surrounding the three stresses) either must contain very few unstressed beats, or the three consecutive stressed beats might be in a little stand-alone section, for instance at the end of the poem.

By way of example I have included a poem of mine (entitled *Leaves*) at the end of this chapter which employs two stressed beats together in several places and three-stressed beats together in the final line. You can look at the poem in class or just read the section yourself to gain a greater understanding of the effects of stressed beats together and of the subtle relationships between rhythmic patterning, meaning and emotion.

When natural beats can change their status within poetry

Here are some examples of how 'natural' stressed beats can change within a line. The words 'thief' and 'black' are normally stressed beat words because they're strong, single-syllable words that contain innate description. In the iambic line: '*the __thief__ was __dressed__ in __clothes__ of __black__*' they still carry stressed beats. However, in the relentlessly busy rhythm of the following line from another of my poems, those two words don't carry stressed beats:

. / . . / . . . / . . /
the __sneak__ thief is __watching__ with his __beady__ black __eye__.

Because there are so many unstressed syllables between stressed ones here, some of the stressed ones become unstressed to avoid 'bumping' against neighbouring stresses.

Conversely, 'as' is a fairly insignificant word and would normally be unstressed, like (twice) in the line: *the __bay__ was __filled__ with __masts__ as __tall__ as __trees__*. However, in the famous Wordsworth poem *The Daffodils* the 'as' becomes stressed (or perhaps one should say semi-stressed) in the first line:

I wandered, __lonely as a cloud__.

This is because it's a regular iambic line (ti-**TUM**, ti-**TUM**. . .) and the 'as' is where a stressed '**TUM**' should land.

An unstressed syllable which changes its status like this, owing to its rhythmic context, is called a 'location beat': it gains status because of where the regular 'metronome ticks' land.

Discovering deeper links between meter and meaning

Using an example poem to discover further links and inspire more thoughtful writing

Before they start to write their own pieces, one activity I sometimes do with able groups from ages 11 to adult is to look at a poem which brings together the rhythmic features we have discussed but also adds dimensions such as extended metaphor, symbolism and other 'layers of meaning'. This also inspires some students to add more depth to their writing.

The poem *Leaves* (on copiable sheets at the end of this chapter) was written after watching a steady trickle of elderly people walking their dogs along a leafy lane behind a school. Through extended metaphor I contrasted the slow, worn-out movements of those people, whose lives were nearly over, with the vital new life of the brightly clad infants whirling around the school playground.

If you read the poem to a group it should be done slowly so they can distinguish the changes in the sound patterning. Apart from finding linkages of meter, changing pace, meaning and emotion, your students should now be able to unearth many of the aspects of poetry already covered in this book, such as questioning and thoughtful observation, descriptive word choice, extended metaphor with sub-metaphors, multiple linked sound echoes, and so on.

Once you have read the poem out, ask which of the two verses feels slower. Although most of the poem feels slow they will realise the second verse seems slower than the first. You can then ask them to identify all the stressed and unstressed beats by conducting before examining the patterns the various beats make. Among several things, this will begin to show why the second verse *sounds* slower and sadder.

Here is the poem with all the stressed beats marked:

Leaden No**vem**ber **mor**ning. **Head**stone **grey**.
Stillness **raked** by the **shrill** of in**fants' play**.
Lively as **leaves** in **wind**, they **swarm** and **spin**
un**til** their **teach**ers **soft**ly **sweep** them **in**.

Fools' gold en**rich**es **worm**-cast **grass**
where **slow dogs** and **slow own**ers **pass**.
On **numb days** like **this**, while **chil**dren **play**,
The **cold old wait** to **blow** a**way**.

The rhythmic pattern is as follows:

```
 /  .  . /  .  /  .   /   .  /   .     /
 /  .  / .  .  /  . / .  /  .    /
 /  . .   /  .  /   .   /     .   /
 . /  .  /  .  /  .  /  .  /

   /   / . / . /   .  /
    . /  /  .  /  /  . /
    .  /  /  .  /  .  /  .   /
    .  /  /  / . /  . /
```

Although the poem is written in five-beat lines (pentameters) and the most predominant foot is the iamb (. /) the feet used vary somewhat. Participants will notice that, in the second verse, there are fewer unstressed beats, no 'bouncy' double unstressed beats, and there are several places in that verse where the poem is slowed dramatically by the placement of two and even three stressed beats together.

If asked what the sonic effect of the three stressed beats placed together in the final line is, students will sometimes notice that the grouping slows the poem down so much at that point it almost seems to pause fleetingly.

This not only makes the final line feel slower and sadder (appropriate to its subject of old age and death) but the third stressed beat in a row causes the rhythm to wait momentarily on the word 'wait'. The rhythm then speeds up slightly with the return of regular unstressed beats between the stressed ones (*to **blow** away)* as if the 'leaf of life' spins away at the end..

In contrast, two unstressed beats appearing together are rare in this poem ('*raked* by the *shrill* of . . .' and '*lively* as *leaves* in'), making those busier and more excitable than their slower surroundings. Sparky students may realise these more 'active' fragments relate to the lively little children.

Marking sound echoes and looking at vowel type

Your group should by now be able to identify many of the sound echoes in the poem and, if you mark and link them all, they will see that every stressed beat has one or several sound echoes on it.

Something to note with stronger groups is the repeating use of 'hard' vowel sounds on key stressed beats, and especially how the hard 'A' (as in 'day') and 'O' (as in 'cold') sounds echo on the double and triple stressed beats, making them seem even more stressed, slow, cold and stiff. (Soft vowels such as 'ah' and 'aw' feel warmer and more relaxed.)

Offering student writers flexibility of poetic form

Tools for controlled creativity

Most curricula require teachers to expose students of particular ages to specific forms of poetry, and students are sometimes asked to create their own versions of these. This teaches them about poetic structures and helps scaffold their poems for them.

It can, however, be too easy to fall into overreliance on simplified 'modelling and copying' routines. As well as absorbing information, children must learn to be flexible and creative.

I often offer participants greater creativity by enabling each of them to select or design a form for their own poem, then attempt to shape their language and its sound patterns to fit that choice.

The following system allows students to make individual choices of structure and covers most forms of normal, sound-based English poetry.

Students are offered three options:

1 Write the poem with the same number of stressed beats in every line.

2 Create or decide on a template for a verse then copy this in each verse.

3 Write the poem in free verse.

Option 1: a regular number of beats per line

Individual students can choose whether they want to use two, three, four or five stressed beats per line throughout the poem. They usually can't hold longer lines in their heads well and the longer the line, the greater the risk of their poems losing rhythm and turning into stories.

It's useful to give examples of two-, three-, four- and five-beat lines and the effects of them. Here's a section of the river poem reworked into various forms. I've kept the same iambic rhythm in them all and the same words as much as possible, to demonstrate differences caused by variations in line length:

Two-beat lines (dimeters):

The tiny stream
comes tinkling down,
it sparks and gleams...

Notice how it 'swings' because of such short lines.

Three-beat lines (trimeters):

The tiny stream comes down
through rushes, reeds and bogs

The three-beat lines seem to 'skip' along.

Four-beat lines (tetrameters):

The tiny stream comes tinkling down
through rushes, reeds and boggy ground...

The longer four-beat lines make it feel more continuous, less jumpy and slightly more serious sounding.

Five-beat lines (pentameters):

The tiny mountain stream comes tinkling down
through tufted rushes, reeds and boggy ground...

The language sounds slower and more 'stately' here than in the shorter-line versions. There's a sense of maturity, thoughtfulness and continuity in the flow of iambic five-beat lines.

Which line length is easiest to write?

Students often ask which line length is the most common. Regular five-beat lines are reputed to be most common but four-beat lines are also common and probably the easiest for novices to write. This is because they are long enough to contain rich description and metaphor yet short enough for young writers to retain and work on.

Students usually progress best by writing two to four lines at a time and conducting possible fragments to check that they contain their chosen number of beats per line and to help create connective flow. While conducting they must always read aloud, or 'out loud in their heads', starting a line or two before the new part.

Option 2: using a verse template

What I mean by a 'template' is deciding how many lines will be in each verse and how many stressed beats (or 'feet') in each different line. *The train journey*, for instance does not have a precisely regular rhythm with the same number of beats per line. It is composed of 'verselets' where the first two lines have two beats and the third has four, so it's a 2, 2, 4 template.

How to build a verse template

Students first decide how many lines they want per verse and how many feet in each particular line. For instance, they might end up with a four-line verse with 5, 3, 4, 3 stressed beats, respectively, in its lines, or with 3, 4, 3, 5 beats instead. They may also decide to choose mostly rhythmic feet such as either 'ti-**tum**', 'ti-ti-**tum**', '**tum**-ti', or '**tum**-ti-ti'. After that they need to keep saying their pattern as they alter their words and ideas to fit it.

Alternatively, individuals can simply write a verse, adjust it until it sounds good, then note down that template in stressed and unstressed beats.

To maintain the rhythmic flow in following verses, writers copy the 'sound reference' of their template verse in tis and **tums**, along with re-reading the words of that verse. Again, new fragments should be 'test conducted' from a couple of lines before them in order to check they have the required numbers of stressed beats, and that rhythm and meaning connect satisfactorily.

Option 3: free verse

Most students in schools tend to write in 'free verse' if they are instructed to write a poem without a form being specified. This is not necessarily the easiest option to do well, however.

Although there is no set number of stressed beats per line in free verse there are still certain variants. Writers may decide to use wide variations in line lengths of between one and five or six beats to a line. Others may focus on one to three beats per line and some might choose three to five beats.

Listening to a developing free verse poem is crucial

Writing free verse well necessitates thinking about the poem's meaning, language and mood while also *hearing what sounds right* at each part and for the poem in general. For example, as in prose, strong effect can be achieved by having several medium or longish lines drop to a dramatic conclusion in one short line.

Writers must continuously try variations in idea, language, metaphor and sound, while also testing how these relate to the sound, meaning, emotion and flow of surrounding parts in general, and the preceding part in particular. It's a complex process, particularly as a writer of free verse has no rhythmic or structural framework to hold onto.

Students must learn to write while keeping the general mood of the poem in mind, and by constantly re-reading each previous part while thinking out the next *and* listening to the 'sound flow' in their heads. Any changes may require alterations to surrounding parts to prevent the rhythm becoming muddled.

When to conduct

To continuously conduct a free verse poem while writing is unhelpful because it can push the poem's subtly altering rhythms into a more regular or formal form into which the writer gets 'locked'.

If writers learn to listen continuously *to what sounds and feels best,* they stand a stronger chance of writing a good free verse poem. Once each 'stanza' or section has been completed, rhythmic flow should be checked by reading it while listening carefully and, if necessary, through testing it by conducting.

Similarly, once the poem is completed, it should be read and re-read to check that the flow of each section is compatible with that of preceding and subsequent sections. 'Remote editing' any poem like this a few days later also helps the writer's brain and ear to detect rhythmic irregularities.

Two versions of the poem *Leaves* follow, and can be either scanned or photocopied. The stressed beats are marked on the second version.

Leaves

Leaden November morning. Headstone grey.
Stillness raked by the shrill of infants' play.
Lively as leaves in wind, they swarm and spin
until their teachers softly sweep them in.

Fools' gold enriches worm-cast grass
where slow dogs and slow owners pass.
On numb days like this, while children play,
the cold old wait to blow away.

The poem with the stressed and unstressed beats marked

Leaves

/ . . / . / .   /   .   /

Leaden No**vem**ber **morn**ing. **Head**stone **grey**.

/ .   /   . .   / . / .   /

Stillness **raked** by the **shrill** of infants' **play**.

/ . .   / . /   .   /   . /

Lively as **leaves** in **wind**, they **swarm** and **spin**

. / .   / . / .   /   . /

un**til** their **teach**ers **soft**ly **sweep** them **in**.

/   / . / .   /   .   /

Fools' gold en**rich**es **worm**-cast **grass**

.   /   / .   /   / .   /

where **slow dogs** and **slow own**ers **pass**.

.   /   / . /   .   / .   /

On **numb days** like **this**, while **child**ren **play**,

.   /   /   / .   / . /

the **cold old wait** to **blow** a**way**.

© 2014, *Write Out of the Classroom, Colin Macfarlane, Routledge*

CHAPTER 6

Essential inputs before students write descriptive poems

A poem must have 'flow'

Inexperienced young writers often create disjointed lists of descriptions or thoughts instead of a poem. This is largely caused by thinking out only one line at a time while forgetting to connect it logically to the lines above. Ironically, having many pages of wonderful descriptive detail from a brainstorming session sometimes makes this fault worse. Many students can become like 'kids in a candy store' and are so excited by the delicious descriptions and metaphors in front of them that they try to throw too many onto the page without connecting them through language that flows.

Trying to prevent such 'listing' occurring is essential before students start writing. I always discuss the difference between this kind of 'wish list for a poem' and a proper poem whose parts are intelligently connected and which flows smoothly. One key thing to tell students to look out for is that a list usually has lots of definite articles and a few indefinite articles down the left hand side of it. If 'the' or 'a' appear more than a few times at the beginning of lines it usually means the writer has been thinking about each line quite separately from the ones above and below. The problem is also sometimes exacerbated by students having been told, incorrectly, that they should complete every line with a comma or full-stop, by poorly disciplined thinking and by inexperience in using connectives.

A bad example

To give students an idea of 'what not to do' I sometimes destroy the first part of my simple river poem by spontaneously making it into a disjointed list such as this:

The tiny stream comes trickling down,
a gull is soaring in the breeze,
the reeds grow out of boggy ground,
the pools are dark beneath the trees,
the hills are steep on either side,
the river pulls the leaves along,
the water's slow where ducklings glide,
an oak is standing tall and strong . . .

Teachers might be happy if certain of their students achieved this level of control of rhythm and rhyme, and perhaps even the limited observational and language quality, but that is not the point I am making here. I wrote this example to show that an un-sequenced list like this is not really a proper poem.

There is little logical organisation of thought or content here, which, in a workshop situation, would immediately be obvious to me or my assistants before we even started to read the 'poem' because we would notice all those definite and indefinite articles down the left-hand side.

An even worse example

The irritating effect of this kind of listing is more obvious in a non-rhyming version because now it has even fewer redeeming features, despite the near-regularity of its four-beat rhythm:

The tiny stream comes trickling down,
a gull is soaring in the wind,
the reeds grow out of boggy soil,
the pools are dark beneath the trees,
the hills are steep on either side,
the river pulls the leaves along,
the water's slow where ducklings float,
an oak is standing tall and proud . . .

Both these bad examples involve a particularly irksome type of list that I term a 'neck strainer' because, not only aren't the descriptive items connected grammatically but they also lack a logical sequence so readers (who become observers of the described scene) have to 'strain their necks in their imaginations' by looking down at the stream then high up at the gull, down at the reeds, over to the pools, up at the hills, down to the current, and so on!

It would, for instance, be much more logical to stick with writing about the stream, or start with that and make links to its surroundings, or begin with a more general view and move downwards to the stream but with some kind of idea and language linking, such as this version in couplets:

Below the gulls that soar so high,
below the hills that touch the sky,
beneath the stunted moorland trees
that shiver in the morning breeze
the tiny stream comes tinkling down
through ruffled reeds and boggy ground ...

The little 'list' at the beginning of this example is 'a list with a purpose' which contains deliberate repetitions to create a smooth movement of the observer's viewpoint, equivalent to the panning 'establishing shot' a filmmaker might use to introduce a locality and perhaps a character within it. In this case the locality is the hills and the principal character is the stream.

Here's another approach, which focuses on aspects of the stream, at least for a while. It uses several small touches of authenticating detail but deepens the descriptions by using extended personification:

The tiny stream comes tinkling down
through rushes, reeds and boggy ground ...
through ferny, dripping, shady places
on it falls and on it races
till it dances out in sun,
full of sparkle, full of fun;
a cheerful child that skips along
and sings her joyful little song!

A poem is not an assortment of descriptions or ideas which lack connection and meaning. It must have 'flow'. I emphasise this concept by telling students that a stream is a good analogy for a poem because it doesn't keep randomly stopping then starting again in different places. It is all connected into one entity, even though sometimes its words run quickly like a river over rapids, drop over fall after fall, or flow slowly like water in a peaceful pool.

Regularly re-reading previous lines while working out new lines is essential to achieving rhythmic and sense flow. Learning to do this while sometimes conducting to check rhythmic smoothness can be a 'eureka experience' for students who have previously struggled to make their writing sound and feel like poetry.

Separating the wheat from the chaff

Generally speaking, 'less is best' in poetry and it is crucial to remind students of this before writing. This is not to imply that a long poem can't be good, simply that a poem's quality invariably gets better with the removal of unnecessary articles, weak words and language, or idea duplications.

Two necessary but apparently opposing factors are at play in poetry creation. The first is the need for freshness and aesthetic value in observations, language and descriptions, figures of speech and ideas. The second is tightness in the work's creation; a concentrated aesthetic quality, a lack of waffle, duplication or illogicality.

Although we want young students to use plenty of rich descriptive language so they develop skills in thoughtful observation and widen their vocabularies, more mature apprentice poets should learn to carefully select, and limit the amount of, descriptive material. For the poet it's like making each poem fit and healthy by feeding it the freshest and most varied words and images to be found and as few junk words as possible in order to prevent it growing flabby and less attractive to the reader.

It is important to point this out to students before they start their writing. I explain that, to a poet, every good word used is precious but overuse of any particular one devalues it, and I often use a metaphor of value linked to supply and demand. I might ask them if there were a glut of trillions and trillions more potatoes grown in the world one year what would happen to the price of potatoes and how much might one then be worth.

I then ask them what a potato might be worth if there were only one or two left in the world. The answer is obvious, so I then tell them to think of each fresh word as being as precious as that rare fresh potato.

To reinforce this concept it is useful to give participants some practical pointers about how to keep lines and language tight and fresh before they start the writing. A few tips follow but more detailed ways of helping students tighten poetic language can be found in Chapter 7.

Cutting out repetition and duplication

To avoid repetition it's essential to remind novice poets to prune as many unnecessary definite and indefinite articles as they can while still maintaining grammatical sense, to seek fresher and richer words where possible (while checking they still fit with the rhythmic flow if they change any), and to be tough about avoiding duplication of words, especially stronger or more descriptive words. Repetition creates weakness in poetry unless it can produce an effect which is better than if there hadn't been any replication.

Some students keep repeating phrases, lines or verses which can quickly bore and irritate the reader. Reasons for doing this are: 1) they gain a sense of rhythmic flow in their heads by repeating identical chunks of rhythm, which helps them keep it going throughout the poem, 2) they have 'poetic arrested development' and are aware mostly of the highly repetitive poetry of early childhood, and ballad or song formats with repeating lines or choruses and 3) repeating can fill a lot of space quickly so it looks and feels like you've achieved more writing than you have!

Avoiding 'key word duplication'

Certain words inevitably tend to keep reappearing throughout students' writing on specific subjects or locations. For instance, the words 'water' and 'river' will keep popping up in poems about rivers; 'waves' or 'sea' in poems about the sea; 'death' or 'blood' in poetry about war; 'leaves', 'red' and 'gold' in autumn poems, and so on.

The first way to avoid this is to have good quality thesauruses available in class and to encourage students to use them on an automatic basis. I believe strongly that young writers should have the best thesaurus available to them that they can cope with for their age, vocabulary and ability. More able students of about twelve years and upwards should start using a good Roget's style thesaurus as soon as possible because these have a wide word variety and the logical interconnections within one can aid thoughtful and creative writing.

Changing the word is one way to avoid the occurrence of this problem of 'key word repetition' but there are others which can also be taught easily. One is to write about aspects or parts of the thing instead so, in a poem about a river for instance, a writer could talk about its surface, bed, banks, currents, depths, pools, falls, rapids, reflections, etc. Even more interesting language arises from making metaphors for the thing or for its parts, so a twisting upland stream might be described as 'a scribble on the hills', a river in its ravine as 'a gash in the land', or, as in an Anglo-Saxon kenning, the river might be, for example, 'the land's blood' or the 'fishes' pathway'.

Similarly, through looking metaphorically at aspects of the stream, its surface could be referred to as its 'cool skin', the slow heaving of its currents as 'gently flexing its muscles', a trout might 'nap on its dark and dappled bed', and so on.

Metaphorical ideas can also be extended to different degrees, so the writer might talk about wind-blown or twig-scratched ripples on the river's surface like this: 'the breeze wrinkles its once-smooth skin' or 'its skin shivers at the tickle of twigs' or 'whorls of hidden currents dimple its glossy skin'. Sometimes these metaphors can be extended to a phrase, sometimes to a couple of lines, a whole verse or even the entire poem.

Avoiding using a key word such as 'water' more than once in a poem about a river can spur a young writer to come up with considerably more interesting observations, descriptions, words and metaphorical concepts. In effect, this process triggers a similar type of 'thoughtful observation' to that of the initial locational brainstorm and is an aspect of underlying thinking that we need students to use automatically if they are to become creative and proficient writers.

Language is the most powerful tool mankind has evolved, so enabling young people to develop greater creative control and accuracy in language and related thinking skills is surely one of the most important things we can achieve as teachers.

Considering the 'I' in a poem

There is much wonderful poetry in the world written wholly or partly in the first person and an able student might create a strong piece like that, especially if it were about a genuine personal experience. However, when writing a descriptive poem, most young writers tend to weaken the piece when they put the 'I' into the words.

For instance, weaker students often write things like 'I can see the . . .', 'I can hear the . . .', etc. This is dead language and tends to distance readers from the scene by making it harder for them to feel they are experiencing the place or event themselves.

I explain this to students before they write their descriptive poems, and usually give them an example such as the following. Instead of writing

I can see the huge waves rearing up like angry bears
and I can hear them roar as they pound the dripping cliffs

the writer could tighten it to:

Huge waves rear like angry bears
and roar as they pound the dripping cliffs

or:

Huge waves rear like angry bears
*and, <u>roar</u>ing, <u>**pound**</u> the <u>drip</u>ping <u>cliffs</u>*

where the two weak single-syllable words of 'as' and 'they' have been reduced to the one syllable 'ing'. We still need one unstressed syllable there to separate the stressed beats properly. The comma now required after 'roaring' also creates a tiny dramatic pause between the strong verbs 'roaring' and 'pound'.

In the final two possibilities only the best language is used, the drama is more immediate and the scene belongs as much to the reader as to the writer because there is no 'I' to make it less inclusive.

Choosing a tense for the poem

As with most poetry, I ask students to write descriptive poems in the present tense. The majority of descriptive poetry (apart from some descriptive narrative poetry) is written in the present tense because it makes the setting seem literally more 'present' to the reader. For 'you', the reader, it's as if you are in the place or event *now*, experiencing its sounds, sights, smells, moods or happenings. It gives you more ownership of the poem's experience.

Another strong reason to promote the writing of most poetry in the present tense is that it helps prevent young writers from slipping into producing a story of sorts instead of a poem, which occurs because stories are normally in the past tense and descriptive poetry in the present. Narrative poems are, not surprisingly however, often written in the past tense.

To rhyme or not to rhyme?

This is a simple but important question which does not have one straightforward answer because it depends on many factors, such as the age and ability of the students; the poetry-writing experience of all or some of them; what you, the teacher, want to achieve on a particular assignment; and how much creative control (and potential for failure) you wish to entrust to each group or individual.

I run workshops and courses (for various age bands) which involve creating rhyming poetry, but students usually have real-time and editing guidance from me and my talented assistants to help the work flourish and to prevent their rhyme choices from damaging their work. In some of them, students work in twos or threes (individually if they are older) on specific poetic forms, such as limericks, sonnets and ballad-style narrative poems. I also run other courses where those with some experience of writing poetry work individually on either a particular rhyming form or a form they design. On others still, we work collectively on rhyming descriptive poetry of various sorts so that dire or limp rhymes can be discarded, both through group voting and guidance.

When I work with a school group for the first time on individual descriptive poetry, I usually try to dissuade students from attempting to end rhyme because it frequently causes them to blight the potential of their writing. Many become so obsessed with the search for rhyming words they put their 'trophies' in even though they clearly don't fit the meaning or mood well, and often to the loss of much richer ideas and language.

Inexpert rhymers commonly pad out lines with weak or relatively senseless word choices just to keep the rhythm going until they reach the rhyming word they have become so committed to using. Sometimes their first verse, or maybe two, is fairly well controlled but brain fatigue combined with lack of rhyming vocabulary and experience take over, so the poem disintegrates into forced or silly 'rhyming for rhyming's sake'.

Rhyming in fewer places

As mentioned earlier, it is worth explaining to students that, if a poem end-rhymes for a while, it shouldn't suddenly stop rhyming because that gives a feeling of 'let down' to the reader. The opposite can work well, however, because it can sound quite pleasant when a poems starts without rhyming then rhyming is brought in part of the way through, or even just at the end. I have written semi-free verse poetry which deliberately doesn't rhyme at the beginning, then slant rhymes to a greater percentage through the poem and concludes with full rhymes. With a good ear, a young writer can sometimes build the poem to an aesthetically satisfying climax like this.

One 'halfway house' I offer to some students who wish to rhyme is to only rhyme a word at the end of the last line in a verse with a word at the end of a line above, preferably two or three lines above. This can be effective because it rounds the verse off in a pleasing way and the young writer stands less chance of losing control of the poem because he or she doesn't need to be fixated with finding rhymes for every line. This can work well for both verses containing identical numbers of lines and semi-free verse 'stanzas' of different lengths.

To enable young writers to concentrate fully on the language, sense, mood and rhythms of a poem you can ask them not to rhyme at all; then, half-way through the session, say you will allow those who wish to rhyme the last word of the whole poem with one at the end of a line two or three lines above . . . or with one on the second last line if they are young students. This is an effective 'cheat' to help apprentice writers end a poem effectively because readers or listeners are left with that rhyme echoing in their heads and the feeling that the poem has more rhyme in it than it actually has.

When to use rhyming dictionaries

I always distribute rhyming dictionaries to students who are working on forms like limericks which depend on potential rhymes to throw up funny ideas for the writer. There are various complexities and formats of rhyming dictionaries. For older and more able students, I recommend the sort that has a high word count and a thick 'rhyme index'.

For more serious individual poetry creation, unless students are relatively experienced in using rhyme, I usually ask them to tell me or my helpers if they want to use a rhyming dictionary so that we can intervene early enough if anyone's work is sliding away from quality language and sense into a weak, 'rhyme-led' effort. Use of rhyming dictionaries in inexperienced hands can make this tendency worse, even when the challenge is to write serious, high quality poetry.

Concept, observation, vibrant language, rhythm, mood and metaphor must come first in descriptive poetry, not the rhymes. I often tell participants that I don't want them to rhyme, for these reasons, but, if someone who has poetry-writing experience strongly wants to then they can discuss it with me first and perhaps even show me something they have written. Differentiation of challenge is important within any group so sometimes I allow a few to try, but quite often a student ends up agreeing not to attempt rhyming on that particular task.

I generally explain to inexperienced students that attempting to control end rhymes will be especially hard for them on this exercise because they will already be trying to achieve so much in the following areas:

- Thinking of and developing a strong idea, direction and form.
- Starting the poem in a suitable and engaging way. This entails finding and

adjusting strong starter lines so they draw in the reader and set up a rhythm pattern or 'rhythmic feel' that the writer is happy with.

- Choosing, retrieving from memory or imagining evocative observations.
- Describing in fresh and powerful language.
- Concentrating language so only the best is used.
- Including new metaphors and similes and extending some if possible.
- Using 'sound echoes' to enrich the poem.
- Sustaining the flow of free verse or keeping up a specific rhythmic pattern.
- Maintaining a smooth flow of meaning, mood and sound patterns.
- Rounding off the poem with a suitable and satisfying ending.

The use of slant and partial rhymes

At this point I usually remind the group about the magical power of sound echoes in general and slant rhymes in particular. If there is time, I explain how their use can replace or partly replace full end rhyming and improve a 'poem in work' rather than damage it by bad rhyming. Slant rhymes are valuable for several reasons:

- Most words have countless other words with which they can slant rhyme, whereas full rhymes often have very limited possibilities or even none at all.
- Full rhymes are frequently quite predictable, partly because there are so few and partly because of overuse. Slant rhymes are mostly not predictable.
- The use of slant rhymes of between about 50 and 90 per cent (see explanation below) can greatly enhance the sound and feel of a poem, often without the reader being aware they are there.
- If a writer end rhymes for more than two to four lines but then stops rhyming, it sounds like the poem has just died. It's as if it's been deflated. On the other hand, a writer can slant rhyme or create simpler sound echoes at the ends of lines then move to non-rhyming without it 'dying', as long as the slant rhymes used are not too near to full rhymes.
- Slant or partial rhymes can be found in the work of many of the best modern poets and most songwriters. Numerous poems end-rhyme with slant rhymes nowadays.
- Many students quickly take to finding and using slant rhymes to enhance their poetry and generally do this without negatively affecting other aspects of a poem.

What is a 'slant rhyme'?

The definition of a slant rhyme varies slightly among poets who use the term but I use it to mean more or less any mirroring of sound between words. As English poetry is based on parallelism, not direct duplication, a word cannot rhyme with an identical copy of itself. I measure slant rhymes as a subjective percentage of rhyme compared to an equivalent full rhyme, so 'water' and 'daughter' would be 100 per cent rhymes to my ear, but 'water' and 'pig' would be zero.

Let's look at the box containing some slant-rhyme possibilities for a word and my ratings for them (which are necessarily subjective as pronunciation varies according to regional accent). Only those words in the central area between the lines slant rhyme as the others obviously fully rhyme or do not rhyme at all.

Slant-rhyme percentages

water / daughter	100%
water / fought 'er	100%
water / otter	95–100%
water / fought her	90%
water / mottle	80%
water / stopper	75%
water / wander	70%
water / naughty	55%
water / splatter	50%
water / lobster	45%
water / whisper	45%
water / waster	40%
water / jester	35%
water / fought	35%
water / watch	30%
water / wasp	25%
water / dot	20%
water /across	15%
water /dog	10–15%
water / pig	0%
water / milkmaid	0%

In the second box are a few 60–90 per cent slant rhymes you can use as examples to start them ringing in your students' heads. You will notice that they sometimes involve more than one word. Ask students to imagine that there are beats filling lines of poetry before your ear lands on each of the two words:

Examples of slant rhymes

mountains / town lanes	while / trial
mountains / mittens	cliff / lisp
bounding / mountain	cliff / slips
meadow / hedgerow	pain / sun
meadow / gentle	pain / shame
raindrop / run up	impede / entreat
raindrop / pin drop	clattering / muttering
shiver / lover	sycamore / waiting for
shiver / silver	forest / tourist
meander / sender	forest / Morris
meander / amber	forest / chorus

A useful little exercise is to take some interesting words out of a piece of writing you find or have been working with, then ask the class to find two slant rhymes for each: one of about 75–95 per cent and one of around 30–70 per cent.

Another valuable exercise is to collect thoughtful description in a locational brainstorm session then write a slant-rhyming collective poem based on that material, using the interactive board or laptop and digital projector. A relatively easy choice of form would be to create couplets (a,a,b,b,) or a,b,a,b / c,d,c,d slant rhymes in each verse. Effective variations of that are to allow full rhymes only between the third last and last lines of the poem, or between the third last and last lines of each verse.

Just as with full rhymes, writers must resist forcing slant rhymes into the poem without them fitting well with the sense, mood, language and sound of the piece. The motto with all forms of rhyming is 'if it doesn't make it better don't use it'!

Initial capitals at starts of lines?

It seems that a sizable percentage of the population think there is still some rule stating that a writer must put initial capitals at the beginning of every new line of poetry. This applies to students too so I feel it is important to explain to them that it's a matter of choice and, for over a century, a considerable proportion of poets have not done it. The misunderstanding is not helped by word processing programs, which automatically place a capital letter at the start of the new line when the writer presses the enter/return key before reaching the right-hand margin, on the assumption that a new paragraph is required. This can be avoided (in MS Word) by pressing the shift and enter keys at the same time, creating a 'manual line break', or by amending the AutoCorrect Options so that a capital is no longer automatically inserted.

I dislike initial capitals down the left hand side for several reasons. The principal one is that, where there are initial capitals at the start of every line of a poem, it is very easy for a reader to miss a tiny full stop and read straight through the beginning of the next sentence by accident. When readers don't spot the difference, the sense gets confused so they then have to go back to discover the missed full stop, or even the line before that, and start re-reading that section in a way that makes sense.

As sound continuity, meaning and flow are crucial in poetry, confusion like this disrupts the enjoyment of the piece. I know this happens because I have read into the first part of 'next sentences' a great many times in poems with initial capitals and have been told by many students and teachers that they have often done the same thing.

The obvious answer is simply only to capitalise where there has been a full stop or equivalent piece of punctuation.

It should also be pointed out to students at this point that poetry frequently flouts the prose rules of sentence structure. This is because full stops and miniature 'sentences' are sometimes used for dramatic effect as well as for reasons involving variations of meaning, mood and sound. Quite often, as mentioned earlier, a 'sentence' in poetry might not include the three fundamentals of subject, object and verb, and might even be as short as one word.

The effect of the natural pause caused by breaking a line of poetry and starting a new one means that it is unnecessary to have the following line begin with a capital letter to underline that pause. Initial capitals can also prevent young and inexperienced readers of poetry from sustaining the flow of an ongoing sentence that runs through more than one line.

CHAPTER 7

Possible additional poetry inputs, editing tips and suggestions about the writing space

Second stage brainstorming

'Second stage brainstorming' involves leading a brainstorm on a subject or setting for a second time, away from the initial location. It is especially useful if there has been a time gap between collecting the data on location and starting to write the poems based on it. I often lead a short session like this with a group just before they start writing because it serves several purposes and I have seen what a positive effect it can have on the quality and complexity of the writing. Here are some of the advantages:

- It brings back the mood and 'presence' of place and experience just before writing.
- Brainstorming 'in retrospect' like this can help participants come up with new ideas and language because they see things from a removed perspective and are not distracted by events happening at the location.
- It can help to widen a brainstorm session that had either been too short or had had to be curtailed due to inclement weather.
- It can be a good place to lead the development of further metaphors on specific aspects, or work more on any areas felt to be underrepresented the first time around, such as using personifications, sound echoes or feelings.

Leading a second stage brainstorm

There's nothing fundamentally different about guiding a second brainstorm except that this is a suitable opportunity in which to ask new questions that might lead to fresh ideas for the concept or direction of individual poems. They might kick-start metaphorical thinking and cause participants to ask more about the mood and feel of the place and how aspects of it might fit into a bigger picture beyond the location.

To write a rich poem, participants need to combine ideas with metaphorical, descriptive and emotional creativity, and a second stage brainstorm session can help to set or reset those approaches in their minds. If there has been a time gap before the writing stage, even of only one night, participants may have lost some of their embryonic ideas and emotional involvement, so this is a chance to help bring back the presence of the place and to trigger individual inspiration.

Any delay before writing gives a workshop leader the opportunity to sit quietly somewhere and work out a list of aspects to cover in more depth and new questions that can be asked in this second thinking session. If participants have scribed their initial ideas on paper and clipboards they simply continue the process in this session, but if someone has been typing or scribing for the group it is helpful if they can also note-take for this session before speedily printing or copying the new material as students settle down to write.

Tips for editing and tightening lines

Culling unnecessary articles

Often, the first way of tightening a section of poem is to throw away or change as many unnecessary definite and indefinite articles as possible. A writer couldn't lose that initial 'the' at the start of my example lines about the stream, however, because the line would then be grammatically wrong and sound like a foreigner speaking English badly:

Tiny stream comes tinkling down,

and that would also be the case in this attempt:

oak is standing tall and strong

This type of line is a common occurrence in young peoples' poetry writing once they understand the concept of tightening language in a poem but don't always sense the grammatical implications of certain apparent solutions. I sometimes refer to this type of writing as one of several forms of 'Yoda Speak' because most students understand that concept.

Pluralising and maintaining rhythmic flow

Wherever there is a plural the article can be thrown away, subject to the effect this has on the rhythmic patterning. So, instead of having 'the' at the start of each line, these could work:

pools lie dark beneath the trees

or

reeds grow out of boggy ground

except that, without a 'the' creating an initial unstressed beat at the start of the second example here, which helps re-set the iambic rhythm, the three potential stressed beats of 'reeds', 'grow' and 'out' can be read in different ways and muddle the rhythm due to possibly 'bumping' stressed beats. One solution, rather than to replace the dull and repetitive article, would be to change 'reeds' to a **tum**-ti double-syllable word and adjust the later words to fit the rhythm, as in:

<u>rush</u>es <u>grow</u> from <u>bog</u>gy <u>ground</u>

except that line is basically just telling us information as if we, the readers, are in a lesson about vegetation, so it could be improved again by saying something more interestingly descriptive and observational, such as (on a windy day):

<u>rush</u>es <u>fuss</u> in <u>bog</u>gy <u>ground</u>

If the writer wants to keep 'reeds' for reasons of accuracy, an alternative approach to dealing with that somewhat bumpy line *reeds grow out of boggy ground* would be to try and change the mundane word 'grow' to a two-syllable ti-**tum** word or two single-syllable words with a weak syllable in the first and a strong one in the second word. The former would then make the line something like:

reeds impaled in boggy ground

or

reeds protrude from boggy ground

or

reeds arise from boggy ground

none of which I particularly like as all of these words sound a bit 'forced' in this context. So let's try the two single-syllable word solution:

reeds like spears in boggy ground

which would then be better re-sequenced to:

spear-like reeds in boggy ground

or

> *needly reeds in boggy ground,*

or

> *reedy needles, boggy ground*

A singular noun, such as in the line

> *a gull is soaring on the breeze*

can lose its article by being changed to a plural, as in:

> *gulls are soaring on the breeze*

or an article might be dropped and another word lengthened to reinstate the article's single unstressed beat, as in changing

> *the <u>curr</u>ent <u>pulls</u> the <u>leaves</u> a<u>long</u>,*

to

> *<u>curr</u>ents <u>tum</u>ble <u>leaves</u> a<u>long</u>*

where we have managed to dispose of two definite articles in one line yet keep the rhythm by changing 'pull' to 'tumble' and have also ended up with a tighter and more satisfying line, a more interesting new word, and an additional sound echo in the 'uh' assonance.

More forms of illogical language sequencing

I talked about 'Yoda Speak' earlier, my term for when students write a line that sounds unnatural to native English speakers and is usually grammatically incorrect. Another relatively common error is when a student (who apparently thinks the language of poetry hasn't moved forward in the last century or so) employs an old-fashioned sequencing reversal in a line. This is often to make a particular rhyming word land at the end of it, as in:

> *Stumbling over rocks went he*
> *to reach the verges of the sea*

I normally point out that the student wouldn't say to his friend about another pupil: 'walking across the playground went he' but, in this day and age, would probably say 'he walked across the playground'.

This is a bit archaic sounding too:

He stumbled over rocks of gold

when nowadays people would say 'golden rocks' instead. With a different colour a logical variation of that might then be:

he stumbled over rocks of brown

which I think you might agree sounds even odder to our modern ears than 'rocks of gold', probably because we have all heard so many old or traditionally styled stories which used the adjective '. . . of gold'.

Correcting rhythmic glitches

If students choose to write in regular or semi-regular meter (non-free verse), editing help must not just suggest using a better word but look at some of the rhythmic implications and solutions of doing this, just as I have in some of the possible tightening solutions above.

It is worth practising writing a few pairs of lines of rhythmic poetry yourself, some with ti-**tum** feet, some with ti-ti-**tum** feet, and others with either **tum**-ti or **tum**-ti-ti ones. Use conducting and say the sound of the foot out loud (e.g. **tum**-ti-ti, **tum**-ti-ti) as necessary as you try to find words for the lines because this will help you find words that fit the rhythm. The exercise will also give you a feel for what your students have to attempt, and will make you more adept at helping on the rhythmic side as well as in language, sense, grammar and flow.

Very often a student writer simply needs a ti-**tum** word or a ti word followed by a **tum** word, because so much poetry is automatically based on iambs, this being the most prevalent foot in normal speech. Quite often the problem is that a writer is attempting to put a **tum**-ti word into the wrong position in a basically ti-**tum** sequence, so they now have two stressed beats bumping against each other, as in this metric example:

*He **notes** the **wa**ter's **foa**my **re**vels*
*and **walks** **o**ver the **po**lished **peb**bles*

where one word can be swapped to fit the iambic 'ti-**tum**' rhythm:

*He **notes** the **wa**ter's **foa**my **re**vels*
*and **walks** a**cross** the **po**lished **peb**bles.*

Editing out duplicating endings and padding words

In present tense poetry, the most common duplication at the ends of words is overuse of the present participle, especially where a young writer is in full flow with several 'vibrant verbs'! The secret is to go for an enhanced variety of texture by changing some of them. For instance:

Crashing waves are tumbling and surging onto the shore,
washing rocks with foaming water,

could become:

Crashing waves tumble and surge onto shore,
washing rocks with foamy water,

or, even tighter:

Waves crash and surge onto shore,
washing rocks with foamy water

where there is now only one 'ing'. I have removed the article and also one of the verbs because, although 'tumble' is a strong descriptive word, it's better to choose between that and 'crash' or there will be too many similar verbs together. 'Tumble' could be chosen instead of 'crash' and is a less common verb, but 'crash' has the symbol-like 'sh' sound and this echoes with the 'sh' in 'shore' and in 'washing', and partially with the 's' sounds in 'waves' and 'surge' and 'rocks' . . . all suitable sounds for the crash and wash of water.

The adjectival form of 'foaming' has been changed to 'foamy' to help reduce the 'ing' duplication. One has to be careful, though, about cutting out verbs in a deliberately verb-based poem or section. Each context requires a different editing sensitivity.

Similar ending duplications can occur with the 'ly' parts of adverbs, and, because using more than the occasional adverb frequently suggests they are being employed to boost weak verbs, there is usually a case in that situation for cutting some of them and for changing the verbs into more vibrant ones.

Helping students learn how to write and control rhythm in poems can be a terrific boost to their self-confidence and even to their interest in poetry in general. However, early experimentation in one area usually brings pitfalls in another. For instance, when young writers first write rhythmic poetry they have a tendency to put in weak padding words to fill lines or gaps in lines, just to make the rhythm work. Teachers can help them spot and change the more obvious words or sections like this, but there are also small, almost unnoticeable words that are used frequently in this way, some of which recur regularly in children's rhythmic poetry. Possibly the most common of these is the word 'all'. It is usually easy to change but sometimes may require a two syllable word and the removal of another single syllable one.

Sensitivity to design when assisting with editing

I generally find that teachers are nervous about suggesting much in the way of editing and improvement in their students' work. This is understandable because one never wants to demoralise a young writer, but this laudable intention should not put people off making suggestions they are confident about. That is why the secret is for teachers to gain understanding and confidence through writing poetry themselves in various forms and why I hope the workshop strategies and editing suggestions in this book are helpful.

Perhaps the most crucial thing to do when helping to edit work, or work in progress, is first to read the entire poem or unfinished fragment before making suggestions, in order to try and understand what design, form or aim the writer may have in mind. Asking the student is important too, so that your suggestions will not disrupt their idea or rhythmic pattern. It may be that the youngster is unconsciously creating a pattern or is varying lines but that these are mostly, for example, pentameters, so you can ask them if they would like to stay in that dominant form. You can then help them to try and reorganise any lines that are unrhythmic, weak or of the wrong length, so as to create a tidier, stronger and rhythmically more satisfying poem.

The 'shock of the new'

To help able young writers experiment and think more creatively, it can be worth mentioning again that poets, like all artists, follow writing 'rules' but also deliberately break them for effect. Examples of this rule breaking might be: the use of 'non-standard sentences', which might not have a subject, object and verb in them, and which could possibly be as short as only one or two words; a complete or partial lack of capital letters; 'cut-down' grammar or deliberately ungrammatical language; over-simple language; an unusual placement of words or text on the page; or perhaps a refusal to repeat followed by a batch of repetitions.

A good example of these types of 'rule breaking' can be to show students 'in Just-', the curious and deceptively simple poem about early childhood by E.E. Cummings, which can easily be found online. It is worth asking your students why he chose to do in that poem each of the unorthodox things mentioned in the previous paragraph, although a thorough poetic interpretation of that text is probably beyond the age group.

'Final lines first'

Starting a poem at the end may seem an odd idea to some, but one clever way of helping some young writers find inspiration, direction and emotional attachment for a poem is to show them how they can kick off the writing process by first creating a couple of stunning final lines. This can have several advantages.

First, when they go back to work out the beginning of their poem and start writing towards those final lines they will be able to 'see where they are heading'. Given enough thinking time, they can then find a sense of direction, and structure evolves more easily in their heads.

Secondly, there should now be better coherence in their poem because the beginning and direction of it will tend to be more logically, structurally or emotionally linked with the ending.

Thirdly, they will already have a stunning final line or two! Thanks to this their poems won't: a) simply peter out at the end or repeat something they've already covered because they ran out of ideas, or b) throw in some predictable, clichéd and probably unrelated 'then night comes and everything falls asleep' type of ending (a variation of the classic infant writer's story ending 'and then they went upstairs and went to bed'). I expect, like most teachers you will recognise these common forms of clichéd ending!

The 'final lines first' technique ... things young writers should bear in mind:

- The final lines must be strong, so students may need to spend some time working on them. Having all the collective material from an in-depth brainstorming session in front of them should give them plenty of initial ideas and rich language.
- The line or lines should contain a sense of conclusion within them.
- They might be slightly 'haunting', evocative or shocking.
- The final lines may be changed partially or completely at any time due to stronger revised ideas or rhythmic patterns evolving during the writing process.
- Possible connectives at the beginning of these lines should be thought of as changeable so as to fit with the flow of the emerging poem.
- Writers should *not* try to connect too quickly but must think hard and plan what they will write about in the intervening verses and how many of these there might be. Again, any plan should be thought of as flexible if better ideas arise.
- Young writers should show you or a literate assistant their proposed final lines before they start, so they can be discussed and improved or changed if necessary.

Let's say, for example that the brainstorm had been at an old watermill on a river, visited on a rainy day. Some students might like the decrepitude and solitude of the place, so some final lines might be:

> so it sits by its river, ruined and unnoticed
> like a tired old tramp
> who has lost his purpose in life.

or

> an outcast now, lost
> in a deep and overgrown wood.
> Silent.
> Stranded in time.

or

> his faint shape hidden in thick foliage
> is a dim reminder of busier times,
> a broken ghost
> that haunts this enchanted forest.

Or some may like to use the river or the rain as their final focus, as in:

> Raindrops spatter the swollen river
> but he has long ago lost the strength
> to draw on its endless power.

or

> he cannot move, he is
> crumbling into the soft soil,
> rain dripping from his rotten stones
> like an old man's tears.

Or more able students might try a rhyming or slant-rhyming couplet, such as:

> though the stream is filled by the hammering rain
> the wheel will never turn again.

Sometimes only one line will be enough to set the inspirational and organisational ball rolling. Something like this, perhaps:

> . . . in the days when the wheel still turned.

or:

No floury dust. No sound. No life.

I hope these are giving you an idea of the sorts of lines that you could model on the board for the group and how they can start the inspiration and growing 'feel' for a poem whirring in a young writer's head and heart. If you are unconfident about trying this, before you introduce it to the classroom you can have fun practising creating 'final lines' with family, colleagues or friends based on an imagined or real setting.

To help transfer the concept to your group it can be particularly effective to brainstorm examples of possible final endings with your students, based on a different, imagined subject so as not to take away their later individual creativity by inadvertently providing them with endings for their own poems. Inevitably many would tend to copy these examples or only alter them minimally. You will get more poetic variety if each student tries to work out possible endings for their poems on their own.

They should attempt to include or suggest some of these: emotion, mood, rich language, a strong metaphor, interesting connections and a feeling of conclusiveness. With less able groups you may need to brainstorm a few possible endings to begin with, to start the ball rolling.

The writing session and the writing space

Where to write?

The first thing to be decided is whether or not to start some of the writing in the location visited. It can be a lovely experience for all involved but there are many drawbacks, and although groups often brainstorm on location with me for considerable periods, I tend only to lead actual writing sessions out of doors in warm summer weather, usually when we are working on short and concentrated forms of poetry such as haikus, and cinquains. I also usually want to include many of the inputs already described, so there often isn't time to do the brainstorm session and all this inputting in one place on the same day.

If the weather is good and you can visit the setting again, or if you are based in a nearby residential centre, it can certainly be a rewarding thing to return to the brainstorming location to do some of the writing. However, many students don't want to do this immediately after all the inputs and brainstorming in one outdoor place. They generally prefer to change scene and return to a comfortable, peaceful place to write, which may be indoors, or perhaps outdoors back at base, working at scattered picnic tables or on a lawn in semi shade where it is easy to retreat indoors if necessary.

Comfort is vital during the writing stage, so having too much sun on heads, varying temperatures, a breeze that blows papers away, inclement weather, biting insects or the noise from a horticultural power tool can all damage depth of thought and creation.

If working in a protected historical site such as a castle, abbey, preserved mine or other industrial setting, it is always worth finding out in advance if there is an 'education room' or other quiet space available for you to work in with your group, where you can retreat out of the weather and distraction to have meals, get warm, supply inputs or start some of the writing. Sometimes it can be valuable to book a visit to a site like this over two days so that you can take time to go through all the stages of brainstorming and supplying inputs on the first day, then return the following day so that students can write on-site and, if old enough, can be given freedom to observe specific parts further themselves, or to work in small groups in quiet and safe corners of the location where they can still be monitored.

Indoors, in schools and residential centres, I like to create a relaxed environment during writing sessions because this really does lead to greater creativity. Usually we stack many of the tables so that those who wish to can work on the

Photo 7.1 Describing a preserved chapel

carpet with all their brainstorm sheets fanned around their clipboards. If we are lucky we negotiate a larger space than usual so that students can spread out all their brainstorm sheets and have more personal quiet space. This might involve using two or more adjoining classrooms or other rooms, a carpeted library or lounge that has been dedicated to their use, or spilling into nearby sections of quiet corridors.

What to write on

Students in my poetry sessions always work on clipboards and on one side of plain A4 paper (often on the backs of old forms or letters) so they are able to move around more freely and won't feel concerned that they are wasting paper if they start different attempts on different sheets, make messy drafts or scatter copious numbers of preferred words, notes and partial lines around the place on different pages.

They are always asked to fan out the brainstorm sheets of words and metaphors in front of them so that other interesting words and ideas will catch their eyes and connect with those already processing in their heads. To help with this process all the sheets that the students, scribers or typists have produced in the brainstorm sessions should have plenty of white space around the words and phrases. This continuous 'availability' of language and idea possibilities counteracts the tendency of many students to narrow and limit ideas or word connections because it is easier for their brains to process them.

We want creative possibilities and originality, not lazy brains, and this system helps throw up truly interesting new language if students are taught to welcome it happening. Working like this produces better results from mundane writers but has also helped many of my most able students become outstanding and original young poets, and several have won significant competitions or had work or collections published. All of them still work in this way.

Computers

I almost never ask my students to write individual poems directly onto computers because there is something about the medium which seems to produce stiffer, less exciting work. On the other hand, students benefit hugely from using computers at the editing stage because of the ease and flexibility of editing on screen, and the 'final look' of type, layout, etc. Interestingly, out of the large numbers of highly committed and gifted young writers with whom I have worked on a semi-regular basis over periods of several years, nearly all prefer to write their poetry on paper but edit on screen, so it isn't just a personal trait.

Ironically, I invariably insist that students use computers while writing stories or other prose of any length because prose flows well on screen, sequencing can be changed effortlessly and sections of text of any size can easily be manipulated and moved around within the work, or 'put aside' and dropped back in later when required. Similarly, notes and complex plans for stories and other forms of prose can be altered, updated or copied onto the tops of evolving sections for reference.

A checklist of possible inputs before students write their poems appears on the following page. All these inputs are highly recommended but, as mentioned earlier, teachers will need to decide whether to input all or part of this material prior to a visit or to include it in a session between a locational brainstorm and the start of poetry writing based on it.

Descriptive poetry: a pre-writing checklist of possible inputs

Things to talk about:

- The special sounds of poetry, in which ways it's a 'sound art' and the relationships between the layout (including line breaks), punctuation, etc., of a poem and its sound.
- Stressed and unstressed beats and the conducting method.
- How stressed beats accentuate the best parts and the musicality of a poem.
- How tempo and mood can be affected by the numbers of, or lack of, unstressed beats between stressed ones.
- Possible general forms of poem and how to achieve these.
- 'Flow' in poetry and how to attain flow in meaning, rhythm and mood.
- Why and how to avoid making a 'list' instead of a poem. Does the content have a logical arrangement?
- Keeping the language tight, losing unnecessary articles and employing interesting and fresh language.
- Avoiding duplication of words and ideas, and any repetition (unless it's deliberate and makes the poem better).
- Keeping the 'I' out of the poem unless it's a poem about a particular personal experience in the past or that of a real or invented character.
- Using the present tense unless it's a story poem or is based on a distinct past experience.
- Your rules for this workshop, if any, on rhyming, not rhyming, partial rhyming, etc.
- The advantages and use of slant rhymes and sound echoes.
- Initial capitals and reasons for possibly not using them.
- Breaking 'rules' of poetry and grammar (although allowing freedom of experimentation is often effective with groups who already have good basic skills).

Things to decide:

- Whether you wish to run a short 'second stage brainstorm' just before writing to deepen ideas and language, and bring back the immediacy of a setting or event.
- Whether you want to supply many of the above inputs before the visit.
- Whether you'd like to start the actual writing on location.
- Whether you want to make an indoor writing space 'informal'.

'Minimalist' poems: a useful poetry form to base on locational brainstorms

What are 'minimalist' poems?

Many years ago I was looking for a concentrated form of poetry that would combine aspects of rhyme with quality language and thoughtful observation. I also wanted it to demonstrate simple patterns of stressed and unstressed beats as well as concentration of poetic language, without being daunting for students or teachers. Because of these requirements I decided it should have a pattern based on short lines of between one and three stressed beats each.

I called the general form 'minimalist' poetry because, although it is descriptive and employs many vibrant verbs, it utilizes a minimal amount of language in each line, forcing writers to discard unnecessary articles, connectives and pronouns. This form, therefore, has some of a haiku's qualities of language concentration but, unlike that Japanese syllabic form, it is longer and is set on English metric sound patterns of stressed and unstressed beats, usually combined with end rhyming.

Within its short descriptive lines a minimalist poem commonly employs Anglo-Saxon-style metaphorical phrases known as 'kennings' where many subjects are mentioned indirectly and often through compound words (such as 'wave-rider' representing a dolphin). A minimalist poem differs from Anglo-Saxon poetry, however, in that it is not narrative and usually rhymes, whereas Anglo-Saxon poetry that included kennings did not rhyme and instead employed alliteration within lines.

It's not as complicated as it first sounds!

The general pattern of stressed beats needs to be decided in advance, with two beats on every line being the easiest and most common. Other example variations might be 2,2,3, 2,2,3, beats per line, or 2,2,2,1, 2,2,2,1.

The position and number of *unstressed* beats in each short line usually becomes fairly obvious, and similar variations of these within lines are best placed in blocks because they sound more natural together and add variety to the rhythmic flow.

The rhyme scheme, if any, should be decided after, or along with, the stressed beat pattern. It is always simple, being usually a,a, b,b, couplets or a,b,a,b, but there are other possibilities such as a,b,c, a,b,c, or a,a,b, d,d,b, in each six-line section. The latter rhyme scheme works well on the 2,2,3, 2,2,3 format and resembles some traditional nursery rhymes in its form and musicality. If you are unconfident with rhyme, the easiest version of all is x,a,x,a, x,b,x,b, where 'x' represents a non-rhyming line ending.

This may all sound a bit complicated to a non-poet but the form is deliberately simple, and, once the poem is underway, following it is straightforward, mostly requiring group 'conducting' while trying to fit 'found' words to the agreed number of swings in each line. The tightness of the lines makes participants concentrate on the best words and learn creative sacrifice, and the hardest part is making them rhyme sensibly, but we'll look at helpful tips for doing this shortly.

Collective or individual writing

With younger or less poetically experienced groups I always favour brainstorming and writing minimalist poetry collectively, and have done this successfully, even with focused 5- to 7-year-olds. The most common bands I work with collectively on this form are ages 7–12 years. With students from perhaps eleven or twelve upwards, it is possible to allow the more able ones to work on these individually or, better, in small groups of say three to five students per poem. Mostly, though, I use this form in collective projects where we brainstorm on location as a group then write together indoors with a computer and digital projector.

Unless one is working with very able teenagers, the quality achieved through collective writing is generally greater than for individual work because a group can take on and maintain high expectations and, above all, the leader can help them to be ruthless about only agreeing lines when the rhymes make sense and help the flow of the poem.

After observing me work on minimalist poems with a group, teachers sometimes try to do the same thing, but without rhyming because they think it will be easier and they are less confident with poetic manipulation. I have nothing against this but I always choose to rhyme this form because:

- the results are much stronger;
- short swingy lines cry out for rhyme;
- students prefer the results and have a greater sense of achievement when it rhymes; and
- this simple form works well as a vehicle on which to experiment with finding and controlling rhyme in poetry while maintaining quality language and content.

Brainstorm variations for minimalist poetry

I like to choose a theme that suits a particular location then spin the brainstorm in favour of it. Successful themes might include subjects such as a stream or river, a lake, a forest, a canal, a railway station, a busy shopping centre, a derelict factory, or cows or other specific animals. The poem may also have a chosen 'slant' that focuses and angles the choice of description, such as 'sleepy', 'joyous', 'tragic' or 'spooky' (see the example entitled *All Hallows' Eve* at the end of this chapter).

For younger students, general themes might be a summer day in a park, a rainy morning, a winter day in the town or country, or just 'watching a suburban street' from the school gates. Looking at life in a busy playground can work well enough with infants, utilising at the ends of lines verbs that come out of the various movements and activities observed. An example using nothing but the verbs as key words in a small section might be:

jumping, skipping,
running, tripping . . .

Easier rhyming tips

Employing verbs, or nouns derived from them, to create rhyming or slant rhyming at the ends of the lines is one of the secrets of minimalist poetry, as in the beginning of my little dolphin poem:

<u>surf</u> <u>skimm</u>er,
<u>fast</u> <u>swimm</u>er,
<u>high</u> <u>lea</u>per,
<u>click</u> <u>squeak</u>er . . .

You will notice the kenning-like way the subject name (dolphin) isn't described directly, but the words are based on what it does. This section could equally use present participles of the verbs, as in:

<u>surf</u> <u>skimm</u>ing,
<u>fast</u> <u>swimm</u>ing . . .

Although rhyming on the verbs or verb-derived nouns can be an easy way both to find rhymes and include vibrant descriptive words, it is richer and more satisfying if there are variations in some sections of the poem so that, for instance, a sequence like the above might be inverted into rhyming on an adverb, like this:

<u>swimm</u>ing <u>fast</u>,
<u>leap</u>ing <u>past</u>,

or (slightly harder) could be varied by rhyming with another non-verb word such as a noun, before returning to a present tense verb, as in:

> *through **night** and **day***
> *you **swim** and **play***

or (again slightly more challenging and interesting) your group could work up a metaphorical idea and then find a way of rhyming it, for example:

> *a **slic**ing **fin***
> *through **o**cean **skin***

or

> ***knife** fin **slic**ing,*
> ***white** foam **ic**ing . . .*

I have emboldened the stressed beats in all the above lines to demonstrate that, although there are two stressed beats in each of these poem variations, the overall sound of it changes with different placements and numbers of unstressed beats. You will notice that wherever the unstressed beats vary, that variation is deliberately matched in the line below, such as **tum, tum**-ti / **tum, tum**-ti, *or* **tum**-ti **tum** / **tum**-ti **tum**, the iambic ti **tum** ti **tum** / ti **tum** ti **tum** or trochaic **tum** ti **tum** ti / **tum** ti **tum** ti.

As mentioned earlier, it is usually best to put variations together in blocks of the same sort and, depending on your chosen rhyme scheme, you will find these groups of lines of a similar unstressed beat variation usually work best in blocks of four or eight lines, or of six lines if you chose the a,b,c, a,b,c, *or* a,a,b, d,d,b rhyme schemes. However, don't panic if this seems confusing . . . if the pattern sounds good it *is* good!

Improving observation and creative discipline

One of the great things about this type of form is that it forces students to look for interesting details and try to describe them in interesting ways, because the poem probably won't last more than a few lines otherwise! So, for instance, when working with young children on a simple playground poem, they could observe not only at what the subjects are doing but also at what parts of their bodies or their clothes are doing, as in:

> *shouting, crying,*
> *pigtails flying,*

or

> *dancing, scrapping,*
> *shirt tails flapping,...*

You might be aware that there isn't a perfect logical connection between the observations within each pair of lines here. It's confusing who is doing what in them, so the sections could be altered and put together like this to show more logical connections and comparisons:

> *dancing, wiggling,*
> *pigtails jiggling;*

and

> *chasing, scrapping,*
> *shirt tails flapping ...*

This is an example of how, even in a simple, minimalist poem about playground activity, there can still be some form of internal organisation of material into logical sections or to fit an overall plan. So, like the text above, which is obviously about some different ways girls and boys behave in the playground, the poem could be built on alternating two lines for girls, then two for boys or, better, into four-line 'verselets' for each, or half the poem for each, drawing out differences or similarities.

In the same way, the first section of the poem could be about children's movements, the second one about other playground activities, the third one about games and fantasy worlds within the real world of the playground, and the fourth could be a little summary, ending in rounding off lines, such as in this x,a,x,a verse

> *So **this** is **where***
> *we **skip** and **run**.*
> *We **love** our **sunn**y*
> *__play__ground **fun**!*

You may have noticed that these lines are identical in the positions of the stressed and unstressed beats except that the lack of a beginning unstressed beat on the final line is made up for here by the extra unstressed one (on the 'y' of 'sunny') at the end of the penultimate line.

Other 'compare and contrast' ideas

When I worked with a group comparing a tiny mill stream with the large and powerful river it flowed into, the first half of the poem focused on minute details, movements, similes and metaphors for the little stream, the second half similarly describing the power, movements, currents, banks, sounds, etc. of the large river, some of it also through metaphor and simile.

In minimalist poems, successful comparison sections can equally be made between places such as: a still pond and a busy stream; an empty playground and a manic one; untouched countryside and a nearby, newly built shopping centre; a quiet park or churchyard and the busy street outside; a station platform between trains, then the burst of activity when one arrives and leaves; an area of shiny new gravestones and one filled with chaotic old ones; peaceful rock pools and surf-driven sea; almost any scene in the dark and also during the day, in rain and sun, and so on.

A satisfying project is to build up a collective minimalist poem over a period by writing a section in the same place outdoors in each season, trying to focus on rich detail and difference, avoiding too many of the usual seasonal clichés and including new metaphorical content each time. Obvious titles for each section could involve the seasons, but it might be better to entitle the poem *Changes* or *Flowering and Fading* or just give a place indication such as *In Bell Wood* then try to avoid any direct reference to the seasons in titles or text. This gentle riddle quality gives readers a slightly greater sense of involvement as they 'discover' the seasonal differences themselves.

Illustrated, or collaged creatively around large print or hand-lettering, a poem like this can make a good corridor or hall display, pleasing and benefitting other students who read it and take in the rich vocabulary.

Riddle quality

Owing to their indirectness regarding the subject, minimalist poems can indeed be almost riddle-like and in some of mine, such as the dolphin poem, I don't put a title at the beginning but include it in the poem at the end. Often the last word is, in a way, the title. Younger students enjoy this aspect, and particularly like it when I simply don't give a title at all but they can work it out by listening well to the poem until it becomes clear what the subject is.

Writing in this way gives an opportunity to have a clear rounding off line at the end which pulls it all together. So, for instance, one of my minimalist poems ends in

rule preacher ...
school teacher!

However, it could also be left as an easy riddle with the simple title 'Who am I?' if it ended in something like:

tireless trainer,
setter of test,
helpful explainer ...
she's the best!

Just as easily, one could 'live brainstorm' a local animal such as a cow, sheep, dog, hen or llama; a tractor working in a rural area; or trains at a nearby station, and give the poem the title 'What am I?' Following a similar visit to a nearby place (for example a park, canal, dock, train station or the local supermarket with its human activity), the resulting descriptive 'riddle' poem might equally well be entitled 'Where am I?'

Preparing for the brainstorm

Preparations for a minimalist poem brainstorm session are the same as for one for descriptive poetry with the exception that you may be focusing more narrowly on one theme or subject and a more limited scale of location. If it's a precursor to collective poetry writing it is exceptionally helpful to have a fast-typing assistant with a portable computer, who stays near enough to hear and capture all the words and phrases supplied by the group. Again, a lightweight fishing or camping stool can be practical in this situation.

Scribing will do as a fall-back but, because you will later want to work collectively on the writing with the words available on a digital projector screen or interactive board, the computer wins hands down. It can also display participants' 'possible rhyming words' in related batches, and a typist can jump back to drop in later discoveries within their relevant batch or area of words.

Older teenagers can scribe on their own clipboards but it's still preferable to have a typist assistant because the students can then be free to concentrate on thinking and answering, and slower scribers don't need to worry about missing out words.

Brainstorming and writing tips

Brainstorming for minimalist poetry

Running a locational brainstorm session for minimalist poetry is similar to running one for general descriptive poetry but with three fundamental differences. The first is that a brainstorming session for minimalist poetry focuses mostly on one subject. The second is that it needs to concentrate on finding pertinent 'vibrant' verbs as well as other related descriptions, and the third difference is that it helps to simultaneously search for rhyming words related to these verbs and descriptions.

Both types of brainstorm session require detailed questioning and thoughtful observation but a session for a minimalist poem often looks slightly less at objects or character and more at what things or people are doing or what is happening to them. A minimalist poem brainstorm in a wood might look at what the trees, twigs, and leaves are 'doing' and to surrounding things like grasses, ferns, clouds, stream, insects, rotten trunks, rocks, light and shadow. Even static things like rocks or stone circles can be 'boldly *standing, wrapped* in moss, lichen-*spattered*, silent *watchers*', etc. so, when writing the poem together later you might have an a,a,b,b form with a section like this:

> slab-capped,
> moss-wrapped,
> ancient boulders . . .
> secret-holders,

or an a,b,a,b form of this, as in

> slab-capped
> ancient boulders . . .
> moss-wrapped
> secret-holders!

Developing the brainstorm

So, in a brainstorm for a minimalist poem, participants are simultaneously looking for strong active and passive verbs or verb-derived words, other interesting descriptive words, metaphorical ideas, multiple rhymes for words from each of these things, and possible sound echoes within or between lines.

Looking at forest grasses, for instance, a group might come up with active verbs such as *swishing, bending, dangling, jiggling, swinging, sprouting, twitching* and *quivering*. To stimulate both descriptive touches and metaphorical thinking, the leader could also ask them to describe these grasses. Answers might be: *thin, fine, wiry, tufted* or *in tufts, dewy, dew-dropped* and *seed-heavy*.

As each strong verb or other word arises, the leader can ask for any rhyming words that fit those or other things in that local environment, so *swishing* might throw up *wishing* which probably wouldn't easily work in the poem, whereas *swish* could produce *wish* which might, with less difficulty, be worked into a poem as it's both a verb and a noun. If there's a little stream near some of these grasses, the word *splishing* might arise, so the lines *streamlet splishing / grasses swishing* could be possible. It helps if you or your typist or scriber are getting all these words and rhymes down in the same general area of screen or paper so they can later throw up useful possibilities of connection while the poem is being composed.

If you have covered slant rhymes or reminded participants about them just before the session, you might get *swishing / brushing* from someone, or *swishing /*

washing. Swinging the focus you could then also ask for anything in that environment that rhymes with *brushing* or *brush* and a student is likely to tell you *water rushing* or *waters rush*. Another might say *waters gushing*, or *forest hush*, so, when you all go inside to write the poem itself you will already have at least four relevant rhyming words from that environment to use within many possible permutations.

You can also ask for pertinent alliterative words to enrich these, and, if nothing is forthcoming, suggest students look for 'g' words to go with *gushing* or 'r' words to go with 'rush' or 'rushing'. If there are still no suggestions, you can ask them to find words which fit aspects of the stream at that point. This might produce words like *rapids, river, ripples*, or, *gravelly, galloping, grumpy*.

So now you can pair up alliterations later as well, as in *gravel-galloping, gushing on gravel, rushing rapids*, or *racing ripples*. Bringing the grasses back in, these might finally end up in the poems in paired lines such as:

> *grassheads brush*
> *it's gravelly gush . . .*

or

> *grassheads brush*
> *the rapids' rush . . .*

Finding slant rhymes can create more rhyming possibilities at the writing stage

It is better, not to exclude any near-rhyme suggestions such as *rush/fuss, brushing/fussing, swishing/hissing* because strong slant rhymes might be used in the poem and they may create 'sideways jumps' to pure rhyme ideas such as *fussing/mussing/cussing*, all of which might sound like odd choices to start with but which could produce interesting ideas: such as the concept of a petulant breeze scruffing up sprays of forest grass seed heads, as in:

> *the breeze is fussing*
> *as it passes,*
> *grumpily mussing*
> *hair-fine grasses*

or a pernickety little stream

> *foams and fusses,*
> *spits and cusses.*

A leader should therefore direct attention particularly towards verbs or verb-based nouns, and generally to language involving action, movements, passivity (*standing, fallen*) and sounds (*sighing, whisper*), while finding deeper descriptions, batches of rhyming and slant rhyming words, and helpful sound echoes. To deepen the brainstorm further, the leader also needs to keep asking for multiple metaphors or similes for most things observed.

For instance, you might ask students what one of the thin grasses looks like or is doing, apart from *dangling* over the water. Someone might say it is *whipping* the water, someone that it is *drowsily nodding,* and someone else that it looks like a little fishing rod. Taking the last, as an example, you can ask if they can remember or think of anything that rhymes with *fishing, fish* or *rod,* and they might come up with *rod* and *nod,* or *swishing* and *fishing.* Later, when you are working on the collective poem, these notes might turn into something (in two-beats-per-line couplets) like:

> *a __grass__ is __swish__ing,*
> *__soft__ly __fish__ing*
> *where __rapids rush__*
> *through __forest hush__*

or, in an a,b,a,b, rhyme scheme, it might end up as:

> *a __grass__ is __swish__ing*
> *where __wa__ters __rush__,*
> *__soft__ly __fish__ing*
> *in __forest hush__*

or, in an a,b,a,b rhyme scheme in a 2,2,2,3 stressed beat form it could be:

> *a __grass swish__es*
> *in __forest hush__,*
> *__soft__ly __fish__es*
> *where __coppery wa__ters __rush__ ...*

I think you will agree that the latter sounds slightly less mechanical and more sophisticated, partly due to the placement of two stressed beats together in the first line (which makes the grass seem to pause before swishing at the end of the line), partly due to the greater space available (which has 'allowed in' the interesting descriptive word *coppery* with its two unstressed beats), and partly due to the tightness of the first three lines contrasting with the little 'liberated rush' of words on the last, slightly longer line.

Deliberate deviation from lines of regular numbers of beats

The trick of increasing or reducing the number of stressed beats in the final line of a section that has had a regular number of beats in all its previous lines can add texture to a poem and supply a feeling of rounding off at the end of the poem, stanza or section. However, to prevent it feeling like the poem almost stops and starts too often, you might suggest writing longer sections than this, with one longer or shorter line at the end of each section.

For instance, the four-line verselet above could have another four two-beat lines in front of it, making it an eight-line 'split' verse of 2,2,2,2, 2,2,2,3 beats. Once you've written a small part collectively you can look at little variations like this with the group, then allow them to experiment with you by saying one or two possible variations of form out loud together while filling in any unwritten parts in 'ti's' or '**tum**'s. Everyone can then vote to choose which of these forms they prefer to stay with for the rest of the poem. This can give students the beginnings of a more 'organic' awareness of possible sound patterns and forms of poetry, something that most are hardly even aware of.

More about writing the collective poem

Working together on the challenge of creating a rich and well-controlled minimalist poem is an effective way to raise expectation, teach patience and determination, and demonstrate the control, memory, creativity and stamina required to combine all the necessary language, sound, form and metaphorical elements of poetry.

It is most practical to collect the brainstorm material on a portable computer but remember to save continuously to a memory stick or external drive as well as to the machine's hard drive because accidents happen, batteries run out, software problems occur and machines break down.

While writing collectively, one can 'toggle' between the document containing the emerging poem and the brainstorm pages, but it is much easier to lead the collective writing fluently if you have an assistant at the keyboard, leaving you free to keep the group continuously focused.

A dream solution is to have two digital screens beside each other, driven by different computers; for instance, the display from a digital projector showing on the wall or whiteboard beside the interactive board. In this way you or your assistant can type the emerging poem ideas on one screen without constantly turning on and off the display of brainstorm words that everyone needs to be able to see. Split screen display is also possible but it's effective to have brainstorm material clearly and continuously visible, and you can scroll up and down those pages to find or add items as required.

We've already looked at variations in rhyme scheme, stressed beats and unstressed beats but the main things are to be flexible in thought, to lead through questioning so that the group is fully involved, and to try and stay one jump ahead of the group by working out possible ideas for lines and rhymes in case the group begins floundering for a while. While staying one jump ahead it is equally important to keep an open ear and mind to participants' ideas, and to try and instil this combination of determination and flexibility into the group ethos.

It's effective and involving in any collective creative work to continuously ask students for ideas, rhymes, new lines and possible variations of lines, and to display relevant words and possible rhymes to enable regular voting on different possibilities. Not only is this 'democratic' creativity, but it enhances involvement, tolerance and teamwork, and produces the richest and best ideas and language within an ethos where the expectation is to achieve the highest quality possible.

Can rhyming dictionaries help?

The answer to that question is 'yes and no': most of the rhymes should come from the brainstorm or be found by participants, because finding them is a skill that can improve with use, and their discovery can also build pride, confidence and involvement. On the other hand, allowing a couple of students to trawl through good quality rhyming dictionaries for possibilities while the group is temporarily stuck can sometimes throw up new solutions or directions. There is nothing to stop leaders and assistants from making suggestions too, as long as students are the primary source.

It is best, however, if participants learn to be flexible and find other ways to rhyme when stuck. This can be through using those tips already discussed, such as inverting lines, finding synonyms or related words to rhyme from, and searching for alliterations, slant rhymes or new metaphors that might throw up easier rhyming possibilities.

As with writing any good poetry, creating a high quality collective poem takes time and is hard work on 'mental muscles', so it is worth considering breaking the writing stage into two or more sessions, to allow for creative recharging to take place.

Photocopiable and scannable examples of some of the author's own minimalist poems follow, along with two collective poems in this style from workshop sessions. All this material is copyright but may be utilised in workshop sessions by purchasers of this book.

Examples of 'minimalist' poetry

The first minimalist poem in this selection of examples is in simple couplets and mostly has a 'push-and-run' rhythm created by having two stressed beats followed by an unstressed one in each line, although this alters near the end. The poem consists of rhyming descriptive kennings and, without its final 'title word', would be even more riddle-like.

surf skimmer,
fast swimmer,
high leaper,
click-squeaker,
deep diver,
wave rider,
smile beaming,
steel gleaming,
sea slicing,
man enticing,
high singing,
joy bringing;
knife fin,
sleek skin,
coy grin . . .
dol-phin!

This little minimalist poem also only gives the subject away in the 'title word' of the last line. Note the wealth of observations described, despite lines containing so few words.

Giant dice scattered on a tablecloth of green . . .
each big, soft, steamy milk machine
is a loud mooing,
cud chewing,
tail swishing,
tongue twisting,
grass cutting,
head butting,
back-scrambling,
slow ambling,
twin toed,
dewey nosed,
easy shocked,
muddy socked,
river wading,
hedge invading,
meadow scented,
fly demented
cow!

The rhythm of this poem was designed to be reminiscent of the amusing, jerky way penguins waddle (like Charlie Chaplin in old films) so this poem has an a,a,b / c,c,b rhyme scheme, similar to some nursery rhymes, until it reaches the final, rounding off verse which is x,d,x,d (where 'x' doesn't rhyme) along with internal (within line) rhymes and alliterations. Although there are only two stressed beats per line throughout the poem, the rhythm holds it tightly on the first two lines of each half-verse by having two stressed beats together to start them, then seems to loosen on each third line, owing to the insertion of additional unstressed beats. The cartoon-like imagery and sound patterns are accentuated when the poem deliberately ends with a clichéd American sitcom phrase.

Penguin

Spring scrapping,
wing-flapping,
rowdy crowder;
vast flocking,
mass squawking ...
who can shout louder?
Egg muffler,
leg shuffler,
dawdling toddler;
tail-suited,
flat-footed
comedy waddler!
Ice-sliding,
line guiding ...
'follow my leader'!
Fishy fun!
Here I come!
Chubby torpedo!
Underwater athlete
shooting from the foam,
landing standing ...
"Honey, I'm home!"

This simple minimalist poem also has a slight riddle quality thanks to its many kennings and a title which only mentions the subject indirectly. Readers or listeners can work out the subject themselves through the descriptive kennings.

Neighbour

wave rider,
wind glider,
ship wheeler,
chip stealer,
bow racer,
plough chaser,
high watcher,
pavement blotcher,
streetlamp sitter,
sneaky flitter,
selfish shrieker,
window streaker,
aerial gymnast,
boisterous guest . . .
noisy
uninvited pest!

To accentuate the 'moving and morphing' quality of the subject, this poem plays with an ever-changing rhyme scheme and different numbers of stressed beats in each line, while still maintaining its sonic flow. To see how it changes, groups can conduct, mark and count the stressed beats in each line, then underline identical rhymes in the same colours.

Clouds

Sedately drifting,
slow shape-shifting,
ever-changing,
re-arranging,
forming, deforming,
wispy and twisty,
pillowy, billowy,
stretched and rounded ...
strangely unbounded.
Boiling up boldly
and fading away;
a paint-store shade-card
in white and grey.
Anything anyone's seen is there
for those with the time and patience to stare.
An invisible artist's eternally changing creations.
Perfect playdough
for young imaginations.

The rhyme scheme in this kenning-filled, descriptive minimalist poem morphs at some points to fit the changing character of the subject and to make its sound more varied and less predictable. It begins with simple a,a, b,b couplets but, on top of the small rhythmic change that underlines its stormy violence in the 'ship shaker . . .' couplet, the rhyme scheme itself morphs from a,a,b,b, to c,d,c,d, where the 'c' is slant rhymed, to e,e,e,e, to x,f,x,f, where 'x' is a slant rhyme or non-rhyme.

Sea

ceaseless heaver,
clear deceiver,
cool inviter,
icy biter;
life renewer,
seaweed strewer,
husher, shusher,
sunset blusher;
toothless chewer,
headland hewer,
cliff-face crumbler
tireless tumbler;
constant creeping,
seashore sweeping,
never sleeping,
secret keeping . . .
harbour lashing,
symbol crashing,
springing, stinging,
shingle flinging . . .
ship shaker,
boat breaker,

sailor taker,
widow maker;
patient provider,
ever defiant;
violent tyrant,
gentlest giant;
sluggish, sudden,
slow and quick;
slave of sun
and 'lunatic';
restless rider,
shoreline slider,
land divider,
wildlife hider;
billowy blankets,
wrinkled silk,
can-can petticoats
white as milk;
glittering, green-eyed
'Dance-All-Day';
baby-blue 'new'
and old man grey.

The following animal poem is a hybrid between a minimalist poem and a relatively conventional one. It has more connectives and so more conventional grammatical and sonic flow than a purely minimalist poem. Like a minimalist poem it makes use of concentrated descriptive language, often rhymes on vibrant verbs and, although it doesn't include individual kennings within it, it has a certain, kenning-like indirectness, such as never mentioning the subject by name.

There are mostly between two and three unstressed beats between stressed ones, creating a rhythm as 'busy' and manic as the subject.

Walkies

Straining on the leather
like a boat in bad weather
tugs at its tether
to escape to the sea;
forgetting your schooling,
impatiently pulling,
dribbling and drooling . . .
a click and you're free!

Floppy ears flolloping,
gulping and golloping,
raggedly rolloping
over the park;
charging at nothing,
panting and puffing,
snorting and snuffing
at grass and at bark.

Slowing now to sniff
with your 'aerial' stiff
as you're catching a whiff
of a curious scent
and you're chancing your luck
in an upwash of muck
as you lunge at a duck
with the vaguest intent.

But your duties are done,
you have rolled and you've run,
and you've had enough fun
(so your owner has said).
So, head's down, it's raining –
who cares about the training!
You're heading home, straining
for dinner and bed!

Examples of group-written minimalist poetry

This piece about a stream was written collectively by a group of students aged from 7–10 years with my guidance. It was constructed around verb-based kennings. Due to time constraints the poem is slightly too much in the form of a list of two-beat line couplets, but shows strong observation skills, thoughtful descriptions, rich language and unusual rhyming, most of which would not have surfaced in a classroom-based workshop session.

Pebble turner's
secret murmurs . . .
softly kissing,
willow hissing;
tuneful tinkler,
crinkly wrinkler!
music player,
gravel layer,
fast-flowing,
ever-glowing,
shingle shooter,
rebel router!
tree hugger,
nettle tugger,
weed nagger,
log dragger . . .
stormy thunderer,
muddy plunderer!
bank nibbler,
landscape scribbler;
cautious creeper,
wildlife keeper,
feather floater,
bobbing boater!
sand streaker,
ocean seeker,
history-tracing,
current chasing,
ripple-spilling
stipples milling,
flower-stealing,
water-wheeling,
dam diver,
drought survivor;
duckling lifter,
dreamy drifter;
chalk shaver,
calm behaver,
mellow tone,
still as stone;
bindweed weaver,
lace-leaf leaver,
wagtail wetter,
rhythm setter;
endless traveller
slow unraveller,
sunshine flowered,
nature-powered,
life-giver . . .
glimmering river.

The following richly descriptive poem was created collectively in a windy rural setting by a group of 9- to 11-year-old students under my direction. As it was Halloween the group wanted to give the piece a spooky edginess so we brainstormed through the cusp of evening into darkness, and participants carefully selected their observations and thoughtfully 'spun' their descriptions to add a sense of creepy unease throughout the poem.

*With this flavour in mind it was written in the unusual form of couplets of alternating two and three stressed beat lines, designed to keep tugging the rhythm back and make it feel more unsettling. The group experimented with various form possibilities, saying them out in tis and **tum**s until they chose a form which felt suitable.*

To add variety and flow this minimalist piece has aspects both of a tight kenning poem and of a looser, more conventional one.

All Hallow's Eve

The dying day
sadly bleeds away,
horizon light
is gnawed apart by night.
A stardust shroud,
is patched by smoky cloud
where hills loom
like sinister waves of doom.

Headlamp feelers ...
fumbling darkness stealers;
squint trunks, bare,
lit by their glancing glare.
Ribbed twigs,
clawed, spidery sprigs,
where spindly shadows
brindle ghostly meadows.

Black-bat leaves
hang from tortured trees ...
shadowy splotches,
blurry, inky blotches.
'Pencil' traces
are creating spooky faces
but window spies
have fiery pumpkin eyes!

A river's sharpness
glints in the dusky darkness
where a black cat slinks,
its eyes like torch-lit chinks.
Twiggy twinkles
pinprick etched-out wrinkles
on half-lit trunks
that watch like hooded monks.

Late-night walkers
followed by shuddering stalkers ...
shadow-shackled
their careless footsteps crackle.
Fingers crawl
on a lamplight-varnished wall;
shapes shifting ...
shuffling, shivering, drifting.

Leaves race,
playing midnight chase,
each a wild
hyper-active child
in this dismal, dreary,
weary, bleary, eerie,
shadow-hurled,
desolate, wind-whipped world

Group poems, their development into other art forms and examples of co-operative work

Location based collective poetry

Although students must ultimately build personal skills and confidence in literacy, and teachers need to assess the development of individual writing, a great deal can be gained from collective writing sessions. This is especially true of such sessions based on group locational brainstorming that is creatively led, because the quality of language and ideas generated can be so high, the manipulation of these so complex and the results obtained so exciting and satisfying for participants, it increases levels of enthusiasm, involvement and skills at all abilities.

As always, it is useful to be supported by an assistant, older student or parent who can type fluently on a computer linked to an interactive board or digital projector, because everyone can see writing developments as they occur, additions and improvements can be made in real time, and you can focus on leading the group.

In a future chapter we will look at suggestions for collective story challenges, but here are a few tried and tested ideas where group poetry writing can be successfully developed into other art forms through collective participation.

Creating 'poster poems'

The first of these multi-media ideas involves brainstorming in an evocative setting, writing a powerful collective poem based on this material and then evolving the result into a large piece of group artwork centred on the words of the poem. Through questioning, the group leader must keep reminding participants at both brainstorm and writing stages to think in particularly visual terms and should pose specific questions that will elicit strong imagery in the poem and subsequent artwork.

Students who have composed a poem usually look forward to creating the artwork as a reward for their hard work. Teachers can either run this stage on their own, in conjunction with their art department, or with a little help from artistically competent colleagues, assistants, older students, parents or friends.

Materials

The easiest and least messy way of achieving good results is to use coloured crayons on paper, with the text and artwork first sketched in pencil. Working with these simple, inexpensive materials avoids incidents with wet paint or grimy results due to charcoal or chalk dust spreading everywhere. Students don't need to wear aprons or other protective clothing and the work can be ready for display immediately it is finished as there is no drying time required.

I have mostly worked with from seven to seventeen students on each 'poster poem', usually with either two or four large Ao sheets of thin white card obtained from helpful local printers or school stocks for each one. Wallpaper lining paper can be a cheap alternative but it only comes in a narrow width, so several sheets must be taped together on the back, and it has a tendency to roll back up. I have also used sugar paper but the medium it is fixed onto must be thick and strong enough to prevent tears or creasing if students lean hard or crawl over its edges.

A large piece of artwork like this can be illustrated while laid out on smooth flooring but, despite instructions to the contrary, students tend to take a short cut by walking on the paper or accidentally crushing art materials onto it. Working bent over on a hard floor can become uncomfortable (especially for adult helpers) so it is best to place the display sheet on a large art layout table or to push tables together and place it on those. It may be necessary to cover tables with smooth cardboard as seams between them will appear in the crayon work unless the artwork card is thick enough to prevent this.

Layout and lettering

It is easiest for participants to understand and be involved in the overall and detailed design if display sheets are first taped together on the back and a precise adult scriber (or neat older student) lays down the lettering before illustrating begins. This can take some time to get right. Sections of the lettering can also be produced on sheets on a computer printer and collaged onto the display, though this can require some experimentation in order to evolve the required font sizes, surrounding white space needed, and so on.

Normally the whole group gets involved in volunteering artwork and layout suggestions as the pencilled-in draft of the display poem is read through slowly. Some students will probably ask to illustrate particular aspects.

All artwork, including the initial lettering, must initially be executed in pencil so it can be checked, changes made and mistakes rectified, and it is best if the title and any stanzas or sections of text have a generous blank area around them to allow plenty of space for large, eye-catching illustration.

'Large' is the crucial notion here because the younger the participants the more minute the illustrations they tend to produce, so leaders and assistants will regularly need to remind them to 'think big', and suggest sizeable spaces to be filled by each main image in order to create text and illustration that can be seen clearly from a distance once the final piece is mounted on a wall.

Enhancing texture and presentation

To increase working space, some areas can be 'collaged' by drawing and colouring bold images (such as key features like mountains, figures, animals, buildings or trees) onto separate pieces of card then gluing these onto the main board. To make central images stand out even more these can be mounted on thick cardboard and cut out before being attached to the appropriate part of the display piece, perhaps with sticky pads underneath to raise them further. It is safest to have such illustrations drawn in pencil then checked in position before being coloured and cut out.

Extra materials may be added for variety and texture and it can be effective to cut leaves and other objects from tissue paper, crêpe, card, fabric, sugar or shiny paper before attaching them to the piece. Groups sometimes also add items such as cotton wool, feathers, twigs, dried leaves or grasses, leather off-cuts, foil, beach shells, and ribbons.

In the final stages of illustration participants can be invited to colour in as much of the background as possible. They must be careful not to affect the readability of lettering, for instance by using dark colours too near to dark lettering. Chubby crayons are inexpensive in high street discount shops and, rubbed sideways, can cover large areas quickly.

For an even quicker outcome, a photo collage can be created around the words, taken from pictures shot at the location, but the photos will need to show what they illustrate in a very clear way because distant things and subtle detail are difficult to capture effectively by camera, even if the pictures are printed off in fairly large sizes. Even with a photo collage it can be more effective to blend photos and text together with a little appropriate artwork or graphics.

Participants find it more rewarding if the final artwork can be hidden from view by a sheet or old newspaper pages taped together, until the time comes for its creators to present it to school or parents. With this in mind it's worth setting aside a little time in which to coach and rehearse the group, no matter what age they are, so they can read the text out together 'slowly, clearly, loudly and with feeling', as part of their unveiling presentation.

Evolving location-based poems into dramatic movement

Another particularly effective way of enhancing your students' rich, location-based poetry is by showing them how to illustrate their work through movement. Unlike a brainstorming and writing session for a poster poem which needs to concentrate much of the descriptive content through visual imagery, creating a collective piece suited to performance through movement requires, at all stages, a mindset which observes and emphasises the movements within a setting, creating a particular emphasis on the use of vibrant verbs.

If a group has had this concept explained to them in the early stages of the brainstorming session they quickly start thinking more in terms of movement and of seeking appropriate language. Of course, interesting visual, auditory and other sensory description should not be left out, but the outcome is stronger if there has been a particular focus on descriptions and metaphors that involve movement.

Creating the movement

The first time you work with a group on producing and refining dramatic movement for words, you may need to 'lead from the front' to start with by showing them subtle ways of moving that 'illustrate, explain and enhance' the words of the first part of the poem. Once they get the idea you can ask them for suggestions and incorporate the best of these.

Producing and performing movement to powerful spoken imagery is a richly creative process and will help develop students' awareness of poetic and language rhythms because they will need to make all key movements coincide exactly with the stressed beats of key words, particularly verbs. In performance, there is always a brief lead-in time to thinking and getting a movement going, so one of the secrets of success is for each performer to have a 'cue' syllable just ahead, on which they actually start a section of movement, which enables key movements to occur precisely on the appropriate stressed syllables, in time with and highlighting relevant imagery.

Whole body movements, including floor work, are required to make the physical side richly reflect the verbal imagery. Performers who are not key to the imagery at any particular instant should freeze with their heads and hands dropped until it is their turn to be involved again. Like this, the audience naturally follows performers whose movements are appropriate to the words at that moment.

Those who haven't led this kind of activity before needn't feel daunted by it but enjoy trying things out while appearing pleasantly confident. Most students will respond by helping refine ideas to make them work more effectively. If there is time between finishing the poem and working on movement, you can read through the text and think about movements or sequences which might be suitable and visually interesting. Better still, you can try moving around a quiet space yourself, testing out movement possibilities so you will have ideas to contribute and more sense of direction when leading the students.

Specific examples of movement creation

Trees in a breeze can be portrayed by several performers standing with their bodies bent or raised in different ways and their arms out and moving in various directions. If the words require a rush of breeze to sweep through this 'forest' they will then need to cascade their movements slightly, so each student's moves follow on from key 'tree(s)' where the breeze starts. Other performers can be the fleet-footed wind brushing and spinning through the 'trees', making their 'branches' toss as they pass.

Similarly, performers might become the sea, rolling and heaving relatively randomly on the floor, before morphing into specific 'waves' together, keeping low as they rush forwards on their feet, rising with their arms curving high and forwards, then crashing onto an imaginary shore before wriggling backwards to their starting positions. It can be especially dramatic if performers occasionally call out a key word along with the reader, to time with a dramatic movement. An example would be the word 'smash' in this line about waves '*maddened monsters SMASH on foam-ripped rock*'.

A 'boat' plunging across those waves could be formed by three or more students, one being the mast with outstretched arms. They can be shown how to bend and rise in sequence to make it appear to roll over the waves in time to the words. All movements and timing depend on what the words of the poem describe at that point.

Tiny sequences of movements can be suggested, worked out and rehearsed little by little, added to the previous parts then run through again and again until their timings become fluent. One of the handiest things to learn is what I call 'the magic position', which is kneeling with one knee up and one down and hands resting on the floor. From this position performers can be still or move, rise smoothly to standing or moving, sink to the floor, roll sideways, or lie on their fronts or backs. It is an essential transitory position as well as a useful 'holding' one for performers who shouldn't be noticed until their time to move arrives.

Movement in smaller groups

If you do this kind of work on more than one piece with your students, you can ask smaller groups to work on their own individual or collective poems then develop movement for these by themselves. Such groups may contain between four and eight students, with all of them involved in working out movement for their piece and one of them reading the work slowly, clearly and loudly as the others perform it.

Natural breaks within a piece or between pieces can also be filled with small sections of an appropriate play, song or dance created by the performers. I have themed and directed many successful shows like this.

For performances I normally ask participants to wear comfortable white T-shirts and black 'bottoms' such as leggings, loose trousers or joggers, as it is less distracting from the words and movement than a variety of coloured clothing. Most people have or can borrow such clothing, or even borrow from the school's lost property collection.

An occasional prop might be used, but most effective of all is to supply, or ask for the loan of, large pieces of fabric such as sheets of varied colours, shiny fabric offcuts, old curtains, and scarves, etc. Groups can create much more variety of movement with these, such as rippling them in the air or on the floor for water or wind, winding and unwinding themselves in them as they spin, covering themselves with white or grey material to be clouds, and so on. Students often become enthusiastic about using fabric in this way once they've see it demonstrated effectively, but it needs to be employed thoughtfully and sparingly so that it enhances, rather than takes over from, performers' own movements.

Presentations and collaborations

Whenever possible, I believe strongly in 'using writing to achieve more than the writing itself' because wider outcomes deepen purpose and bring a greater sense of achievement to young writers. It is part of what educationalists sometimes refer to as 'reasons for writing'.

Sharing, displaying and celebrating excellent collective or individual writing leads to raised quality expectations and heightened confidence. Evolving it into visual art or movement can deepen this essential sense of achievement and stimulate a stronger drive to observe, think and write interestingly and creatively.

These sorts of extension of creative writing can also be the basis of small, informal collaborations with school art or drama departments, or with an enthusiast from within the greater school or local community. IT, art and drama departments may also be happy to assist in making an edited video of the performance with the words of the poem as soundtrack, or a video which tracks the words in text and sound while cutting in appropriate illustration, video shots or 'stills' taken at the brainstorm location which inspired the piece in the first place.

A particularly notable audiovisual presentation I was involved in producing came at the end of a location based project I led which involved able students of around 12–13 years of age working, on several occasions, in the evocative environment of a semi-ruined abbey. Participants brainstormed with me and worked intensely on poetic sounds, forms, on deepening meaning, writing, re-writing and editing.

They were lent digital cameras with which to record aspects of the edifice described in their final poems. Once all the writing was perfected, I tutored and rehearsed them in vocal delivery before they were each filmed reading their complex pieces at a lectern.

For the evening presentation to families and educationalists, the material was edited together on the final day and touches of discreet linking music were added. The results were displayed across a large 'video wall' in a lecture theatre at the site via two computers and linked digital projectors. The videos showed each student reading their poetry in one portion, the words scrolling slowly in synch on another, while beautiful photographic imagery appropriate to each part of the poem was displayed on softly changing 'sub-screens'. The effect was mesmerising and showed what can be achieved in multimedia with suitable IT assistance.

Examples of collective poetry

A few collective poems written by student groups follow. These are included here to demonstrate the high standard of observation and writing which can be achieved through using the world outside the classroom as inspiration. Although these have been created by relatively able students, the secret of the language quality is in the following: well-paced and thoughtful brainstorming; an interesting, language-rich location as inspiration; inputs on poetic sounds and form; enough time to work in depth at each stage and, above all, the creation of an ethos involving the highest possible expectation.

The following three collective poems were each produced by groups of sixteen 9- to 11-year-old students of above average ability. The first, brainstormed beside a canal at night, was evolved into a giant poster poem.

Reflections of night

The dying sun showers the horizon in flames.
It gathers the vibrant colours of day,
storing them in the cellar of night
till dawn breaks silently into the dark
and scatters them sleepily across the sky.

But now the fire of sunset fails,
volcanic embers smoulder away
and fade into dull ash.
The last survivors of lilac light
are swamped by a storm of darkness,
their lonely spirits shiver above,
bleary stars clutched by ancient oaks
like pearly drops of precious memories.

Late dog-walker's faces are softly slapped
by the wind's icy palm.
Spidery shadows marble the towpath
or contort into forest monsters,
and chinks of light mosaic a tangle of branches,
spilling ghostly patches
of dim illumination.

Luminous ladders of reflected light
plunge the canal's gloomy depths
where the elegant silhouette of a lone, majestic swan
slowly patrols the sinister waters,
cutting through glowing, rippled rails of colour
like scissors through a swathe of rumpled cloth.

Lit windows of houses hang in the dark
like empty picture frames.
Their lights wink out, one by one
as sleepy townsfolk drift away,
abandoning hectic lives for night
as they sink into dreams of day.

Brainstorm session words for Reflections of night

puce   lavender   lilac pink   burning pink eels cut/swim across the sky
         streak the sky   fiery   the sun showers the horizon in flames
like spilt paint bleeding   spindly silhouettes like pastels power smudges   smeared
         smudged chalk smooth   glowing   fire glow   the failing fire of sunset
         volcanic orange   amber embers turn to the ashes of night
         trees streak the orange like ashes on embers
the ashes of day   a faded denim sky   translucent blue   a bruising sky
light sinking   drowned by night   drained away   drooped into darkness
Pavements empty roads still full   late workers returning home
         bunches and packages of cars   chains of cars playing follow my leader
street lamps amber glow   peachy light   flooding
bathing the street in amber glow buttery light   garage-empty with welcoming lights
a package of warm light   glaring headlamp eyes of cars   lights pierce the night
   dazzling eyes tear through   cars flow   a river of cars
   weave through the streets   purring   motorbike purring tearing the silence
ripping the night   showing off in the empty streets   boasting their arrogant roar
             roaring with arrogance   Belisha beacons flash a warning
/blinking a warning   midnight dog-walker shuffling down the street
dark arches forbidding   foreboding shadowy arches   rippling water

wind tickled surface of the water   light flecks the rippled surface   rippling like eels
seething like eels   lights firework the face of the water
ripples dancing from duck to dawn   spidery shadows   dark   gloomy   mysterious
ominous unknown   intriguing but uninviting   lifeless but threatening   contorting
shadows contort into monsters by night   blurry stars   pinprick stars decorating
   the treetops   cradled in the trees   trees clutch the stars like lost memories
   pearl drops   precious memories faeries of the night   perching like dew drops
silhouettes of ancient oaks clutch the stars like precious memories   bleary   blurry
         spooky sombre   icy wind biting the cheeks   pricks the skin
slaps you with its icy palm   shadows marble the towpath
      scaled shadows like the shed skin of a snake   a lone bobbing light
      trees contorted like the faces of lost souls   the colours of day drained
      washes away   bleached out   night has murdered the colours of day
stolen the colours of day   kidnapped   reflections seethe like a mass of eels
windows of houses are like empty picture frames deprived of their stories/lives
         strange squares   blacked out   internal reversal
         trapped sunlight escaped from the houses   leaking from window cages
         branches brambles trapped and tangles
chinks of light in a mosaic of tangle shattered branches   ghostly patches of
                                                              illumination
   a haze of lights a distant whirl of cars like a gusting wind   sounds hover in the air
   a dull metal sheen   a dull lead sheen   a sheen of lead
   water guttering in the dark   indistinct   obscure   forms and figures
shapes and shadows anticipate lurk peep through the trees slivers of silver flicked
flecked   light silhouetting branches   silvering their tips   half silvered branches
mysterious lights   deserted path   a lonely road of night
villagers have abandoned their dreams/ their lives / their hopes for the night
a fuzzy other world dark and inverted   leaves up-lit by artificial light
an unnatural inversion of day   a light show   streaming light tiger-stripes the water
         spearing stabbing   shimmering   glistening   the lock leaks
         ladders of light probe the depths ropes of light descend
shivering light spilt across the water   embroidered with a lurex of silver thread
woven into the water   coloured ribbons
a weft of light bars the water tiny sequin stars glitter tiny specs like spilt ... gliding
effortlessly parading   patrolling   regal a royal scavenger   majestic
cutting through the water   a heavy canvas   ribboned with cloud
patrolling behind the empty pub   drifting serenely effortlessly   drift aimlessly
survey their pub-side patch   bars of light that follow you like the warped eyes of
                              a painting
      orange reflections scuffling feet   walking in space   moon walking
      swallowed by the gaping maw of night   bus shelter, a human fish-tank

The brainstorm sheets

The above sheets of words and metaphors were typed directly onto a laptop computer during the brainstorming session along the canal towpath at sunset. The sheets are reproduced here in a slightly concentrated form to save paper and printing costs. During the writing session these words are displayed to students with more white space around them and ragged margins. This not only allows participants to re-find words or phrases they are looking for more easily but also helps them make more 'accidental connections' between words, which can create new phrases and fresh idea connections.

Normally, more sheets of words are produced in one brainstorming session but this was a well-focused group who had just had recent experience of brainstorming in a different daytime setting for a movement poem, so their language and ideas were very well targeted. You will note how visually orientated the language is here, because the group knew they were going to produce a visual art 'poster poem' from the final piece.

Endless variety from the same location

In order to demonstrate how different each brainstorming session and each poem can be, here is another poem by a similar age group, again written at night, at the same time of year and at the same location. The observations and language are totally different, as is the unusual form of the poem, which is in semi-free verse, largely based on four beat lines with the last line of each stanza rhyming with one of the previous ones:

Midwinter walk

Frosty asphalt sparkles like sprinkled glitter,
the bustling road is bright with amber light,
shadowed cars are purring past, sweeping through the gloom,
but the dark canal, unseen below,
is lonely, calm and quiet.

The reflected moon gently bobs,
a restless boat on troubled waters
held by the lock's gigantic gate
that form an imperfect, inverted world
where mirrored houses softly wobble
like jelly on a plate.

Bickering coots shatter the silence,
frantically flap on the inky complexion,
skidding and skimming and scraping the surface,
their sudden ripples ruining the smoothness,
carving black bars on a window's reflection.

Tethered like horses
patiently awaiting their riders' return,
narrow boats doze in hibernation
where the ice-capped canal, glazed and grey,
cowers away from the lights of civilization.

A crested wave of frozen foliage
cascades across the deserted towpath
where spider-lace necklaces, jewelled with drops,
loop and droop, snagged and caught
on pipe-cleaner twigs that are softly fuzzed with frost.

Crumpled sedges, bent in mourning,
weep for the death of the summer sun.
Ducks stand on the edge of the ice,
motionless, dark and dumb.

Ice-sculpted swans dream on the water,
their heads tucked under their wings,
or drift through the night like snowy queens of the winter,
casting rippled rings.

A 'movement poem' by the same group

Here is a 'movement poem' by the *Midwinter walk* group, this time in regular four-line verses, rhyming a,b,a,b, with each line containing four-stressed beats (tetrameters). The group invented the second word because they felt it sounded better and was more accurate than any 'official' word.

The scene was unusually still so the children had difficulty in finding many moving things to include, but they still worked out successful ways to illustrate the words in performance.

Winter's kiss

A froudy sky is frowning down
on a wintery world, upholstered in white:
hardly a movement, hardly a sound,
frost has wrapped the land up tight.

Silver sunlight seeps through mist
spilling pallid light on the plain.
Grass and leaves are crystal crisp.
A peacock print on the window pane!

Slender birches, radiant with winter's
soft and snowy silken veil,
are shedding showers of shining splinters—
a wispy web, porcelain pale.

Beeches etch a milky sky,
the tips of their twigs are dipped in white
where raucous rooks flap and fly
like ragged spirits of the night.

Spiders' webs, heavy with frost,
sag like hammocks or loop like lace;
beaks peck, leaves are tossed,
blackbirds rummage at a frantic pace.

Aglow with the brightness of their hearts,
their colourful clothes cheering the day,
their 'train-tracks' run through frosted grass—
the scuffed traces of children's play.

Beech roots claw at rock-hard earth
where a fox has left its pungent musk,
a pheasant shrieks for all it's worth
and blusters away in the deep-frozen dusk.

Useful poetry forms for writing on location: 'reflective haikus'

About haikus

As many readers will know, a haiku is a short, three-line form of poetry which originated in Japan and is based on syllable counting rather than on a sound pattern of stressed and unstressed beats. There are various schools of haiku writing in Japan, and nowadays in other parts of the world. Each of these has its own conventions.

It is often said that the total number of syllables in a haiku must invariably be seventeen, with five in the first line, seven in the second, and five in the third. However, as Japanese syllables are very different from syllables in English, it can mean that haikus translated from the Japanese into English often end up with fewer syllables per line.

It is not within the aim of this book to discuss different forms of haiku or their history, but readers who are interested in knowing more will find plenty of information online, and attractive books of translated Japanese haikus are available.

What I love about using haikus in poetry workshops isn't just that they are short and therefore manageable within restricted time limits, it is the tightness of their writing. It enables me to show young writers that, in good poetry, not only is every word valuable, but every syllable can be too. I explain that a haiku should be a poetic equivalent of an exquisite miniature painting; a tiny work of art which is so limited in size that every part of it must be as perfect as possible, otherwise any weakness will be obvious. Like a miniature painting or a faceted gemstone, it has to be crafted carefully because one weakness will spoil its perfection and hence its value.

Why 'reflective haikus'?

In the UK, haikus are commonly written in school by students of around ages seven to nine, largely because, compared to other forms of poem, they are considered quite easy to write, being very short, and the activity also teaches children about syllables, fitting writing into a specific space, and about including the odd descriptive word. A Japanese haiku master might spill his precious ink in shock if he learned that children are being introduced to the subtle art of haikus in such a way!

Of course I understand why the form is utilised like that at those ages, but my experience and that of teachers I have discussed this with is that such young children don't particularly enjoy the activity or understand the point of it, and the outcomes of the exercise are limited.

If presented imaginatively to older groups, however, the conception and creation of more subtle 'reflective' haikus can demonstrate the values of tightness in writing, in quality of language and concept, and in the satisfying 'roundness' of well-executed ideas. It can be a creative, challenging and satisfying exercise for any age from around 9 or 10 years-old to adult, and more able students particularly love it if there is a philosophical or emotional aspect to the challenge. Participants usually wrestle cheerfully with the ideas and language in haikus because the shortness of the form means they are not daunted by the scale of what they are dealing with.

During extended courses I have often used haiku writing 'on location' as an introduction to creating well-controlled, evocative and thoughtful poetry. When I have taken a group to a stimulating location on a pleasant day to brainstorm and write thoughtful haikus, I have always found that, not only have students always responded superbly to the challenge but the activity has raised the originality, quality and control of their brainstorming and writing of longer poetry on subsequent days.

Just for information, I should perhaps mention here that some traditional schools of haiku in Japan reject the use of metaphorical language and every descriptive word used must already be listed in a huge book of 'approved' words. However, in that situation the object of the exercise is different and more 'Zen' oriented in its appreciation of the natural world.

Our purpose, through writing 'reflective haikus'is to teach and develop:

- thoughtful observation skills;
- originality of concept and description;
- concentration of language and tight writing discipline;
- creation and extension of metaphor;
- the value of vibrant language even down to syllable level;
- the discreet power of sound echoes in poetic writing;
- the satisfying depth gained through introducing more than one level of meaning;
- confidence in 'taking creative chances' in writing; and

- confidence through reaching an exceptional quality of vision, depth and perfection in writing within a manageable space.

Session logistics and locations

This is an excellent activity for a warm, dry day from mid-spring to early autumn. It is essential to take extra layers of clothing, sun hats, sun cream, water bottles, clipboards and plenty of plain A4 paper, and perhaps a snack to keep people going, because the process usually takes several hours. Along with the usual offsite gear such as first aid kit, mobile/cell phone and a throw-line if working near water, I normally carry a couple of lightweight plastic tarpaulins in my rucksack for students to sit on if the grass is damp, or participants carry plastic bags.

Places where I work on this type of form are usually redolent or interesting, such as: by a town canal lock in a place thronged with walkers, fishermen and summer bargees; by a tumbling stream in a flower-carpeted valley; in quiet, overgrown churchyards; beside a muddy creek scattered with tide-stranded boats; on a hillside at night with a full moon peeping through a tunnel of clouds and village lights dusted below; or beside a boating lake in a town park. Other urban locations could be a quiet corner of a shopping mall or market square, or near a dock or marina.

After outlining the purpose of our visit and explaining that we are there to find exciting ideas and language which people wouldn't see or think of if working indoors, I first lead a 'thoughtful observation' session with students scribing on clipboards, often with an assistant typing or scribing as a backup to prevent slower scribers panicking. This brainstorm uses similar types of questioning as in a descriptive poetry session but focuses on building a complex and detailed collage of ideas, descriptions and metaphors about a *limited* number of aspects on view.

Starting the process

Once I feel we have enough good base material for students to start from while also creating variety between individual pieces, I explain what haikus are and read them several of my own. I start with simpler, largely descriptive ones, looking in depth at word choice, sound echoes and slant rhyme, simile, metaphor and personification, and at what ways had been found to make them more concentrated through changing dull or unimportant words, and losing unnecessary articles, connectives or 'dead' syllables such as the 'ing' part of a verb. I explain that, although traditional haikus don't rhyme, the use of sound echoes and slant rhymes can lift them to a new level and raise the profile of key words or word roots.

Working in this way, I move steadily from largely descriptive haikus to more metaphorical ones, then to relatively philosophical ones, and we discuss what writing 'reflective' haikus entails. I sometimes make this preparatory input indoors before the visit if concerned about a group's concentration being spoiled by working too long in strong sun or a cold breeze, but it is best to move quickly from this input to writing while the sound and feel of the form and brainstorm are fresh in participants' heads.

It's important for leaders to explain they will be happy with powerfully descriptive, perfectly fitting haikus, but stress that a greater challenge is to create more than just a strong description. The addition of simile or metaphor will take a good haiku to a new level, and extending the metaphor or personification in some way can raise it again. Best of all, is when the haiku is powerfully descriptive and the metaphor within it can suggest a deeper idea or mood; something that leaves readers thinking.

Expectation

This exercise is particularly about expectation. Leaders need to show that they are hoping for the highest quality writing in each haiku, no matter how long it takes, so it should be emphasised that it's quality not quantity which is required. I always point out that it's much better to produce only one or two brilliant and clever haikus in a session than a greater number of weak or mundane ones. To help set the benchmark I insist that students aim to write lines of *exactly* 5, 7, 5 syllables and explain they will need to adjust their ideas, metaphors and language to fit with that form.

It's essential to explain that students will only achieve original results if they continue the process of thoughtful observation themselves during writing, ask further questions about the environment and more again about interesting ideas that come out of this. The significant thing we can teach in creative writing is not simply about how to fit syllables into a haiku ... it's about how to develop a creative, flexible and enquiring mind!

Improving a reflective haiku attempt

An example sequence

Just as in writing longer descriptive poetry, one of the most common weaknesses in penning descriptive haikus is when a writer 'lists' descriptions, rather than building one coherent idea, description or metaphor. One can often spot that a writer falling into this trap has been thinking out each line separately because there are full stops or other punctuation marks at the end of each line.

Here's a typical bad example:

The cows are walking like drunks.
A plane is crossing the sky.
The stream is gurgling.

This is a boring list of unrelated descriptions, the syllable count in the first line (seven) is too high, there is an irritating triple repetition of 'ing' endings, and four unnecessary articles in only three lines. There are almost no pleasant sound echoes despite the (probably accidental) 'aw' sounds in 'walking' and 'crossing' and several 's' echoes. The language level is poor, the observations mostly mundane and its only slight saving grace is the simile 'like drunks'.

Here's a slight improvement:

> Cows stumble like drunks.
> An aircraft scratches the sky.
> The stream is gurgling.

The syllable count is correct now but the attempt has still ended up with a list of three disparate descriptions on three separate lines. Its qualities are the slight extension of the descriptive personification in the first line (by adding the drunken movement word 'stumble'); the metaphorical choice of the verb 'scratches' for the aircraft; assonant sound echoes between 'stumble', 'drunks' and 'gurgling'; and the sibilant alliteration and consonance between 'stumble', 'drunks', 'scratches', 'sky'; and 'stream'. It could be slightly improved by changing the aircraft image to something more linked with the cows and also on ground level, such as in this attempt:

> Cows stumble like drunks.
> Swallows skim across the field.
> The stream is gurgling.

Now the items described are more within the same physical area but it is still a list. There may be a connection between the things described but it's not made clear. Qualities are the descriptive personification in the first line and sound echoes such as the assonance between 'stumble' and 'drunks' and slightly with 'gurgling'; the sibilance between 'stumble', 'drunks', 'swallows', 'skim' and 'stream', and assonance between 'stream' and 'field'.

In the next example the list is at last breaking down and the first two lines now have logical 'flow':

> Cows stumble like drunks
> through sloppy mud and boulders.
> The clear stream gurgles.

This is also better because there's an interesting juxtaposition between the filthy mud and the clear stream. The middle line is much more descriptive and shows why the cows 'stumble like drunks', and an attempt has been made to improve the observation and description of the third line, although it still doesn't relate to the content of the first two apart from the juxtaposition mentioned, which may not be deliberate. There's also a fairly satisfying compound slant rhyme on the final word 'gurgles', which is echoing partly with 'drunks' and partly with 'boulders'

In the following version the telltale full stops have vanished completely and it isn't a list anymore:

Cows stumble like drunks
through sloppy mud and boulders
to sip spring water.

Now the haiku has become one logical entity instead of three. The description of what the cows are doing runs throughout and the personification simile is playfully added to by the addition of the bovine 'drunks' stumbling off to sip 'spring water'. This adds potential for more thoughtfulness and amusement for the reader, who might subconsciously link the cows to drunken humans in a night club. <> The juxtaposition between the mud and the clear water is maintained and the piece is tighter because all the articles have gone, as has the dead 'ing' of 'gurgling'.

Other qualities are sound echoes such as assonance between 'st*u*mble', 'dr*u*nks' and 'm*u*d'; and sibilance between 'stumble', 'drunks', 'sloppy', 'boulders', 'sip' and 'spring'. There's also assonance between 's*i*p' and 'spr*i*ng', and between 'sl*o*ppy' and 'w*a*ter', which lands satisfyingly on the haiku's final word.

Squeezing in more 'reflective subtlety'

Another creative direction might play more on the extended simile by attempting to make the location description fit both cows and drunks effectively:

Cows stumble like drunks
lost in a tumbledown world,
searching for a drink.

The cows now sound more like compulsive human drinkers and a curious philosophical touch has appeared with the line 'lost in a tumbledown world', which might suggest the disorder and emptiness of a drunkard's life, or hint that some people drink compulsively due to feeling 'lost' when their world is in chaos. Some readers may be surprised that a child could write something involving such a thoughtful adult concept, yet I have seen many ten-through-teenage students develop similar ideas in haikus based on well-brainstormed locations.

A slight drawback with this last version is one that sometimes appears when students try to fit very subtle concepts into those three tiny lines. By making descriptions perfectly fit the metaphorical and philosophical side as well as the 'real world' side, they may have to sacrifice part of the 'show' quality of the description. In this case, although the line 'lost in a tumbledown world' is curious, it is less specific in its description of the 'real' world than the former version 'through sloppy mud and boulders'. One solution is to try and change the middle line to keep the double meaning yet include more authenticating detail, and another is to give the haiku an explanatory title. These are subtle challenges which can help build flexible minds.

Here's a possibility for the first of those options:

> Cows stumble like drunks
> between rocky obstacles,
> searching for a drink.

The line 'lost in a tumbledown world' is more evocative, however, and could be explained well enough if given an apt title.

Titles for haikus

Traditionally, haikus don't have titles but I allow students to add them if they make the piece more interesting, amusing, thought-provoking or intelligible. A title for a reflective haiku can help describe or 'signpost' whatever is required for the reader to make full sense of the piece. In the 'tumbledown world' version above, for instance, the title might be something like *Cattle among rocks*, or perhaps better: *In the canyon* (if that was its location). The latter is better as it leaves a little something for the reader to work out and it doesn't mention either cows or cattle, while, like the first title suggestion, it also makes sense of the 'tumbledown world' line.

Repeating any key or relatively strong word in the title and in the body of a haiku seriously devalues the word when readers reach it the second time and, because haikus are so compact, it would also damage the piece itself. So, for instance, putting the title 'Cows among rocks and mud' would ruin the slightly earlier version where the words 'cows' and 'mud' already appear. Similarly, 'Cows among rocks' would be bothersome when the next line starts with 'Cows stumble . . .'

The title *In the canyon* also has additional subtlety because it hints that a drunk might be 'stuck in a rut' or at least a deep place from which only a limited number of directions are possible. *Cattle in a canyon* is alliterate and doesn't repeat the word 'cows', but it does repeat the *idea* of cows and doesn't fit as well with the metaphorical 'drunken human' side as *In the canyon*.

Making logical line breaks

Another common flaw is to break lines in illogical and unpoetic places in order to make each line have the correct syllable count. To correct this, one or more lines will need to be reconstructed until the breaks land in sensible places. A haiku writer needs to have a sense of natural grammar and of natural rhythm, and creating haikus is an excellent way for students to learn where a poetic line break is logical and 'feels right'. For instance:

> Seagulls swirl like the
> beginnings of a winter
> blizzard out at sea

has the correct number of syllables per line but the first two lines have been forced to break in rather odd places. The following would be more sensible and stronger:

> Gulls swirl like the start
> of a wild winter blizzard
> on steely wave-tops

Cutting down 'seagulls' to 'gulls' and shortening the three syllables of 'beginning' to the one of 'start' positions the first line for a logical break, saves precious syllables which can be filled with additional vibrant and descriptive words, and also avoids repetition of 'sea'.

Instilling a constant awareness for improvement possibilities

Thinking deeper, the word 'wild' might be considered redundant here as blizzards are relatively wild by nature. The part about a 'start' is neither strong nor significant so the first line might be tightened further to something like 'a blizzard of gulls'. 'Winter' could also be cut because blizzards generally happen then. This would leave free syllables in the last two lines in which to describe the scene in a more evocative way, such as:

> A blizzard of gulls
> swirls in a feathered frenzy
> on grey steel wave-tops

If you compare this version to the very first one the difference is clear. You will notice that the best words (gulls, blizzard and swirl) are about all that has been retained, but we have made spaces for other strong words and fragments such as 'feathered frenzy' and 'grey steel wave-tops'. The simile 'like the start of a winter blizzard' has now been compacted into the word 'blizzard' which is now a metaphor describing the gulls' activity. Metaphors are stronger and more compact than similes, and leave a little more for readers to do intellectually, which increases their sense of involvement with the work.

Out of interest, by removing the weak word 'of', the first line could be tightened still further to 'a gull blizzard swirls ...' hence releasing another syllable in the middle line which can now be filled by a vibrant word there instead (e.g. 'in a fast, feathered frenzy', 'mad feathered frenzy', or 'shrill feathered frenzy'). Even this one small word addition can create a deepening of authenticating detail:

A gull-blizzard swirls
in a shrill, feathered frenzy
on grey steel wave-tops

This version could have a thoughtful touch added in the form of a title such as 'Competition', 'Bullies' or 'Freedom', the latter possibly the most subtle.

This process of reworking using the strongest words as a base illustrates a useful editing tip which can be explained to young haiku writers in particular and to apprentice poets in general. It is simply that, if a writer is finding it hard to radically alter an unsatisfactory haiku or a section of poetry, one solution is to pick out only the richest key words or roots of words, copy them onto a different area of paper, score through the weak version to release it from one's mental focus, then work afresh with some or all of those key words, testing new ideas, vivid words and metaphors. It's a way around the problem of 'being too close to the text to see a new direction'.

Staff skill and expectation

Ideally, any assistants you have with you will have learned about and experimented with writing 'reflective haikus' beforehand (perhaps along with you) so you can all move around the workshop helping individuals with suggestions and editing tips. This should of course involve praise for specific strengths and ideas but also be combined with an obvious resolve to seek and use powerful words and syllables, original similes and metaphors, sound echoes, some thoughtful philosophical content if possible, and a distinct mood or flavour.

By initially examining 'reflective haiku' examples through discussion and leading questions, I allow young writers to discover how much subtlety in observation, language, sound, thought and skill can be packed into those three tiny lines. This always seems to fire up individual drive to achieve higher quality results and students usually settle into the challenge with quiet gusto.

Examples of 'reflective haikus' with notes

A number of the author's own haikus follow, along with notes on their composition. These examples are duplicated on photocopiable and scannable pages at the end of this chapter. All the haiku examples are copyright but readers of this book may use them in workshops along with the accompanying notes.

Example haikus and notes are presented in a sequence of increasing complexity of metaphorical and conceptual content. Group leaders can use as many of these examples as they think fit for their students' age and ability, but it's better if a fair number are read out and studied in order to model the processes before individual writing begins.

I advise asking students to discover the points in the notes through leading questions. Not only does this involve them more deeply with the input and raise their confidence but it also leads to greater retention of the concepts, higher aspirations, and awareness of further tools for individual creativity.

Demonstratively checking the syllable count on your fingers during a second reading of each of the first few helps set a sense of line length and form in the minds of participants.

> *On the still river*
> *crazed whirligigs skim and spin,*
> *skating on silver*

A small rural vignette here, which will be understood by those who have watched shiny 'whirligig' beetles whizz around on the surface of ponds or streams. There are several sound echoes at work on all the key words: the 'ih' sound (as in 'still') in six places, the hard 'ay' in 'crazed' and 'skating', the 'im' and 'in' in the second line, and the 'l' in 'still', 'whirligigs' and 'silver'. There is also a strong compound slant rhyme on 'silver' which comes from a combination of echoes with 'river' and other words.

I like to speak out the final two lines clearly then ask students what they *sound* like, and some students always realise the sound is like the movements and scraping of skates on ice. This is caused by rhythmic variations combined with repeating 's' and 'z' echoes.

> **View from above**
>
> *Like cheerful beetles,*
> *gleaming cars scuttle and swarm,*
> *devouring our earth.*

Students will recognise this is a straightforward, extended metaphor with an ecological message. Sound echoes are 'ee', 's' and 'our', but the last word is deliberately devoid of musical echo to make it feel negative and 'dead'.

> *Raw red building bones*
> *mesh a fleshy sunset*
> *with skeletons of steel.*

This is about the partly built skyscrapers rising in New York when I lived there many years ago. I ask students to explain the 'structure of a body' metaphor but I sometimes have to explain that 'raw red' is like the colour of bones with some flesh or sinew still attached, and that steel girders used in building are often treated with a reddish oxide coating, so it isn't just the sunset which causes them to be that colour.

There are obvious alliterations in pairs here, such as on 'r', 'b' and 's', but there are also deeper sound echoes on 'eh', 'esh' and 't' sounds.

> *Her hair peeled and pulled,*
> *the old willow lady weeps*
> *for children's mischief.*

This apparently simple personification deliberately leaves a couple of small points for the reader to work out. The first is what it's about (which participants quickly realise is a weeping willow tree) and the second is why she is crying 'for children's mischief'. Some students usually realise this is because branches have been broken and lower twigs stripped of their bark due to children swinging on them. It was, after all, written about a willow tree in the grounds of a school!

The sound echoes are the 'p' and 'w' alliterations, the similar sounding words 'peeled' and 'pulled', the 'il' sounds in 'willow' and 'children', 'I' sounds throughout, and 'ch' sounds in the last line.

> **Cathedral façade**
>
> *Dark, soulless windows*
> *where weather-blinded saints guard*
> *the stone face of God.*

It's interesting to ask students what emotional sense of the place this haiku gives them or if it feels like a modern Christian environment. I then ask what message the outside of the building seems to have been designed to tell the people around it when it was built. Sparky students may come up with it being a statement of the power of religious belief and of the church establishment, which, of course, was true at that time.

It may be necessary to explain the double meaning of the word 'façade' to students. Sound echoes are 'oh', 'ay', 'ah', and the slant rhyme between 'guard' and 'God', which makes that final word stand out more dramatically.

> **Buzzard**
>
> *The soft hunter wheels.*
> *Its sad squeals echo the hills.*
> *Shrill siren of death.*

I would prefer this haiku not to have its title rather than spell it out, but it may be needed in order to avoid confusion with other possibilities. The 'siren' is, of course, the plaintive cry of the predator as it sweeps across the valleys, hunting. The choice of this word suggests police or ambulance sirens, also associated with death or murder.

There are 's' sound echoes throughout, but more significant are the rhymes and slant rhymes linking 'wheels', 'squeals', 'hills' and 'shrill' and the fact that there is deliberately no rhyme or sound echo on the final word. When I ask older students about this, someone usually realises that, after all the sound echo 'musicality', the total lack of any on the word 'death' makes that final word feel 'dead'.

It can be interesting to read out the middle line slowly and clearly then ask students what the word 'echo' seems to do, sound-wise, within the text. The answer, of course, is that 'eh-ko' seems to echo like the effect it names.

Keen young writers gaze
intensely at white paper
full of reflection.

After explaining that this haiku was written in an outdoor workshop session I sometimes ask groups if they can work out what the weather was like that day. If they have figured out the double meaning in the last line they will realise that bright sunshine was reflecting onto the writers' faces from their papers while they were 'reflecting' thoughtfully on their ideas! Having another 'layer of meaning' can move a descriptive haiku into the 'reflective' category.

Light fingers

As rooks fuss awake
you steal into my still room
to take and bring dreams.

Double-meanings play a part in this one again, from the puns in the title to the different possibilities for the meaning of the word 'dreams'. If you ask your students leading questions such as 'what time of the day is it in the haiku?' some may eventually work out that the 'light fingers' are thin beams of early morning sunlight entering through gaps in bedroom curtains. Students may need to learn that the idiom 'light-fingered' refers to someone with a tendency to steal things, but they should be able to work out that the morning light takes away the dreams of sleep but brings daydreams of what that day may bring.

There are sound echoes on 'ay', 'ss', 'st', 'oo', 'i' and 'ee' sounds.

Gaunt pylons march,
grey slaves dragging aspirations
in both directions.

This was written on a hillside in an official Area of Outstanding Natural Beauty and muses on technological 'progress'. Students often realise what this image is of, but questioning should help them discover more depth. For instance, does the choice of the word 'gaunt' fit the haiku's subjects as well as their metaphorical personae? Why choose 'grey'? Why choose 'march' when electricity pylons don't move? Why are they 'slaves'? They might mention 'chain gangs' here.

If asked in what way are pylons 'dragging aspirations in both directions?' students may realise it's contrasting the benefits of technology with the damage (such as global warming) that it causes.

There are sound echoes on the stressed beats in the form of the 'ah' sounds in 'march', 'dragging' and 'aspirations'; the 'g' sounds in 'gaunt', 'grey' and 'dragging'; the 'ay' sounds in 'grey' and 'slaves' and 'aspirations', and the slant rhyme of 'aspirations' and 'directions'.

Fading

This old signpost points
to many far-off places
where it cannot go.

If your students have studied several of these haikus by now it can be interesting to see what they understand about this one. If they need help, you can suggest they look for one or more words which might provide clues. If they are still puzzled, they should think about the title and the description of the signpost, helping them realise it is also about the immobility and 'living in memories' of old age.

Cold snap

Fiery leaves of words
drop on dank earth around them.
They have reached autumn.

Another extended metaphor, which is about the final stages of a close relationship. The double meanings of 'cold snap' and 'fiery' are keys to unravelling the meaning but also provide the writer with different language from the clichéd 'colour words' that children employ in autumn poems. Again, the poetic use of the full stop in the middle line and the short final line can be discussed.

Apparition

The moon is a ghost,
her pale face suffocated
by thin, jealous cloud.

Students can describe the view seen by the writer before explaining the metaphor fully.

Swollen

Fern fronds line its path
but the cool stream cold-shoulders
its cheerleaders' dance.

Groups may again need to look for key words to explain this metaphor. Signposting words are 'swollen', and the idiomatic 'cool' and 'cold-shoulders'. They can also be asked to describe the initial outdoor scene the writer saw. Hopefully they will realise that the metaphor of the stream in spate is about the arrogance of power or celebrity.

Greyscape

Bleak beach. A dog barks.
The couple throw it pebbles
far from youthful waves.

The use of full-stops to slow down the tempo and concentrate description is even more obvious in the first line of this haiku. This helps accentuate its slowness, the bleakness of the scene and its message. 'Signposting' words are the title and the words 'far' and 'youthful'.

As is obvious, it was written about an elderly couple walking their dog along the top of a wide, empty beach at low tide. Their figures seemed small and lonely in the vast bleak landscape and it made me think about how they were past the period in their lives of having their children around them and how far they were from their childhood, again signposted by the final line's double meaning.

Most of the sound echoes are on explosive consonants or hard vowels. They are on 'b' (three times), 'ee', 'p' and 'ar'. There are slant rhymes on 'bleak' and beach, as well as 'couple' and 'pebbles' but there is no sound echo of any sort at the end of the last line, so as to make it end with a wistful tone.

Sad saplings

Their roots seek comfort
but, feeling out for soft earth,
find only cold stone.

This was composed in a wood where young trees seemed to manage to grow out of solid blocks of rock. Students may need to think about the title before they spot that the personification relates to children brought up without affection in their lives.

Sounds are deliberately soft in the first two lines, particularly with the use of soft vowels and soft 'f' and 'th' sounds. Contrasting that, the haiku ends in an almost staccato way with the hard 'oh' in 'only', 'cold' and 'stone' ('jabbing out' on the stressed beats of those three final words).

The grumpy farmer
shoos writers from the footpath.
Beware. Talking bull.

Hopefully the ironic element here will be apparent to older students. An aggressive ex-city landowner who appeared during our peaceful countryside writing workshop insisted that my small group didn't have the right to sit on or even brainstorm along the public footpath across his land, which of course was ridiculous.

The play on the 'beware of the bull' idea will be understood by older students, as will the mischievous double meaning of the final word. The farming metaphor is bolstered by the choice of the verb 'shoos'. I can't remember if I thought up the phrase 'talking bull' or if it arose from the collective brainstorm but, like all words and ideas discussed in a sharing brainstorm session it became 'communal' language to be used by any of the participants.

Reflective haikus as 'beach art' or other 'land art'

It adds another dimension to a workshop to 'publish' students' writing through some form of art, print or presentation. One popular way of doing this is to celebrate the haikus artistically in some form at the location where they were written.

For instance, a deserted or relatively quiet beach or shore is an excellent location in which to inspire, write and 'immortalise' your group's reflective haikus. I have done this with groups on several occasions and students have always loved the experience and put even more effort into perfecting their concepts and writing because they knew there was going to be a greater outcome.

With careful timing, participants can have brainstormed, written and edited one or two excellent pieces by the time the tide is low, so they can then inscribe their finished haikus in clean sand, and perhaps illustrate or decorate them with 'found' materials, ready to be photographed and later displayed on a school wall, website or in a computer slide show on a screen in the school's reception area. Photography and displays might include views of the students at work and specific subjects which inspired them, along with pictures of the finished pieces.

Apart from suitable clothing, sun protection, water bottles and, possibly, packed lunches, **for 'beach art' reflective haikus you will need:**

- a fully charged digital camera (preferably more than one);

- lots of blunt knives for inscribing effectively in damp sand (metal ones from school canteens are usually perfect);

- a small step-stool, splayed-leg 'gym horse' or aluminium stepladder to photograph the pieces from, so as to picture the words from a good angle and keep them all within the frame;

- thick chalks to inscribe on slabs of rock, concrete, timber or tarmac, or for writing titles or key words onto flat stones;

- clipboards, pencils, lots of old, plainA4 paper;

- large plastic food bags to cover clipboards loosely if there is any possibility of rain; and

- a fine, long-handled floor brush, which can be useful to brush out photographed text to make space for new text, or to correct mistakes.

For photography purposes it's helpful if participants leave space between their own beach haikus and their neighbours' but, if sand space is limited, you can photograph individual pieces as they are finished then brush the sand smooth, ready for other writers to inscribe theirs.

Given enough time, this is a highly enjoyable and creative activity. Key aspects mentioned can be illustrated in the sand close to the text, a view of the text within the environment may be used to back up images mentioned in the words, and objects such as pebbles, seaweed, string, driftwood and flotsam can be used to decorate or border a haiku.

For instance, along with her lovely haiku about a dog's pink tongue lolling out as the frustrated animal stared up at unreachable gulls, one 13-year-old inscribed a dog's bone beside the title and finger-pressed some 'paw prints' across a corner of the photo frame area of sand. Another haiku, describing sand caving in like brown sugar where toddlers had left 'sweet traces', was inscribed beside a couple of tiny footprints in the damp sand. Others have drawn relevant waves, clouds, trees, and so on, or have bordered their work with small pebbles, looped strings of seaweed, shells, twigs, etc.

Text must be inscribed neatly and cleanly in individual letters, with lettering kept relatively close together so the haiku will fit readably within one photograph. Individual haiku lines should be kept intact to aid readability, rhythm and meaning, and students may need reminding that punctuation matters, even in beach haikus!

For those far from the sea, it's possible to scribe and illustrate reflective haikus with chalks onto the asphalt of the playground, walls or rock, or to carve them into snow. Some may letter all or part of their haikus using found materials, or natural resources such as twigs, gravel, sand or grass blades, as long as the text stands out against the background.

Haiku lines can be scribed with board markers onto 'banners' made from inexpensive wallpaper lining paper held up by plant sticks, with each line fixed into the ground and photographed within a view of the inspirational location. A 'prize-winning entry' or two might even be painted onto a school wall as part of a more permanent illustrated 'haiku mural'.

Parentwood

Trees that grow no more
cradle sand between their arms,

holding it in place.

Bright, white terrier
stares, sun-stencilled, at the sea's
routine lunacy.

Examples of reflective haikus

On the still river
crazed whirligigs skim and spin,
skating on silver

Buzzard

The soft hunter wheels.
Its sad squeals echo the hills.
Shrill siren of death.

View from above

Like cheerful beetles,
gleaming cars scuttle and swarm,
devouring our earth.

Keen young writers gaze
intensely at white paper
full of reflection.

Raw red building bones
mesh a fleshy sunset
with skeletons of steel

Light fingers

As rooks fuss awake
you steal into my still room
to take and bring dreams.

Her hair peeled and pulled,
the old willow lady weeps
for children's mischief.

Gaunt pylons march,
grey slaves dragging aspirations
in both directions.

Cathedral façade

Dark, soulless windows
where weather-blinded saints guard
the stone face of God.

Fading

This old signpost points
to many far-off places
where it cannot go.

Cold snap

Fiery leaves of words
drop on dank earth around them.
They have reached autumn.

Greyscape

Bleak beach. A dog barks.
The couple throw it pebbles
far from youthful waves.

Apparition

The moon is a ghost,
her pale face suffocated
by thin, jealous cloud.

Sad saplings

Their roots seek comfort
but, feeling out for soft earth,
find only cold stone.

Swollen

Fern fronds line its path
but the cool stream cold-shoulders
its cheerleaders' dance.

The grumpy farmer
shoos writers from the footpath.
Beware. Talking bull!

Useful poetry forms for writing on location: *'syllable cinquains'*

Enjoyable and challenging!

Cinquains are small, highly concentrated poems which are well suited to individual brainstorming and writing on location. They are called cinquains (from 'cinq', the French for 'five') because they have five lines. The main modern form of cinquain is loosely based on the way Japanese haikus and tanka employ a specific number of syllables in each line. However, the effect is different because its sequence of longer and longer lines ending in a dramatic short one can suit tongue-in-cheek ideas as well as deeply reflective ones.

Although five line poems already existed in English and several other languages, the modern form was re-invented in the early 1900s by the American poet Adelaide Crapsey, who arranged the numbers of syllables per line as 2, 4, 6, 8, 2, in that order. Crapsey's form was not just based on syllable counting but also comprised an accentual pattern of 1, 2, 3, 4, 1, stressed beats per line, in that sequence, usually in iambic (ti-**tum**) rhythm.

This can produce beautiful, reflective, Zen-like results and you are welcome to attempt the full Crapsey form with very able older students. I have found, however, that for most students, just fitting a smooth flow of rich, concentrated language, meaning, logic and impact into the 2, 4, 6, 8, 2 syllabic pattern can provide enough challenge and satisfaction, and this is what I refer to as a 'syllable cinquain'. If certain participants work well at fitting their ideas into the official syllable count, after a while you might choose to suggest they attempt to include the 1, 2, 3, 4, 1 stressed beat rule too, to see if it improves their results, but I find that insisting on an exact stressed beat count in each line is unnecessarily restrictive for most students.

To clear up possible confusion, it's important to mention that there are several types of 'cinquains' in existence, including a version sometimes used in US schools which is based on the number of *words* in specific lines, rather than the numbers of syllables, but we are not looking at that form here.

How to inspire cinquain creation on location

Even basic 'syllable cinquains' can initially feel challenging for young newcomers to this kind of poetry but they will find it easier if the form is explained and modelled with examples, then a collective cinquain is brainstormed and written before participants set off on individual writing.

As with 'reflective haikus' it can help to brainstorm a few selected aspects of a location and some ideas in detail together for around 15–20 minutes in order to pull up the quality-of-language expectation, but an older group which has already worked with you on location in ways described in this book might be able to wade straight in themselves once they have heard some examples and understand the simple format. It always helps to ask everyone to jot down 2, 4, 6, 8, 2, at the top of their clipboard sheets, otherwise some will lose track as they write.

If students are stuck for an initial idea you can ask them which object or aspect of their environment they might like to write about, suggest they jot down some good descriptions of it and its features, then help them to start asking thought-stimulating questions< such as 'what metaphors come out of it?', 'what does it remind me of?', 'how does that link to feelings, human situations?' and so on.

Some examples of 'syllable cinquains'

I have deliberately chosen 'syllable cinquains' of mine here, rather than some with only a strict stressed beat structure. Nearly all of these cinquains are based on inspiration from locations, and students can be shown that there is often a thoughtful aspect, sometimes triggered by a 'twist in the tail' in the short final line.

Adelaide Crapsey's cinquains always had titles but I like to allow student writers to choose whether to give each one a title or not because sometimes the last or first lines can act as a title, and sometimes a title can act almost like an extra line, adding sense or value to the piece.

Arrival

Slowly,
the river twists
through endless flat meadows
(horse-scented or ribbed with cut hay).

Dying.

Harvest

Proudly
the loud tractor
drags back its catch of hay.
The fat cows will not go hungry.
Nor us.

Predator

Eyes blink.

A shadow wafts
through night-swamped forest.

Softness unfolds talons which crush
small bones.

Prey

The mouse
seems so little
as it fidgets about.
Does it think of the sudden owl
as God?

The bather

She sinks
her huge body
in the tepid water.
Ecstasy is simple for a

hippo.

Spring

softness
cascades over
sweet curvaceous meadows,
dusting impatient forest tops
with joy.

Old soldier

This bent
green sentinel
clings to its windy hill,
a proud survivor of Nature's
class war.

Heaven scent

The cow
wades in May green,
flicks a teddy bear ear,
twitches her superstar lashes

and farts.

Like bugs
leading small lives
on water's fragile skin,
we dance fast to try and avoid
black mouths.

The doll
crawls to a chair,
stumbles around the room,
runs through sun and dark woods; falters

and falls

On dark
tattered bushes,
berries wait for winter's
sweet ecstasy of greedy beaks.

Trapped sun.

Comedy

"Ha! Ha!"
laughed the people
at the poor, silly clown . . .
and even more on seeing his
sad frown.

Goldfish
rise to greet me,
wrapping my fingers in
bright rings of anticipation.

Old friends.

Achieving more than description

Cinquains can say more than literal descriptions. In the first example above, the shock of the final word might suggest it is about a polluted river but, on deeper reflection, may also raise the thought that even something which seems eternal (such as a river) carries its own mortality, just as the river 'dies' when it reaches the sea.

Personification or other forms of figurative language can enrich these small poems and participants should be encouraged to use potent description and, if possible, metaphor. Sometimes a metaphor or simile can involve only a part of the piece, such as in the Harvest cinquain, and sometimes the metaphor can be extended throughout the five lines, as in *Old soldier* and the penultimate piece involving the doll metaphor. After you read or display each of the examples for them, students should be encouraged to identify these figurative aspects so that they should hopefully think beyond simply literal terms while writing themselves.

I encourage participants to use different widths of blank line space, if they feel it necessary, because this makes them more aware of layout possibilities and how rhythmic flow is affected by them. There are several examples in the list which use blank lines, and asking students why they are there can help young writers to think more about variations of sound patterning, and particularly the use of pauses in poetry. With this in mind, it is important to pause slightly longer on these blank lines when reading the examples to the group.

The 2, 4, 6, 8, 2 syllabic form of a cinquain naturally creates a climatic or anti-climatic 'building up then collapsing' effect, which can turn the final short line into a sort of punch line. This can enhance a serious or mysterious concept, as in the cinquain ending on the words 'black mouths', a thoughtful concept as in the one finishing with the words 'trapped sun', or a mischievous or humorous ending such as in *The bather* or *Heaven scent*.

Students may be shown that sound echoes are used to enrich most of these, such as the cinquain about berries with its 'ah' assonance in 'dark', 'tattered' and 'trapped'; the 'ee' sounds in 'sweet', 'greedy' and 'beaks', and the 'b' alliteration in 'bushes', 'berries' and 'beaks'. In the final example I have even included a syllable cinquain that rhymes.

Observing and working directly on location is a great driver of originality, language and inspiration for cinquains, but the writing can be continued in class if you don't feel your students have had enough time on location to do the challenge justice. In winter or inclement weather you might be able to make arrangements to take a group to a large covered space with a rich environment, such as a main railway station or airport, a covered market, shopping mall or museum. These kinds of environment can introduce rich elements of human activity and interaction into the descriptive and metaphorical mix.

How locations can improve story writing and generate amazing plots

Moving students on from clichés and copying

Students must learn to observe and describe accurately, interestingly and thoughtfully before they can create believable worlds through their writing. Although reading, writing and creative classroom teaching can build language confidence and help drive this development, working exclusively within the 'insulated box' of a classroom, where little of the world can be seen and where little changes, can also restrict it.

Children have a relatively small stock of personal 'world experience' on which to draw, so their ideas, story plots, characters, settings and descriptions inevitably rely heavily on what they have come across in books, television, films and games. Because of this, when they are asked to write original stories solely within the classroom environment, we risk guiding them more towards copying than creating.

A well-read student usually writes better than a less privileged one because the former will have learned more about the world and have been exposed to more stories, richer language and subtler plot lines, though much of that knowledge is second hand. Personal experience is different. It is mentally 'available' because it's visceral and linked to other associations through place, time, mood and emotion. When thought about and noted down, it helps writers 'see', think, imagine and describe more originally and effectively.

Originality is a relative concept but a writer really starts to blossom when he or she has begun to observe the world through 'writer's eyes' and describe it in a developing and increasingly individual 'writer's voice'. Thoughtful brainstorming in rich and varied environments can help drive that process and I have seen much dazzling student writing based on out-of-classroom sessions to prove it.

Collecting the building materials for a story

In previous chapters we have looked at locational brainstorming methods for poetry, which can deepen thoughtful observation, widen vocabulary and drive originality in ideas, authenticating detail, description and metaphor.

Story workshops can also be greatly enhanced by similar location-based sessions where language and ideas are brainstormed. Obviously these don't require inputs on poetic sound patterning but instead benefit hugely from the inclusion of techniques which can inspire and develop truly original plots and characterisation.

Before we look at ways to improve plot lines in stories, it should be stressed how, at the inspirational stage of story writing, the process of observing and collecting descriptive data in one or more locations will provide new and richer vocabulary and figurative language for the story, raise expectations of the quality of language required, and improve the believability of the story setting through the use of well-chosen and subtle authenticating detail. Even if some participants don't set parts of their story plots in the actual environments brainstormed, this activity will make them more adept at selecting and describing 'authentic' key and background detail.

Students should learn that professional novelists spend an enormous amount of time both researching subjects for their future books and observing people, places and situations, while collecting copious notes, ideas and descriptions on it all. The multi-prize-winning novelist Ian McEwan has described how much he researches the subjects and environments in his books. In an interview he explained that, for one book, he had 'shadowed' a top surgeon for over two years, even spending considerable time in operating theatres with him in order to describe convincingly what his own fictitious surgeon's life is like. Even highly acclaimed and experienced novelists need to brainstorm on location!

How not to think up a plot

An essential element of creating proficient young story writers is to teach them how to evolve original, logical and fascinating plots. This important aspect of creative writing is often weakly covered in schools because many teachers have little knowledge in this area.

Acquiring the tools to write interesting and intriguing plots is essential in order for a young writer to grow confidence in his or her work. When students can create strong and original plots that they are proud of they will work harder at writing the story well. It is common logic . . . which writer will want to work extra hard on the language, setting and characterisation of his story if he senses his storyline is feeble?

I often begin a story plot workshop for older students by asking participants at random to make up and tell each line of a story in turn as quickly as possible. No matter how able the students are, the results of this deliberately impossible exercise are invariably dull, boring and either achingly predictable or illogical and silly.

Participants always acknowledge that this quick-fire story plot is dreadful, which is just what I want because the activity breaks down any inhibition to contribute and, most importantly, the group has just given me a perfect example of how not to write a story! We always analyse the results in a way that breaks the 'thinking stream' down into stages of single thoughts.

An awful example

For instance, their story might start with a man walking along a road (the most common default story beginning produced when people are under time pressure to contribute) then, as the man rounds a corner he sees something unusual. A UFO lands in the middle of the road beside him, then the man panics and starts to run away down a side street. The door of the UFO slides open and little orange men start running after him. They begin to make a bizarre yodelling sound. The man turns to look back and so doesn't see an open manhole and falls into it. He then drops into a smelly sewer and gets carried away in the flow ... etc. This is a terrible story plot so far, but it is typical of the sort of instant line by line story produced by many groups.

When we break down a group story like this, or even an 'instant' story produced by one person, we see that young writers have a first idea, which we might call 'A'. This makes mental connections and suggests a next idea 'B', which leads to another idea 'C', and so on. I call this type of story an 'And then story' for the obvious reason that one thing happens and then another thing, and then another, and so on. It is common for young children to make up and tell a 'story' like this with the words 'and then' connecting the idea steps.

If asked why the first idea was that there was a man walking along a road (or whatever it was) even older participants usually answer that it was the first thing that came into their heads and they had needed a starter idea so that they could ponder what would happen after that ... and then try to make it more interesting.

Although an instant group story like this is not exactly how an individual writes if given enough time, this sequential 'A, B, C ...' thinking is typical of the sort of initial thinking process I have observed from virtually every student during story plot workshops. Left untouched, a plot of this sort leads to boring, clichéd, predictable stories. As young writers sense this they often then drop in random or silly happenings in an attempt to kick start more interesting directions in the story, such as having the UFO randomly land in the street, the fact that the aliens are orange rather than the usual 'default' form of green, their odd yodelling sounds, the man falling into the randomly open sewer, etc.

Of course, given enough time, more creative young thinkers will start changing these ideas around further to try and make a better story, but because of the way they are programmed to think they will still struggle to come up with a plot that is original and at the same time unpredictable, logical and enthralling.

What causes 'sequential thinking'?

Several things create this type of thinking, which, depending on how it is used, brings disadvantages or advantages. We mostly think sequentially because 1) we live our daily lives with time always running in one direction, 2) cause creates effect and, 3) much of what we teach young people re-enforces this process. Think of maths (2 + 2 + 3 = 7), or science (take this chemical then add this other chemical then heat them and you will get these other chemicals), or geography (tectonic plates float on liquid magma, some can then bump into each other, the collisions cause stress ridges, which become mountain ranges, etc). We can't help it . . . we think, we live and we mainly teach A,B,C thinking.

There are other effects which tend to make inexperienced writers produce predictable and clichéd plots. The first of these is called the 'availability effect' (also called the 'availability error' in issues of judgement). The availability effect is probably caused by the way our brains produce 'synaptic routes of thought', which become more like familiar main roads (rather than unknown or lesser-known side roads) when they are well travelled or have been travelled recently.

This is why young writers (and also adults) tend to think first of ideas and connections they already know well, such as things they have heard or seen many times, or have known since they were very young. It's also why they tend to copy aspects, ideas, characters, settings and plot devices from programmes, films, computer games, books, newspapers and word of mouth stories they have been in contact with recently, or repeatedly, or which had an emotional effect on them.

Indeed, rather in the way that recent details of people, places and happenings somehow mix themselves into dreams, anything that has recently been seen or heard tends to find a way of connecting itself into a person's thinking during the search for new ideas for a story plot.

For example, in the case of that sequential 'instant story plot', the contributor who mentioned yodelling had very likely seen someone yodelling on TV or had recently read about Swiss yodellers, and the person who mentioned the open manhole had probably seen that occurrence in an animated film or cartoon. When I make students aware of the effect, they suddenly start to notice that many of the things we or they have talked about, seen or have done recently keep popping up in our collective brainstorming sessions on plot possibilities.

We can't stop making connections

Another related aspect of human brain function is that our minds are remarkably effective at finding possible connections between things. I have sometimes performed the party trick of asking participants to write a list of unrelated things, characters, places, etc., on a flip chart and then, after scanning the sheet, have almost instantly made up possibilities for several different plots using these random entries. It's surprisingly easy to do and I have developed and refined workshop methods utilising this process which regularly help students create unusual and curious plots.

The trick is to start from apparently unrelated things that we do not normally think of as being connected, because any connections then formed by making up associations between them will tend to be new ones.

I refer to our natural ability to connect diverse things as 'webbing'. I expect it derives from our ancestors having been constantly on the lookout for cause and effect, an essential process for learning and survival but, in common with the availability effect, one that can work both for and against the creation of original story lines.

Let's look at how we can use these two natural thinking tendencies to work to our advantage in the formation of original plots.

Creating original story lines: understanding 'x-points'

In sequential thinking, a thinker starts with thought A then proceeds to thought B, and so on. Unfortunately, due to the 'availability effect', each stage tends to throw up obvious connections, which leads to predictability.

I realised a long time ago that whenever I had fashioned an interesting and original plot I hadn't been thinking sequentially. Instead of having tried to find a beginning for the story, I had begun with thinking about at least one interesting event, situation or moment and then had wondered how that might have come about. I have since talked to several professional story writers about this and they have told me, often with a touch of surprise, that they realise they mostly work in a similar way.

The 'intriguing moment' can be anywhere in the story. It should be fairly limited in descriptive detail so as not to restrict possibilities, but it needs to contain enough detail to make it intriguing, because, above all, *it must make one want to ask questions about it.* As the writer doesn't initially know where this dramatic or curious moment may fall within the sequence of the final story, I call this moment an x-point.

Here are a few examples of effective x-points:

- A man is hanging upside down from a bridge with a rope twisted around one leg and is very slowly spinning around. The bridge is unusual in some kind of way.

- Someone is jumping about in a form of excitement on the final tee of a golf course and something is lying on the grass nearby.

- A teenage girl is sitting crying on hay bales in a barn.

- A wide trail of flattened long grass and other vegetation leads across a steep hillside and on into the distance through fields of crops.

- Three young children are laughing as they play in a remote forest clearing in the middle of a pitch-black, moonless night. They have no torches or artificial light.
- A girl is sitting on a limb of a huge, solitary oak tree. A small spade is leaning against the tree and a flowering plant is protruding from the short meadow grass nearby.
- Inside a deep cavern which runs off a barred and abandoned mineshaft there is a dusty piano. Suddenly it starts to make soft, slightly musical noises.

X-points can create non-sequential thinking

If you relate one of these x-points to a group and then ask them to tell you more of the story, some participants will initially try to continue the plot from that point on and, because they are still thinking sequentially, the results will be weak and predictable. However, if you keep asking for ideas, someone will soon come up with a noticeably better and more logical idea and this is almost inevitably because the x-point has begun to work its magic and make that student question in a particular way.

And here's the amazing secret. Sequential thinking runs forwards in time (this happened and then that happened, etc.) but an x-point works by pushing plot writers to *think backwards* in time. Because an x-point is intriguing it stimulates people to think about what might have brought about such a curious situation.

Using x-points effectively helps writers to work out the bulk of their story plots backwards, thinking through many possibilities at each stage so the stories are more original and less predictable for the reader who, of course, reads the story forwards. Plots can also be much more logical and plausible because the writer keeps thinking: 'So what caused that? What came *before* that moment of the x-point? Why did that previous thing happen?'

Let's look at this in more detail, taking, for example, the x-point about the piano in the cavern. Just look how many initial questions it can bring to mind:

- Why is the piano in that cavern?
- Where did it come from?
- How did it get there?
- Who, if anyone, put it there?
- Why was it left behind when the mine was abandoned?
- When was it put there?
- Is there anything special about it?
- What causes it to make those sounds?
- Why do the sounds start suddenly?

- Do they start at any particular time?
- When was the mine abandoned?
- Why was it abandoned?
- When was the piano last played?
- If it was played there, who played it?
- Who listened to it?
- Why is there a cavern in the mine?
- What did they mine there?

Introducing 'story excuses'

In being stimulated to ask questions about an x-point what we are really doing as writers is attempting to find a believable reason for that intriguing situation or moment to have come about. We are creating possible 'story excuses' for what the x-point describes *in order to make it seem more possible or plausible.*

It's often said that good creative writing creates 'suspension of disbelief' by making invented characters, situations, happenings, settings and even entire made-up worlds seem believable. X-points are fundamental to that principle.

Because a story plot driven by x-points is largely formed backwards, by seeking good reasons for why something occurred at each stage, the writer is constantly searching for believable story excuses for what happened before something, and then for what happened before that in order for it to have caused that story excuse, and so on. The process generates plausibility in each scene, builds strong 'story logic' throughout the work, and also produces amazingly original and creative story lines.

Teaching the importance of 'story logic' and believability in creative thinking is more essential than ever nowadays because most young people, especially boys, grow up immersed in animation, films, television and computer games filled with computerised special effects in which actors and animated characters do things which defy conventional logic. Within areas of these media there is a culture of unquestioning acceptance of impossible, distinctly visual concepts and plot clichés.

At the simplest level, this involves a character who falls off a cliff and freezes in panic in mid air before dropping below or, equally incredibly, peddles his legs so fast in the air he can turn and 'run' back onto the top. Many young students struggle to understand that characters should not randomly do something unbelievable or out of character in a written story, or that readers tend to stop suspending their disbelief when a problem is suddenly 'solved' by unexplained magic, by the random inclusion of some unexplained and unlikely technological device or because one of the human characters just happens to be an alien or a vampire. Many students are so used to these cinematic and computer led clichés and 'plot cheats' that such types of occurrence seem almost 'normal' to them, and so they often fail to work much on the believability and sense of an inherently unbelievable situation.

Working with story excuses for x-points helps solve this because apprentice writers learn to question what might have caused each step by questioning backwards in a creative but logical way. Thinking like this, they can't just throw in sequential clichés, or make randomly dramatic or 'useful' things happen in the plot, or have situations suddenly exist without a believable explanation.

Teaching students how to make up strong x-points

It is important to begin by first demonstrating and explaining sequential thinking to students so they can understand not only how most young people try to think up story plots but also how they can change this and dramatically improve their ideas. Asking them to make up an 'instant' verbal group story is a useful way of showing youngsters how they tend to think sequentially if you break it all down into constituent parts and give each a letter in sequence, starting with 'A' for the first thought. Otherwise, if time is short, you might just try to do this by using my UFO storyline example to explain the way common sequential thinking works, noting and lettering each thought in a step-by-step, forwards direction on the board.

Next you will need to explain in depth about x-points: what they are, and how by generating story excuses they make the story more logical, believable and unpredictable. You can tell students an x-point example of your own, or from the list above, and ask the group to say which 'before' questions might arise from the situation in that x-point.

After they have given you several good questions and you've noted them on the board, the group can vote for the two they think are best and most interesting, before making up and sharing believable story excuses for those questions. When you have elicited a good batch of these, select one or two which seem most interesting and believable, then ask the group to make up several story excuses for those in turn, and so on for a few stages in order to give the group practice in 'thinking backwards'.

Students should be told that they must always try to think up a few story excuses for each stage because that way they can then choose the best to ensure they have discovered more unusual and better quality fragments for the plot. If they are stuck for questions to help them find story excuses at any point, they simply need to ask themselves the 'five w's and an h' questions: Why? Who? What? Where? When? and How? If you show them the list of possible questions that I provided above for the 'piano in the mine' x-point, they will be able to find all six of these one word questions within them, some of them several times.

Creating individual x-points

Once you feel your students have a good grip on the basic concepts of x-points and story excuses you can ask them each to think up a strong x-point and write it down. They may need a little time to do this as it will be a new and creative challenge for them, and you'll need to remind everybody that an x-point needs to make people want to ask questions about what might have happened before that point in time. It's important to explain that x-points generally work best if they don't involve obvious story clichés such as a hand clutching a bloodied knife, a message in a bottle or a vampire rising from a coffin. After all, one of the main advantages of using x-points is that they create interesting and unusual story lines, so starting from a clichéd x-point is self-defeating.

I find it helpful to have the group or class rate and discuss which are the best x-point ideas supplied by participants and why. If the group functions well together, they might also suggest ways of changing a couple of the weaker ideas to improve them. Discussion should include why some of their x-points seem more original and why those stimulate interesting questions.

Once participants each have a strong x-point you might decide to allow them to start building up individual story plots based on these by thinking backwards. At this time you may need to remind your students to search for interesting and believable reasons for the situation in their x-point being as it is, through asking things like: *What* might have caused this situation? *What* was the person doing before? *What* is in/on/under something there? *Who* is this character or *who* else might have been involved, or *who* caused something to happen, or *who* is watching this? *When* might this have happened (day, night, time of year, anniversary, special event, during a snowstorm, etc.)? *Where* is this place or *where* did this thing or character come from or *where* were they going to? *Why* has someone or something done this thing? *How* did this character/object/animal get here, or into this situation?

Through using 'five w's and an h' questions students can usually find surprising numbers of questions to ask about a good x-point, and asking enough questions will then open up myriad fascinating possible story excuses to enrich the plot and keep it logical.

Crafting x-points on location

X-points can of course be created effectively in class, but it's even easier to inspire students to be truly original if they are encouraged to think them up within an interesting environment. Taking young writers to a stimulating location to work on ideas for them means that most participants will produce x-points and subsequent story lines that they would never have even thought of in class, and this can help wean then off the usual clichéd ideas that come easily to mind when there is little other inspiration around them.

Photo 12.1 Creating x-points on location

I have always found that many writing students produce spectacular story ideas during and after brainstorming and discussing possible x-points out of the classroom. Any interesting location will do as long as it does not contain too much distraction. It's even better if a location contains diverse sub-locations where you can lead your aspiring writers in thinking up x-points related to different parts of the environment because this will ultimately produce more varied story lines from your group, and ideas from different sub-locations often cross-fertilise each other to create even richer and more unusual plots and settings.

In one instance, I took one group by minibus to a tall upland pine forest on a rainy summer's day and shared x-point ideas based on the deep forest, a remote hillside bench, an evocative and misty wooded valley, an idiosyncratic sculpture park in the woods and a lonely and tiny moorland chapel. On another occasion we walked around a mixed environment of rugged coastline, rocky beach, stream, marsh, and twisty miniature woodland.

Suitable locations for x-point sessions

Anywhere varied and interesting will do: town parks, streets, boating lakes, grave-yards and churches, shopping centres, a fairground, hills and valleys, farms, canals, rivers and estuaries, coast and sea, woodland and meadow, derelict places, building sites, markets, museums . . . the list of possibilities is endless. A leader needs to sense how diverse and stimulating any one location is and to plan to move participants on to other nearby locations or sub-locations as required, so as to include enough variety of inspiration for the group's stories.

It's important, however, not to spread a brainstorm too thinly for this can cause students to lose focus. Intensively brainstorming x-points and their initial story excuses in a few places is generally more effective than brainstorming less deeply in more places. Locations with interesting medium-range views as well as nearby detail can contain more possibilities, but a little wander around an area will often flush out interesting places, objects, happenings and real-life characters on whom stimulating x-points can be based.

If possible, it can be worth deciding which are the best locations and sub-locations beforehand and to make up a few default x-points yourself in case the group struggles to get their ideas going. A brief preliminary visit like this can be more inspiring to do with a friend or colleague and might be accomplished in advance while making a visit risk assessment.

Making up powerful x-points is a highly creative activity, so the environment only needs to act as a starting point and students should be encouraged to think in terms of 'what if'. For instance: What if there was the sound of a child sobbing on that play-park roundabout in the middle of the night? What if a few of the cows in that field seemed considerably larger than normal? What if a small plane suddenly crash-landed in the field, scattering cattle, and two teenagers in fancy dress stumbled out of it?

An example x-point produced in a specific setting

A good example of this type of thinking was when a group was brainstorming x-point ideas with me at the top of a steep escarpment in summer. One of many x-points that came out of that session was the one in the list about the long grass having been flattened in a bizarre trail, stretching away across grassy downland and distant fields of crops. The idea came about because children had been making shorter trails by sliding down the hill. This kind of original idea is typical of those inspired by the real world and would rarely occur in a classroom environment.

Many story excuses were created to explain the curious idea of a cross-country trail of beaten vegetation but one that particularly stands out in my mind was that it had been caused by a huge, saggy, balloon-like creature, rather like a gigantic airborne jellyfish. The trail had been caused by a cow (or a character) having been dragged along the ground by the creature's long, dangling tentacles.

You may notice that, like this one, *good story excuses are, in effect, x-points themselves* because, in turn, they immediately create a desire to find reasons for their being how they are. So, for instance, the giant floating creatures may have been alien attackers, or they might have been created by future biotechnologists to move heavy things around. Or maybe the scene was on another world with a denser atmosphere.

How did it lift the struggling cow over the hedges? Perhaps it just crashed them over them, or it suddenly created more lifting gas, or ejected stinking water, or had fleshy manta-like 'wings' on either side to help alter its altitude. Each of these possible story excuse 'solutions' again creates its own interesting questions, and following the backwards trail of these helps develop an imaginative, yet logical, story.

Once most members of your group have individually created or chosen one or two interesting x-points and a few related story excuses that they, and you, are happy with, you may consider briefly brainstorming some local descriptions and metaphors that could end up being used to enhance stories based on those x-points. Students can then take their x-points and a base of rich language ideas back to class to work up their story plots.

More aspects of working with x-points

Employing multiple x-points

Referring back to that interview with the writer Ian McEwan confirms this writer's way of 'thinking backwards'. When asked about his planned next book he explained that the plot had come about from three notes he'd jotted down at various times, and they were all, in effect, x-points. One was the idea of someone having held a secret for so long that they now couldn't even tell it to people close to them, even if they wanted to. The other two were about completely unrelated things but McEwan had obviously asked many questions about each of these and also asked himself, eventually, whether any of the developing plot ideas that came out of these possible story excuses could also be webbed together.

This shows how a writer often employs more than one x-point to make the main story richer and more complex, and also enriches it through the generation of linked sub-plots. The trick is to think out various possible story excuses for each x-point separately to start with so that any eventual connections between them aren't clichéd or predictable. Inevitably our natural 'webbing' facility will start finding ways to alter and connect these possible and still malleable 'proto-plots' and incorporate them into a more complex, and probably longer, story.

Using more than one x-point is challenging for younger or weaker students, but some might do this naturally if they sense their single-x-point storyline might be too thin. More able teenage or adult students often want to add a second or even a third x-point and can do so successfully as long as they initially treat each separately to avoid falling into sequential thinking. They need to make up simplified chains of possible story excuses for secondary x-points to begin with before allowing the ideas produced by the various x-point chains to web together.

Due to our natural 'webbing' ability these disparate chains of ideas often start linking together while the thinker is only partially through this process. Although it is sensible to try and stay true to each chosen x-point because this can help defeat the slide towards cliché and predictability, the entire process is just a tool for finding inspiration, originality and believability, so specific story excuses thought up can be altered as necessary to fit with the emerging combined plot line.

If any student writers have been derailing the process by ignoring potentially good story excuses and falling back on 'safe' and familiar sequential thinking and TV-led clichés, the weakness can sometimes be solved by giving each of them a second, apparently unrelated x-point, which they then have to develop using new story excuses and finally weave into their story in a logical and believable way. It's challenging but can exercise, and bring discipline to, a creatively lazy brain.

This is also a useful activity to give to pairs of 'thinking buddies', or when teaming up a student who is good at the process with another who needs a little help in breaking away from clichéd thinking.

Photocopiable illustrations showing the thinking processes behind developing a plot line through the creation of x-points and story excuses based on them can be found at the end of this chapter.

Fitting an x-point to various genres

It is surprisingly easy to place an x-point into more or less any genre of story writing, and trying this out for a small part of the brainstorming session is a valuable exercise for young writers. A leader simply has to take one or two strong x-points from that session, mention a different genre from the ones they have been discussed in so far, then ask participants how they think it might fit into it.

So, for instance, we've already seen how that odd trail of flattened grass might fit into a science fiction story, but how about an historical one? Could it be a trail caused by a tight group of cavalry? Where a large boat was being dragged across the land and carried over the hedges?

How about a comedy story? Perhaps the trail might have been caused by incompetent bank robbers, who had stolen a huge quantity of banknotes but could only find a king-sized duvet cover in which to drag them across the countryside as they tried to make their escape in the night. Or perhaps the grass flattening was the result of some crazy characters riding on a wide piece of plywood pulled by an elephant they had liberated from a zoo?

A detective story? Maybe the trail was made by eco-terrorists who were testing a way of flattening and destroying areas of genetically modified crops.

A whodunnit? Perhaps a body had been found but, after much enquiry, it transpired that it wasn't a murder because the suspicious death had been caused by a hot air balloon accident, when a temporary failure of the burner had forced the basket to drop too low and trail across the countryside, causing bizarre injuries and death to someone who then fell or was thrown out of it miles away when it was airborne again. Perhaps the occupiers were doing something illegal such as drug smuggling at the time?

Romance *and* cowboy genres? The tracks might have been made by a sheriff's posse on the trail of an honest deputy who had been wrongly accused of a train robbery in which his boss had taken a pay-off. Maybe the deputy had escaped in order to save his future lover whom the train robbers were trying to kill because she was the only credible witness?

Given a strong x-point, many wonderful story ideas can be created in any genre.

Solving minor difficulties in fitting an x-point within a genre

One of the few difficulties that might arise is when an x-point appears anachronistic compared to a chosen genre, such as might happen if the x-point contains a modern device like a computer, but the writer wants to create a story in an historical genre.

There are several ways of dealing with this. The first is to change the device in the x-point to something relatively equivalent for that period, such as changing the computer to an abacus, a fountain pen, a scribe's office or a ledger clerk. A second possible route would involve using the x-point in its appropriate time period while also writing the historical element, so the computer might be used by someone in modern times to research the stories of their ancestry, creating two parallel and possibly linked or 'echoing' stories. In a similar type of parallel story, the computer might be used in an analysis of archaeological samples to reconstruct an ancient town or habitation where a character from the earlier period lived.

Another resolution would be to write a zany time-travel story such as has been used frequently in television science fiction and comedy sci-fi series, but the most obvious solution would simply be to create an x-point which does not have modern or anachronistic content.

I hope, by now, you will have seen that an x-point can work well in producing fascinating and subtly linked story plots in any genre, with the slight exception mentioned above, but even that has effective and often interesting solutions.

Developing the story

This book is principally about techniques which make use of the wide inspirational and language potential of out-of-classroom brainstorming sessions for creative writing, rather than a manual which looks in minute depth at the art of writing a story. However, here are some essential pointers that have helped students in many of my intensive writing courses.

Once young writers have at least one or two x-points (depending on age and ability) and have created a backwards chain of clever, interesting and logical story excuses, a large portion of an interesting and original plot should have developed.

Once most of the plot has been decided there are still various story planning aspects that need to be worked out, notably:

- any essential *background* to the story and its characters;
- how and where *the start* of the story will be for the reader;
- a powerful, logical and believable *ending*;
- the *final sequence of scenes* and their settings; and
- *character development.*

To familiarise themselves with any necessary story background, plot creators simply need to work backwards, finding good story excuses until they have made sense of everything necessary. This often means that they have to work out the 'back story' before the chronological point at which the story is going to start. Writers may need to know this background information themselves and must remember to drop essential snippets of background information into their writing, either as a third person writer, a narrator, within dialogue, in characters' thoughts, or as flashback.

This brings us to the second bullet point, because each young writer will need to choose an intriguing or gripping first chapter which, in chronological terms, could be from before the main story starts, at the time it starts, or after it starts. The essential thing about beginnings nowadays is that a writer needs to hook the reader as quickly and as strongly as possible, so that the reader desperately wants to read on to find out more.

For readers, a good beginning should be a bit like a strong x-point because it should make them want to have questions answered. This may be in the form of something intriguing in the story setting or the plot, in the characters or the way they behave, or through drama and suspense. There must always be a sense of something, or several things, remaining unexplained so far, but this should be so fascinating that readers crave to know more.

Choosing an ending

By now each young writer will need to have decided on the ending of their story. It is important to wait until the rest of the plot has been worked out through a backwards sequence of story excuses because all this knowledge will help them to decide on a good ending. This is the only point in the process of plot creation where writers may need to think forwards, but, because they now have a wealth of story plots and backgrounds in mind, they can create endings which fit logically with their stories and with the 'feel' of each one.

Occasionally the original x-point also turns out to be the final part of the story, but even if the x-point falls very near the end, the writer still has to add a satisfactory ending after that point.

If young writers are able enough, they should be encouraged to think up several possible endings. They should also look at the possibility of adding an *additional twist*, as long as it makes the story better, or leaves the reader with a satisfactory feeling of finality, even though this may include a curious sense of still wanting to know more about the future or past.

'Chronological order' and 'story sequence'

The sequence of scenes chosen can help in keeping this 'hold' over readers, so scenes can be chronological, jump forwards or backwards in time, or past scenes can be dropped into the present via characters' conversations or thoughts. So that a young writer can hold a complex story in his or her head, as well as make changes to the way the plot is presented to the reader, I strongly encourage each student first to note it down as a chronological sequence of events in bullet points. The writer can then choose how to bullet point the 'story sequence', i.e. the order of plot events as they will be revealed to the reader. Due to the flexibility of copy, cut and paste options, this can be achieved much more quickly and effectively on computer, as can the writing and editing of the story itself.

Before and during the actual story writing it helps greatly if students jot down notes about their main characters and try to find characteristics about their appearance, behaviour and speech which fit and deepen their fictitious personalities. Again, the flexibility of working on computers makes students more likely to keep this process up and to alter writing, notes and bullet points as they have better ideas.

Photocopiable and scannable sheets follow, which illustrate the stages of creating x-point stories. The final photocopiable page may be used as a teachers' 'crib sheet', or be displayed or given to students so they can check off their progress on it. As well as being a useful aid to students, a story development 'tick list' like this can help teachers quickly keep track of individual student's progress during the period of story creation.

Thinking routes for an X-Point story plot

The following diagrams demonstrate how ideas for story excuses 'leapfrog' ideas backwards on each other and can also cross-link to create richer plots. As shown below, to find story excuses simply interrogate the x-point with questions, using 'the five Ws and an H'.

Story excuses based on the x-point of a man hanging upside down from an unusual bridge by a rope are presented here in simplified ideas chains. *Each chain must be read backwards from its end* in order to understand the thinking processes involved. These are not logical sequences of a storyline, but are brainstormed ideas and possibilities, some of which will be discarded during the formation of an original, realistic plot.

The beginnings of a possible basic plot resulting from these ideas & possibilities:

A drunk man tried to cross a massive, unfinished bridge because he'd missed the last bus home and he knew his wife would worry. Because it was dark and he was drunk he accidentally stumbled into a coil of rope left there by some workmen, tripped and fell over the edge with the rope wound around his leg.

Ways to develop a more complex & subtle plot

- Look for more story excuses 'before' these: the more backstory possibilities, the richer and more believable the plot and characters.
- Web-in more unusual concepts by doing another brainstorm.
- Brainstorm another X-Point to enrich it further and help create a sub-plot.

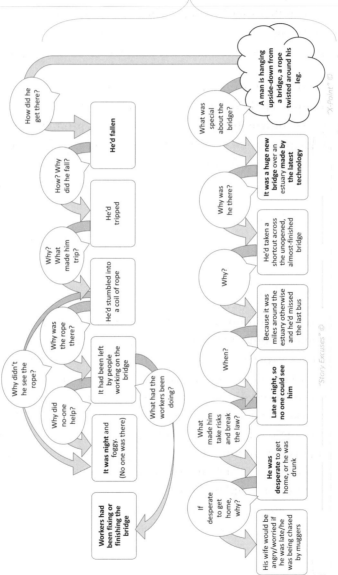

Diagram 12a Thinking routes for an x-point story plot

Graphics by Katie Wilkinson.

© 2014, *Write Out of the Classroom, Colin Macfarlane, Routledge*

Another brainstorm of the same X-point

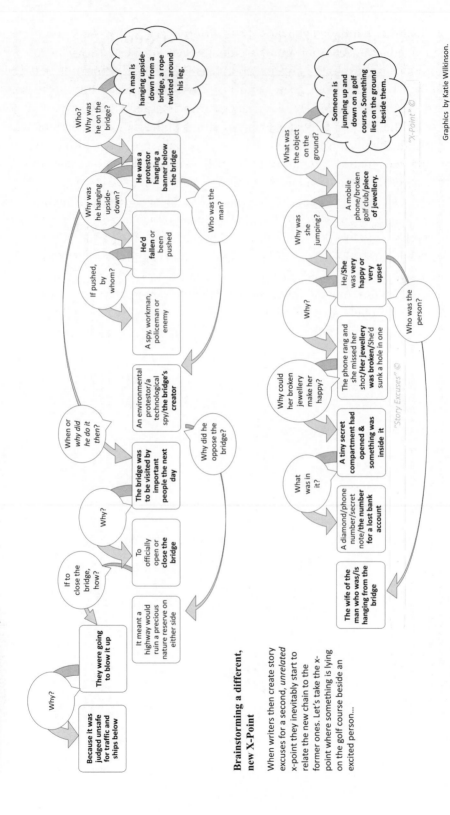

Brainstorming a different, new X-Point

When writers then create story excuses for a second, *unrelated* x-point they inevitably start to relate the new chain to the former ones. Let's take the x-point where something is lying on the golf course beside an excited person....

Diagram 12b Another brainstorm of the same x-point

© 2014, *Write Out of the Classroom, Colin Macfarlane, Routledge*

Graphics by Katie Wilkinson.

Combining plot ideas arising from both x-points

In collective discussion, students, aged 12–15, found the above story excuses for the two x-points. Due to the natural tendency for ideas to 'web' together, before they had created much of the second x-point's chain of story excuses, the following rich, composite plot began to appear to them. Story excuses they used are emboldened in the two diagrams.

A wealthy man, who owned a major construction company, had dreamed all his life about bridging a huge span of sea between two countries. He had his company spend a fortune developing a totally new technology capable of this incredible feat. The company eventually won a contract to do the job but, as the massive new bridge neared completion several years later, a problem was discovered with the revolutionary design. The owner spent all the company's money and all his own in trying to rectify the problem but, although he was sure they had found a solution, investors became frightened off and refused to put any more into the project, so the bridge was to be blown up as it was considered a danger to shipping in its current state.

The distraught owner decided to try and prevent the destruction of the bridge by attaching a massive banner beneath it at night which said 'This beautiful bridge can now be fixed. Stop its senseless destruction!' He knew that the world's press and television would be covering the dramatic event next morning and hoped that if he tied himself to the banner they would not be able to blow it up with him there, and public outcry might save the bridge once they'd interviewed him on TV.

Early next morning the man's wife was finishing a round of golf. When she swung her club the jewel-encrusted bracelet (which had been given to her on the morning of her wedding by her late mother-in-law) flew off and hit the ground. A secret catch released, springing open a tiny compartment beneath one of the stones, and inside was a piece of folded paper with a number on it.

When she had been given the bracelet on her wedding day, the bridegroom's mother had told her 'this is more valuable than you can possibly imagine and one day I will tell you why'. Unfortunately the groom's father and mother were both killed in a private aeroplane accident shortly afterwards and so the secret had died with them.

It was known that, as the bridegroom's parents had escaped occupied Europe during WW2, their massive family fortune had been hidden in a secret numbered account in a Swiss bank, but nobody knew the number except the groom's parents. When the owner's wife looked at the paper she realised that written on it were the details and secret access number for the 'lost' family fortune.

She tried to phone her husband at home to tell him the wonderful news that he'd be able to save his bridge, but he didn't answer. She realised he had gone out late the night before and she hadn't seen him that morning so she immediately called his mobile but unusually got no answer on that either (because it had fallen out of his jacket pocket as he dangled upside down).

From this point the final part of the plot was created forwards...

Very concerned that he didn't answer his phone and taking into account his recent fragile state of mind, she knew there was only one place she might find him. She jumped into her car and rushed to the bridge where she discovered him hanging upside down beneath it. He was unresponsive (because people fall unconscious when upside down for long) and she assumed he had committed suicide because of the imminent destruction of his life's work.

Angry at the irony and crushed by her loss, she stared at the tiny piece of paper in her hand before letting it flutter away towards the sea. She spun as if to walk away but turned back, closed her eyes and followed the paper towards the ocean far below.

A sequence of story creation using x-points

- Create an x-point that is intriguing and makes you want to ask lots of questions about it.

- Make up a variety of interesting and believable 'story excuses' for the x-point by repeatedly asking the 'five w's and an h' questions.

- Chose the best one (or two) of these story excuses and make up more strong story excuses for that story excuse, then story excuses for that one, etc., thinking backwards like this until most of the plot is in your mind.

    Optional:

    - *Create another unrelated x-point.*

    - *Make up some possible story excuses for this, then story excuses for these excuses. Try not to become too fixed yet on any one route.*

    - *Think about how both sets of 'floating stories' (story possibilities which are not finally decided yet) can be altered to fit together as one greater story if necessary.*

- Ask more questions about what might have happened before that until you have a good sense of the 'back story' (i.e. what happened before 'the reader's story' begins).

- Decide on an intriguing beginning that will 'hook' readers and make them want to know more. You may want to start with a dramatic scene in the story and then jump back in time to the real beginning, or write a special scene for this, or start with a fascinating or powerful scene in the past and jump forwards to the real story beginning.

- If you are sure about your plot-so-far, carefully think of several possible endings for your story then choose the best one. See if you can think of a clever additional twist to that ending.

- Work out the *chronological sequence* (what happens after what *in time*) of happenings, scenes and settings in your story and put them down in bullet points. Some things may be happening to different characters at the same time. You may be able to use different colours for different characters if this helps or, to help sort it out, you might make a short note of each scene on a card and place these on the floor in sequence, with scenes occurring at the same time beside each other.

- In bullet points, work out the final *story sequence* (the order in which you decide to present the scenes and happenings to the reader). Think about whether you want to change the chronological sequence at the beginning or elsewhere by using 'flashbacks', time jumps, characters' thoughts or mentions in dialogue so the reader can still follow the plot.

- Think hard about your characters and make and alter notes about them before you write and during writing. Try to find things about what they do, what they say, how they dress, etc., which fit their personalities.

- Write slowly and thoughtfully and keep thinking about what the reader needs to know. Through well-chosen and interesting description, try to *show* your readers all the most interesting or dramatic scenes instead of telling them about them. Use '*tell*' mostly for less interesting scenes, simple connecting scenes or things from the past the reader needs to know.

- Read through the completed story, improving and editing as you go.

Location-based collective stories

As we have seen, observing and thoughtfully brainstorming in interesting locations can make a significant improvement in the quality of language, inspiration and ideas in most forms of creative writing, and this is equally true of working on collective stories for younger students. The process can dramatically 'switch on' their language awareness and raise personal expectations.

The brainstorming process has been well-covered in previous chapters so I won't go into it further here except to point out that, in the case of collective stories, it has two main goals in mind. The first is to stimulate and collect a wide variety of rich descriptions and metaphorical language from the environments visited. The second is to inspire a variety of possible plot ideas that can come out of those environments.

So, as well as asking participants to observe and interestingly describe aspects within the environment, leaders also need to encourage students to keep asking 'what if?' questions to share with the group as it moves around a location. In effect, the group needs to combine a hunt for rich and interesting language with a search for potential x-points.

Later, when working on the collective story back in the classroom, the developing plot may well only feature those brainstormed environments in one or two scenes, so it is unnecessary to brainstorm language as widely as for individual descriptive poems. However, the act of observing and interestingly describing general settings (with a few aspects of them being covered in subtle detail) will supply some related vocabulary and raise the students' level of language aspiration when writing the story.

Using a portable computer on location

Portable computers are perfect for data collection while brainstorming on location for a collective story. Having an assistant type every word and idea onto a computer means that students are free to concentrate on looking and thinking, and every one of those wonderful observations, descriptions and embryonic plot ideas can be taken back to class and immediately displayed through a digital projector so the group can start work on developing the plot and then the writing as soon as is practicable.

Your typist should space the words and lines well and continuously save to memory stick as well as to the computer as a precaution against battery or technological failure. Carrying a clipboard is a sensible back up plan.

Democratic story writing

Getting it started

The most effective way of creating collective stories is to employ what I call 'democratic story writing'. What this means is that participants (including any adults) give and discuss suggestions for plot or language possibilities, which are all typed up on screen in front of the group. Once the leader thinks there are enough strong suggestions, students (and any adults present) vote for what they think are the best by a show of hands. This works incredibly well as long as students are reminded to vote for what they genuinely think is the best idea and not to vote with people just because they are friends with them.

A helpful way to start the classroom session is to ask students to tell you any story genres they can think of, then list these on the whiteboard. Hopefully they will come up with quite a number but they may need some adult help. Participants are then given two or three votes each which they can use to choose which genres they would prefer for the story, and they can only vote once for each genre. It's probably best to discard any limited genres such as cowboy stories.

When the votes are counted you can agree to try and fit the story to the two, or possibly three, most voted for of these genres. This means the story might be something like: an adventure story with comedy, a humorous horror story with a touch of romance, a science fiction story with a detective story element.

Growing the plot

The plot needs to be evolved next and this is best done by thinking up 'an interesting or curious moment or happening' (an x-point) and then asking questions about it so that much of the story is worked out backwards (see previous chapter). One of the advantages about having brainstormed on location is that the young writers should have come up with quite a few interesting and original ideas that they would never have thought of in class and, hopefully, by the time they are all back in the room ready to work out the plot, some of these ideas may already have emerged as front-runners because they are so fascinating or unusual.

If you have led a vote on possible genres for the story, participants should be asked to try and make initial 'story excuses' for the two (or even three) most popular x-points which might fit into one or more of those genres, especially into any genre that was a runaway winner in the vote. If group members show good thinking, aspects from both sets of story excuses may end up in a story, making the plot richer, but you can always discard the weaker one if the group finds it hard to connect both emergent plot lines.

Once the plot has been agreed the group will need to think about possible endings, but don't necessarily have to decide on any particular one at this stage. They will also need to vote on the number of main characters, whether all or some are children, teenagers, adults, animals, aliens or whatever suits the plot best. They will probably not cope with more than three main protagonists because writing all the action and dialogue for more takes up a lot of time!

All this can be typed up virtually in real time by your literate assistant and quickly arranged into a series of notes (in sections such as 'characters', 'settings', 'background', etc.) and a chronological plot sequence, which can be displayed and referred to continuously throughout the collective writing process, or changed slightly if better ideas come along.

Writing the story

Following that, it's simply a case of choosing and writing a fabulous beginning that will hook the reader, then working on by encouraging students to put forward strong ideas, words, metaphors, phrases and even whole sentences. The leader's job is to ask questions of all this, to elicit the best story and language ideas from students, to 'lead from the front' by helping piece these together into sentences, and to run 'instant voting' as required throughout the process. A quality thesaurus can be allowed to move casually around the room with students occasionally asked to look up additional suggestions on behalf of the group.

After a while, a well-functioning group often needs to vote less frequently because participants have a growing sense of which choices are best. Votes will then mostly occur when suggestions are more or less as strong as each other. (You may have to throw in an occasional casting vote!)

Writing a high quality collective story like this can take some time and is best worked on over a period, perhaps on certain days of the week. If strong teaching help is available from within school or by a literate parent, sections of the story can be developed by this person leading small groups, and the 'story-so-far' can be periodically shared with the class to keep everyone up to date so other sub-groups can keep developing it in their own sessions.

For teachers who struggle to find enough time, just writing the plot and a reasonable chunk of the story collectively can be enough to embed the advantages of the process, but it is much more inspiring for a class or group to have completed the entire story and eventually presented it to the rest of the year group, school or parents.

This is another 'cream on top' language activity in which every good idea, plot twist, word and metaphor is reinforced by being found or thought about, discussed, typed and voted for, so the best ideas, thinking processes and language elements are repeatedly brought to the fore and potentially embedded in young minds. Everybody contributes, stronger students are stretched, weaker ones pick up processes and vocabulary, and everyone feels valued through their suggestions and democratic involvement.

CHAPTER 14

Location-inspired fictitious diary writing

The creation of strong writing within a diary format is relatively challenging at most ages. Principal reasons for this are that:

- in such a tightly 'reported' form, it is harder to illustrate exciting interaction between characters than when writing in the form of a 'live action' story apparently taking place in real time;

- diary writing is further limited because it is usually presented in consecutive sections of recent past events and normally from only one character's perspective;

- partly due to the lack of a clear 'beginning, middle and end' story format, students can tend to ramble in their writing and fail to grip the reader. A diary entry can be nearer to 'stream of consciousness' writing so it's easy to ramble and forget to 'paint' vivid scenes;

- students can forget to describe as richly as they might in a normal story format because they are more involved with getting the form right;

- a young writer's lack of experience of, and confidence in, this format can sometimes cause them to be less enthusiastic and feel less inspired than if writing a story;

- students' lack of knowledge of a chosen character or subject area can narrow their writing even further in this restricted format than in a story;

- students can get muddled between past and present tenses; and

- young writers are so used to third person stories they sometimes find it hard to write in the first person from a different person's viewpoint. 'I' in children's own writing is commonly reserved for the reporting of their personal experiences.

From a teacher's point of view these difficulties and restrictions are a list of strong reasons why young people need to be challenged by this format, and the good news is that brainstorming diary writing in interesting and evocative locations can alleviate several of these problems. The process can raise descriptive and figurative language levels and aspirations, while settings and events chosen can be more originally, convincingly and closely observed in the writing.

Enthusiasm and inspiration are increased through the feelings of discovery and 'reality' gained on such a visit, and knowledge about the diary subject's life, difficulties, habits and environment can be increased in a more lively and vicarious way than if only discussed in a classroom.

Diaries based on historical locations

One obvious cross-subject diary project is to base the writing on an imagined character or characters who might have lived or worked in the past at an historical site you visit, or in a similar setting elsewhere. The diary can be based on 'real' or imagined characters in a novel or story studied in class, or can just as easily be linked to a history project.

It isn't, of course, necessary to link a 'historical' diary to any particular book or project because young writers can fill in realism details through personal or small group research on the internet or in books, and especially through gaining the quality of 'live' authenticating detail and metaphorical content that comes from creative observational brainstorming sessions in a relevant setting.

The places visited may be relatively intact, as in the case of a stately home, a monastery or a preserved industrial site such as an old mine, a working watermill, or a 'living museum' where people sometimes act historical parts. Conversely, the original edifice or major aspects of the site might have largely vanished, as is often the case with locations such as battlefields, hill forts, ruined castles, 'plague villages', flattened industrial areas and in-filled canals.

In either case, the relevant background information provided plus the results of collectively brainstorming both observed and imagined material on site can be supplemented by a small amount of student research and the employment of young imaginations ... all important skills to develop. However, finding a location which still has a reasonable proportion of the original buildings, features or atmosphere can aid strong writing, owing to the richness and originality of observable 'reality' detail that can be woven into the narrative, and by curious story ideas that can grow from questioning those features.

No matter where you are based there is always some location of historical interest to inspire: castles, ancient houses, graceful parkland, old parts of town, preserved or half-ruined industrial sites or buildings, themed museum exhibits, Victorian schoolrooms, old train stations or 'steam events', harbours, antiquated farms or settlements where humans once lived, and so on.

Diaries based on non-historical settings

Creative diaries can be based on, or inspired by, any location, whether or not it has obvious historical connections, but as always, the richer the environment selected the richer the language and ideas that can flow from the brainstorming process into the writing.

Here are some fictional diary writing ideas I have used successfully. The first is normally for ages 11 or 12 and upwards but can be taken down to lower age bands, especially if the work is pursued collectively.

'Disaster diaries'

The process of creating a 'disaster diary' can successfully enthuse boys as well as girls if it's well presented to them. This is largely due to the dramatic scenes that can be triggered in young imaginations as well as in those of potential readers. The disaster covered can be anything from a plane or train crash to a dam bursting or a landslide, to an epidemic or to people becoming shipwrecked and cast away in a remote place. The concept of remoteness or isolation in setting can be helpful in some of these choices as it means that help is not at hand, or at all, so characters have to survive for some time on their own or on their collective wits.

Good material to combine with location work can be press cuttings or internet research about a particular disaster. This might, for instance, be a plane crash in a remote place, a huge forest or heath fire, or perhaps a volcanic eruption. As mentioned, having characters cut off from easy assistance means that your writers will need to work hard on brainstorming a particular locality in depth, and on developing character and interaction between characters.

To create enough interesting human depth and interaction in the narrative it is best to specify a minimum of three main characters, but of course, having many more principal characters makes writing logistics complex, so perhaps three or four is about right, depending on age, with two or three for younger children.

Following through 'questioning trees' to combine emotion with description

We've seen that the thoughtful brainstorming of different locations creates richer observation and language. Led carefully, a 'diary' brainstorming process can also generate plot ideas, useful story 'problems' and convincing micro settings, as well as ideas for characters' survival, and competition or collaboration between survivors. On top of seeking exciting observations, language and metaphors from the real location, a group leader needs to keep asking detailed questions about where or how characters could survive in that environment, what they might do to try and save themselves, how they might collaborate, what they might disagree on and which actions they might take.

All interesting answers are best followed up by questions designed to elicit further vivid language and metaphors from participants that describe characters' more precise sensations, reactions and outcomes linked to experiences in those environments. This process builds potential story plot lines; more believable actions, reactions and interactions between characters; and richer 'internal worlds' for characters, as well as stronger and more diverse language.

For example, if the brainstormed possibility arises where fictitious characters attempt to build a shelter with beach rocks, branches and old plastic sacks or leaves, a leader could ask how well this structure would keep out the rain or wind, what it would look, feel or smell like inside it, and invite participants to describe the discomfort of sleeping in it, what rainwater leaks would cause, sound and feel like, and so on.

'Disaster diaries' – a 'castaways' example

A popular workshop format of mine at residential centres near the coast begins by taking a group to a rugged shore, ostensibly to brainstorm descriptive material for a poem or story. A message in a sealed plastic bottle is soon 'discovered' in a rock pool as we move across the area. Depending on timings and tides this prop has either been placed in advance, or sneaked into position behind participants' backs by my discreet assistant or a 'passer-by' the students will not recognise.

The bottle, partially weighted down by pebbles to make it float upright, has some strips of bright plastic tied around the top as if to draw attention to it. Inside, a 'message', suitably scrawled on a ragged fragment of tea-stained paper, or the back of a frayed and 'sea-stained' product label, informs finders that a small group of amateur sailors have had their small boat wrecked in a storm or through having been being run over by a massive tanker at night (be creative!). It mentions the castaways have been stranded on a desolate little island which we can some-times see on the horizon. The writer has scribbled 'no-one knows we're lost!', and the message is always dated a few days previous to the workshop.

Setting story parameters

I next set the parameters of the diary format, including the minimum and maximum number of main characters, and stress that the students' writing must grip the reader from the outset and that diary entries need to create a vibrant sense of place (through well-observed details and powerful description). There must also be tension created between at least some of the characters, and inter-esting narrative complications. A strong sense of the personalities of the 'diary writer' (or 'writers') and the other characters must emerge.

With this in mind, we continue our brainstorm of the similar surroundings on our shoreline. This will now include discussing possible survival options involving materials, wreckage and wild foodstuffs available, possible major interactions between characters, etc.

This format has produced many powerful diary stories, not all with happy endings ... a few have even ended with the writing apparently becoming a dying scrawl! The best contain quite subtle interactions between protagonists, sometimes with the surfacing of latent talents, emotional or mental states, hidden rivalries, surprising secrets and even love interest complications, so it's worth asking for, and pursuing, plenty of suggestions about these aspects from groups of suitable ages.

Most fundamental of all at any age is to keep reminding writers that plots need to be backed up by the use of relevant 'show'; that is, closely observed description, some of which might result from in-depth group brainstorming at the location. Participants should be encouraged to paint a high quality of authenticating detail into all areas, including character, moods, action and events, and not limit it to the physical environment.

If it is good weather and you have enough time (some teachers make the initial part into a whole day project outing in summer), placing participants into pairs or 'ideas buddies' near the end of the planning process can stimulate and deepen individual plot ideas, a process which can also work well later at school.

'Animal diaries'

Animal diaries are especially suitable for individual writing at ages 9–12. Collective or partner work around the age of 8–10 can also produce diaries of remarkable quality.

Once students are familiar with diary formats and have been shown some examples (see photocopiable page after this chapter) it is best to proceed through a few sub-locations to discuss what animals might live there or survive there if they were lost in those environments for some reason (story excuses required here!)

One potential drawback to this process, especially with younger children, is their lack of precise knowledge regarding particular animals: their detailed appearance, traits, individual and social behaviour, etc. Having plenty of facts about this contributed by the leader or group members during locational brainstorming will increase this knowledge and help writers to include more authentic detail and micro settings.

Although an animal diary inevitably involves anthropomorphic writing, where, for the purpose of human storytelling, some at least of the animals need to think and partially behave like humans, it is still essential to make the characters' behaviour seem as much as possible like those of the actual animals, otherwise the reader may stop suspending disbelief and find the story silly.

As well as showing students some general diary examples, reading out small sections of anthropomorphic stories such as *Watership Down* and *Attila the Hen* will help them understand this concept, as can looking at the close reference paid to particular types of animals' behaviour and environment by writers, artists and animators in films such as *The Lion King* and *Finding Nemo*. Showing and discussing small extracts of these can demonstrate to students how incredibly well animal movements, behaviours and settings have been researched for these works and how a writer (who is unable to show readers any such spectacular visuals) must observe especially well in order to generate appropriately convincing and vivid pictures in a reader's imagination through only the creative use of words and metaphors.

Knowing animals' characters and settings well

The descriptive quality of the writing will be stronger if young writers are already familiar with the look and behaviour of any animals featured, and if the habitats in which they are going to set parts of their stories have been richly brainstormed in advance. Unusual animals or those that can't do many interesting things should not be considered, whereas commonly known creatures such as foxes, lost cats, rabbits, mice and, possibly, badgers could be chosen, as could other well-known animals that can do complex and relatively 'humanistic' things, such as escaped monkeys or chimpanzees.

Something else to avoid is allowing boy writers to feature, as principal animal characters, odd creatures they like or own, such as tarantulas or snakes, or to allow young girls to write diaries about their cute kittens or sweet ponies because, speaking from experience, they will inevitably forget to include either genuinely interesting and dramatic plot complications or original, descriptive settings.

Narrowing options to increase descriptive quality

Although it means giving young writers less creative freedom, it's sometimes easier for the leader to choose one or two types of animal for the project in advance so that collective brainstorming can be more targeted to those creatures. Creating a couple of basic story 'set-up' situations featuring particular types of animal can help. Examples of this would be to tell students 'story set-ups' such as the following:

> *While the driver was changing a punctured tyre on the circus (or zoo) lorry, he left a door open for a moment and Chooko the Chimpanzee escaped into the countryside, lolloping away between the trees on a steep, deeply wooded hillside.*

or

> *Scriffle the Squirrel's part of the ancient wood was felled by men with chainsaws and he had to escape along a hedgerow.*

You can specify two or three different types of central animal characters for your students with which they are liable to have reasonable familiarity. This means you can guide mini brainstorm sessions for those particular animals and for available locations as possible settings, which can greatly increase the quality of observation and descriptive language in student writing.

Writing 'from the animal's viewpoint'

During the outdoor brainstorm session participants can be led to look at the different ways in which a creature might perceive the world, compared to humans. This could mean discussing what it would see and note at its scale within that brainstormed landscape; what senses it would use and how differently it might describe various sights, smells, feelings, tastes and sounds; what individual animals' 'personalities' might be like, and how an animal character might 'think' about things and situations in ways that seem believable for that animal but still comprehensible to human readers.

An animal's description, metaphor or simile for something needs to be 'accessible' to the animal as well as to us, so it must be based on something the animal could encounter. For instance, baby puffball toadstools in the rain might be described by a squirrel or fox as 'round and shiny as river pebbles', or 'white and smooth as pigeons' eggs', which would be descriptively original, understandable by human readers and convincing in connection with those creatures,

Familiarity with verbs specific to the creature's movements and habits is essential, and placing participants who have chosen the same animal into sub-groups to brainstorm specific verbs and descriptions before writing can be helpful. Imagining that creature doing various activities in each sub-location visited should bring a variety of strong and appropriate verbs to the fore.

The photocopiable pages at the end of this chapter demonstrate how a story based on the second 'set-up' idea mentioned above might begin. It is written in conventional story format and incorporates the types of 'animal-specific' metaphors and verbs mentioned above. The latter part shows students how the same story might appear when written in diary format.

Characters, locations and plot

Plots are usually richer and more complex if they contain more than one central animal of the same sort so there can be interesting interactions between them. Introducing other species (including humans), known of or unknown to the main character(s) also gives scope for curious and gripping plot complications as well as for further well-observed writing. In a story about a rabbit, for example, introducing a fox or a domestic cat would enrich plot possibilities and interest. It might also be interesting to introduce a fox or stray cat into a story about a small escaped monkey, or inquisitive squirrels, or a friendly or unfriendly dog.

To create a wider variety of plot ideas it helps to brainstorm aspects of a few different sub-locations in relative detail, particularly if some of these are very different from each other, such as dense woodland, shore, hedge-bank, outbuildings, a cliff or rock-fall, a busy road, a field of tall maize, suburban gardens and sheds, drains, streams, or a small cave.

It can be counterproductive, however, to look at more than three or four sub-locations with a group because students may be tempted to create a 'too easy' sequential story based on simply racing or escaping from one to another to the next. It should be emphasised that a strong, relatively *non-sequential* plot is vital and that settings (and descriptions of them) must be selected to enhance a story's 'reality', believability and its hold on the reader.

Using simple x-points to create stronger plots

To allay weak sequential writing it is important to give young writers a simplified concept of x-points before they work on their plots. Ask them to think up one or two truly 'curious moments' that don't involve their chosen animal characters but that can be set within any locations they might use. Please refer to Chapter 12 to learn more about x-points and how to use them. You may need to model and share ideas for random intriguing x-point situations so they can grasp the concept.

When individuals have told you their 'curious moments' ideas you can request that they ask 'story excuse' questions about why that moment, event or situation might have occurred. Once they have found a possible plot section developing around that 'curious moment' you can ask them to think about how any of these x-point-driven happenings might involve some of their animal characters. After a while you might also need to put students into pairs of 'ideas buddies' to develop these nascent plot ideas. It's surprising how quickly reasonably strong narratives can surface from this simple process.

'Alien diaries'

Alien diaries can partly be treated like 'lost animal' diaries in that your young students need to find story excuses for why aliens have appeared in those earthly locations, then they can treat the characters as intelligent lost creatures who nervously explore their new surroundings, seeing everything through oddly un-human eyes. Their views of, and interactions with, wildlife, aspects of the natural environment and with humans and their world can be amusing as well as exciting, sad, frightening and heartwarming.

The location-based 'alien diary' format can appeal to a wider age range than 'animal diaries' (say from 8 to 16 years of age) because the endless potential ironies of human life shown through alien eyes can amuse older students as well as younger ones, depending on how the project is presented and how brainstorm sessions are angled.

Young writers enjoy allowing their aliens to invent appropriate-sounding names for things we take for granted, while also describing earthly creatures and objects in detail in a way that means readers can understand what they really are.

Students learn more about their own language by making up new words which sound like the things they are describing.

Again, especially for older students in this age range, having three or even four aliens in the diary story will allow for more interesting interactions, emotions and plot twists, but the important thing is that these characters also interact in an engaging way with the 'real' environment and that that environment and those interactions are both interestingly observed and understandable, even if sometimes described in fairly alien ways.

As in all diary forms, young writers should work out their story plots and sequence them in detailed bullet points *before* they start to write their stories in diary format.

Adding a humorous side to diary writing

As you will imagine from these alien diary ideas, there is plenty of scope for humour in many sorts of diary. For instance, having incompetent urban bank robbers thrown into hiding and attempting to survive in a rural setting could provide many amusing antics and experiences: aliens could cause chaos through misunderstanding human ways or by using peculiar human or alien technology; a chef could keep blaming the restaurant owner or waitress for filching newly baked pastries, when the culprit is really a crafty monkey or squirrel sneaking the goodies out of a high window; the smug 'professional survivalist' among a group of castaways could tell everyone the 'correct' way to do things then amusingly fail at achieving them.

Diaries certainly do not always have to be serious. For instance, a visit to London's Hampton Court linked to a project on the Tudors could inspire either a conventional diary of a cook or chambermaid, or an amusing one, purportedly by the cook or manservant of Henry VIII who sees everything 'from the inside' through ironic eyes. A diary could be 'written by Henry VIII' in which, in-between affairs of state, he contemplates why he has gone off each current wife and fancies a new one. He might muse on all the things that happened that week or year that annoyed him about his current wife . . . and his wife might write an equivalent diary listing all the things he has done to annoy her.

Instigating aspects of this type of ironic humour in writing is a good way of involving boys. When they learn to combine skills in humorous writing and plot-making with subtle, location-brainstormed descriptive details of behaviour, time, setting, clothing, buildings, gardens, etc., not only will their writing improve dramatically but also their the hunger for and retention of knowledge about the setting and subject.

Timings of diary entries

Diary entries can be timed as appropriate, but will usually coincide with there having been plenty of action. This could mean that some entries are days or weeks apart, others separated by only hours or even minutes. Most animals have fast or busy periods in their lives so some of their entries can be relatively near to each other in time compared to others.

A castaway fighting to rebuild a shelter flattened by a gale, or making a failed attempt to swim off the island, will obviously only have been able to write those sections *after* such traumatic events, so there might be longer gaps than usual in their 'survival diary' entries at those points. It is a combination of logic, narrative action and the ability of the young writer to imagine their characters' situations which must dictate the frequency and variability of entries.

More than one 'diary author'?

An interesting challenge for older students is to create two diaries covering the same events but purportedly written by two different characters. They might even have similarly timed diary entries, but what works best is when they have very different viewpoints.

This is a good introductory way for young writers to learn how to write from the perspective of what is known as the 'unreliable narrator' because juxtaposing differing viewpoints of the same events in diaries exposes the human unreliability of one or all of the diarists. The effect can be more amusing, ironic, illuminating, intriguing, touching or tragic than with single diary narrations, depending on the characters' personalities and the situations encountered.

Just by way of simplistic example, working collectively, younger students could create the diary entries of one of the Three Little Pigs and also the diary of the aggrieved and hungry Wolf.

Ten to thirteen year olds who have visited and brainstormed a Victorian classroom might create a plot then write a story as if the events, feelings and opinions had been simultaneously noted down in the diaries of one or two of the children and also of the strict teacher, perhaps trying to catch out a culprit who has caused apparent mischief.

Older students might write diaries of commanders of opposite sides at the site of a siege, or juxtapose the euphemistic diary entries of a general in the First World War with the descriptive, gritty reality to be found in a trench soldier's account of the same hopeless military operation.

Creating fictitious 'dual-diaries' can be useful vehicles through which students can learn to separate and develop different characters' 'voices' and select appropriate language for these. This is an excellent form in which they can experiment with describing settings, happenings and human interactions from differing viewpoints. Learning to distinguish these helps children to 'imagine inside others' heads', something they are often weak at and something they must learn to do to become strong writers and mature adults.

Diary of an African Elephant

Monday

This morning dawned really sunny, the first of the boiling days of the summer season here on the African savannah. I spent the morning sheltering from the burning heat under one of those tall, flat-topped trees that taste so good. I love swinging my trunk through the tall, dry grasses there as it tickles me in a funny way.

We all trouped to the water hole to cool off at midday and I spent hours wallowing in the lovely, gooey mud to keep the irritating flies away. Mud dries so fast in the heat and, as it cracks, it itches strangely all over my back so I had to scratch it this evening against a rough tree trunk.

Tuesday

I was woken early today by my little elephant calf playing around and throwing twigs about with his tiny wobbly trunk. He's so sweet the way he gambols happily and can't quite work out how to stand properly on those knobbly little legs yet. I'm trying to show him how to eat leaves and pick them himself from the tree, but he can't quite manage to grasp them in his trunk. He'll learn soon! I stroked my trunk along his back for hours this afternoon as he suckled and then I showed him how to spray water over his back at the waterhole to keep himself cool.

He kept missing himself and spraying it over other elephants instead, which was rather funny, but the big bull elephant wasn't very amused at the sudden shower and flapped his enormous ears at us in warning. He's rather a grumpy, old elephant, but he does have to worry about the rest of us all the time. As our leader, he has to decide when we all move somewhere new if food's running low, he has to protect the herd from danger and now he has so many little baby calves like my own tiny one to worry about too.

Wednesday

This morning it was so hot we all headed straight for the water hole. I think I might be turning into a hippo as I love to spend so much time in the mud! We've had to wander far afield to find fresh grass today because, where we've been staying, all the tall grasses are drying out in the heat.

We'll be moving up to moister places soon. I love rambling around searching for food with my trunk, it's very relaxing and lets me spend some time alone with my calf away from the centre of the herd. The flies are really becoming annoying here now, I'll be glad when the bull announces that it's time to move on.

Thursday

What excitement we had today! We were all standing around under our usual favourite trees, peeling off leaves and bits of bark to nibble, and relaxing together in a big, contented group, when suddenly there was the crack of a rifle and a dark green Landrover appeared in the distance, churning up huge clouds of beige dust. It was a band of humans trying to kill us and saw off our tusks –we call them poachers.

They crashed and bumped over the rough grassland towards us and we didn't know what to do. Our bull was going to attack them with a huge log he'd grasped in his trunk, but they stayed out of his reach and started trying to aim their deadly rifles at us.

Just as we were all trumpeting in fear and flailing our trunks about, trying to hide our young ones behind us, a big flying thing with a top part that spun round and round appeared from behind and landed between us and the Landrover. Lots of humans in dull green outfits rushed out of it, shooting and shouting, as they attacked the poachers in the vehicle on the ground. Within seconds they had gathered them all up before they took them away into the sky in the strange, clattering machine.

They saved our lives, but it's dangerous here now that poachers know where our herd is. We'll have to move on tomorrow. It's about time to anyway because the water hole is beginning to dry up.

Friday

We've found a lovely little spot to rest in tonight on our way to cooler climates. It's a peaceful glade between thick, scrubby trees which I've never seen before but taste fantastic. I even persuaded my baby calf to try one and he liked the taste so much he pulled another leaf off the tree to eat all by himself. I was so proud of him I picked itchy insects out of his hide as a special reward!

Hyenas have been circling around all day, but there's nothing for them here. We're too big for most other animals to attack us and the humans are far away now. I wonder if we'll find that stand of delicious bushes in the narrow ravine we passed through last year. I've been thinking about them for days!

© Ayesha Wyatt

Comparing conventional story format with diary format for the same narrative

How a story based on the 'set-up sentence' about Scriffle the Squirrel might begin if based in conventional story format:

The grinding scream of the man machine terrified Scriffle. Its angry, mad voice seemed to rip through the still air of the woods, making leaves shiver as if autumn had come early.

Horrified, the squirrel felt his hiding place start shuddering, the way the old willow tree near the railway bridge shuddered when a train passed. In a blind panic, he bounded away along strangely purring branches and leapt wildly from a dipping twig of the huge oak, just in time to see the massive and majestic tree sway slightly behind him, then topple crazily towards the brambly clearing.

The safe treetop sanctuary he had so often escaped to smashed and splintered onto the damp forest floor as easily as a dropped bird's eggshell might smash on a branch below.

How could his high and hidden world ever feel safe again?

The same story put into diary format: (the text below illustrates how much descriptive detail can be included effectively in a diary version of a story)

Monday, 8.40 am

I had heard them coming long before they'd arrived at the woods. One of their heavy metal monsters roared and revved its way up the misty valley to the bent gate where the smooth, grey, monster-path ended.

Rough man voices echoed between tree trunks as metal ground on gravel, and doors thudded like the thud of thick branches dropping onto mossy soil.

Monday, 8.50 am

I wasn't especially worried as their bootsteps drew steadily nearer through the still wood, panicking the scatty blackbird in Lower Copse and making nervous pigeons clatter away between the highest branches above the patient rows of tall pines.

I still wasn't anxious when I heard man grunts nearly beneath me, and metal clinking the way pebbles do when a deer crosses the stream edge. I had seen man beasts pass below me many times before and heard their angry machines growling in further reaches of the forest.

To be on the safe side, however, I dropped the cob of juicy farmer's sweetcorn I'd been eating, scampered along a slender branch of a rowan tree then sprang across to a leafy twig on the ancient oak where I'd hidden safely many times before.

Monday, 9 am

Men with baggy, bright yellow skins had stopped beneath my special oak and dropped heavy metal things onto the leafy ground. As they clanked and clattered about I scurried higher up the ancient oak's reassuringly rough and chunky trunk and hid in a 'v' of branches towards the top, my fluffy tail flicking nervously the way a leaf dangling into a stream is constantly tugged by the current.

Monday, 9.10 am

It was terrifying! A man machine coughed and spluttered like a sick cow. Then suddenly it began to scream, a furious, grinding scream as if it wanted to attack everything around it.

Its crazy, enraged voice ripped through the still air of the woods, making leaves shiver on their stems around me as if autumn had come early.

Monday, 9.20 am

I grew very frightened but the yellow-skins kept moving about on the grass around the great oak, so I just hid there between the branch and the trunk as I always do.

Except this time something was different. The yellow-skins didn't lumber off into the forest as they usually do and my hiding place suddenly started shuddering the way the old willow near the railway bridge does when an express train passes.

In a blind panic, I bounded away along strangely purring branches and leapt wildly from a dipping twig of the great oak, just in time to see the massive, majestic tree sway drunkenly behind me, then topple like a dying giant towards the brambly clearing below.

The secret, protective world I had so often escaped to smashed and splintered on the damp forest floor as easily as a pigeon's eggshell might shatter on a branch below.

My high and hidden sanctuary has been destroyed. How can I ever feel safe in my leafy kingdom again?

Endless possibilities: taking out-of-classroom writing in more directions

I hope readers who have not previously taught outside the classroom in any depth will soon recognise how working with the limitless resources provided by the 'real' world:

- is highly inspiring;
- dramatically improves observational skills;
- increases thinking, creativity and knowledge;
- helps children learn at a deeper, experiential level;
- improves vocabulary and the use of figurative language;
- can assist hugely in the development of rich, convincing and original writing.

Of course, when utilising this powerful resource, teachers need not limit themselves to the genres and forms described in this book.

Even thoughtfully brainstorming a street from the school gates, or the pond area and its overgrown hedgerow, can enliven story scenes. Taking students to people-watch in a public square or shopping centre and interestingly describe the clothes, gait, behaviour and interactions of passers-by can generate brilliant ideas for story characters and trigger unusual plots.

A class might collectively write a lively song lyric from brainstorming in an animated locality such as a shopping street, market, playground or train station. Alternatively, they could create a moody lyric based on an evocative place or moment, such as sunset over a lake, a ruined abbey or a misty scene. They can then enjoy creating a melody line and chorus for this with you, before rehearsing and performing it in assembly as the words are displayed on a digital screen.

Projects can vary from short writing exercises, such as creating amusing limericks, riddles or songs triggered by objects, places or situations encountered outside, to larger projects such as crafting travel literature based around a locality.

Literary travel writing

Creating quality travel articles is an activity which students aged from eleven to adult enjoy greatly with me, both on courses and in schools. It can also be a stimulating and creative choice for English exam coursework.

My literary travel writing workshops have always involved guiding intensive group brainstorms in several different settings within a greater locality. Localities I have used successfully include small country towns, an area of hills and the hamlets within them, semi-ruined abbeys, coastal and resort areas, a seaside steam train and the places linked by it, a dramatic castle with its surrounding village and countryside, and an interesting section of a city.

Organising such a project needs only a little research and pre-planning. Groups can walk or be minibussed around selected parts of their local town, pausing to brainstorm buildings, parks, notable edifices, museums, amusements, shopping areas, sea or river fronts, hidden alleys and courtyards, and the way locals act or behave to participants and others. In the UK and other countries, organisations such as The National Trust, English Heritage and National Parks often offer school membership and free educational visits.

Leading a workshop, I stop regularly to guide short brainstorming sessions as students note ideas and language, or my assistant types them on a portable computer. I sometimes negotiate a cheap meal in a café or restaurant, which not only helps bond the group but is a source of human, culinary and experiential material for the writing.

Modelling the genre

The project should begin by reading and discussing strong extracts from varied travel books, internet items or quality newspaper articles. These should be chosen carefully and supply variations of style and approach, mixing-in a variety of authors, for example Paul Theroux, Bill Bryson, Charles Dickens, V.S. Naipaul and Michael Palin. There are lists of literary travel writers on Wikipedia and endless books, blogs and articles available online.

Following this, most of the first day will involve brainstorming in varied locations. Subsequent sessions are reserved for further inputs and writing.

Aspects to cover in travel writing inputs include:

- form;
- the use of first and third person;
- non-chronological writing;
- 'hooking' the reader by writing a captivating introduction or selecting an intriguing moment, fact or experience to relate at the beginning;
- considering leaving a full explanation of the introduction until later;

- using rich and apt description;
- 'honesty' of narration;
- working-in an 'angle' or theme;
- including 'found' places, characters, happenings, quotes, anecdotes, inscriptions, epitaphs, signs, etc.;
- embedding aspects of local history and geography;
- adding emotive touches through the narrator, people encountered; local historical events, evocative moments, etc.;
- making thoughtful narrator 'asides';
- tone and language choice;
- giving the article a satisfying 'roundness'; and
- creating an apt and pleasing conclusion.

'News journalism' outside the classroom

Creating fictitious news stories, acting them out in dramatic scenarios and reporting on others' scenarios through 'interviewing' the performers is an exciting and engrossing way of learning journalistic skills as well as those of story plot creation, interview techniques, and so on. Using parts of the school buildings and grounds, neighbouring parks, interesting locations or residential centres brings life and depth to this hugely popular and challenging activity.

It is beyond the scope of this book to describe how to run journalism scenarios and workshops, but detailed information on how to set up and run such sessions is provided in a book by the same author, entitled *Hit the Headlines*, which is available online and from good bookstores internationally. The publication is also featured on the website of the educational organisation the Council for Learning Outside the Classroom (www.lotc.org.uk), which promotes the advantages and proven effectiveness of learning in diverse environments beyond the classroom walls.

Keep thinking!

As I hope you will have seen, enthralling and powerful writing projects inspired and informed by the world outside the classroom may involve almost any form of factual, semi-factual or fully creative writing. These can be stand alone writing challenges or may tie-in with other subject areas or coursework.

Writers don't live in classrooms. The endlessly varied and fascinating world we inhabit is what generates endlessly varied and fascinating writing. Results obtained from employing the techniques explained in this book are frequently described by teachers as 'amazing' when compared with those generated by purely classroom-based work.

The 'real' world is a massively diverse and powerful educational resource – and the only limits to exploiting it effectively are the limits of a teacher's imagination.

The End

Glossary

Except for those marked with an asterisk, the following terms used in this book have been created by the author over many years to explain and describe key aspects to students of all ages. Many teachers and students now use parts of this terminology and all others are free to do so as long as the author is credited in any publication or broadcast in which they appear.

Term:	Meaning:
'and then' stories	Weak, sequential story lines caused by thinking of one event after another.
authenticating detail*	Well-observed descriptive detail which makes a setting or situation feel 'real' to the reader. See also 'reality detail'.
availability of metaphor	Students, especially more able ones, often do not provide readers with 'a door' into a metaphor they've created, so the reader either fails to recognise it as a metaphor or fails to understand it. This can be solved by 'signposting' in some way within either the work or its title.
backed-up self-scribing	An arrangement where students scribe brainstormed ideas and language on clipboards, but needn't worry about missing any material because it is simultaneously typed or scribed by an assistant.
conducting	An effective method, invented by the author, of finding the location of stressed beats in poetry

through swinging an arm in a loose, horizontal figure of eight in time with the words. The stressed beats occur at the crossover point of the downswing. The system also flags up possible rhythmic inaccuracies to writers of poetry.

'cream on top' activities	Group activities where the best ideas and language 'rise to the surface' and are multiply reinforced.
door into the metaphor	See 'availability of metaphor'.
'five w's and an h' questions*	The essential questions (Who? What? Where? When? Why? and How?) that students can ask of an x-point in order to produce interesting and believable 'story excuses' to explain it.
found data	Descriptive or informational material acquired directly from the environment, usually during a brainstorming session.
locational brainstorming	Collective questioning techniques that utilise interesting locations or settings in order to generate inspiration and develop 'thoughtful observation' skills, personal awareness, wider vocabulary and rich figurative language.
minimalist poems	Closely-observed, short-line poems loosely related to kennings which keep the use of mundane words such as articles, connectives, etc ., to a minimum. Other types of 'minimalist' poems exist, such as in 'concrete' poetry.
naming*	A term for identifying and poetically describing things, situations and experiences.
orbital vocabulary	Vocabulary an individual is aware of but which is not used by them.
questioning trees	A metaphor for the way a good facilitator can subtly lead groups through thoughtful observation processes and model those thinking processes for young writers to continue using themselves.
random word insertion	A surrealist-type technique where interesting but random words are thrown into the mix with

	'found' language, often creating stimulating new ideas and word combinations.
reality detail*	Well-observed descriptive detail which makes a setting or situation feel 'real' to the reader. See also 'authenticating detail'.
reflective haikus	Haikus with an added dimension of extended metaphor or an underlying layer of meaning.
second stage brainstorming	Further brainstorming, remote from a location previously brainstormed, usually with a short time gap between sessions.
show not tell*	A term commonly used in poetry workshops, indicating that a poet should mostly *show* readers the situation or setting through subtle description and authenticating detail rather than *tell* them it is so. Stories generally use a mix of show and tell, but with much more of the former.
signposting*	Giving readers clues that lead to the discovery of underlying or metaphorical meaning in a piece of writing. This is sometimes achieved through using words with more than one meaning or through symbolism, subtle titling, and so on. See also 'availability of metaphor'.
sit-upons*	A school's term for pieces of waterproof sponge that individual participants can sit on while brainstorming out of the classroom.
slant rhyme*	Imperfect rhyme, 'near-rhyme', or strong 'sound echoes'. Much modern poetry and many song lyrics use slant rhymes. Slant rhymes can be less predictable and restrictive than full rhymes.
sound echoes	Repetition of similar sounds within poetry and other writing. Alliteration, assonance, consonance, sibilance, and slant rhyme all fall into this category.
sound families	Groupings of words where similar sounds within them suggest related qualities (such as wetness, speed, noise, softness, etc.)

story excuses	Possible reasons why a plot situation or 'x-point' might have occurred. Creating story excuses involves thinking what might have happened before this moment in order to have made it happen. Their use creates more original, logical, unpredictable and believable storylines.
story sequence	The most effective order in which scenes of a plot unfold for the reader, as opposed to 'chrono-logical order' which lists plot events in time sequence.
sub-location	A part of a general setting or site visited which is worth stopping at in order to brainstorm ideas, words and descriptive data found in, and linked to, that place. An inspirational out-of-the-classroom visit usually involves pausing to brain-storm in several sub-locations.
thoughtful observation	The process of observing, thinking about and noting the world in detail, which is essential to vocabulary development and to the creation of strong descriptive writing, Locational brainstorm sessions are designed to model this process for writing students and assist each in developing an individual 'writer's eye'.
user vocabulary	Words which are known and used by an individual.
vital presence	The visceral experience of physically and emotionally experiencing a place or situation which, combined with questioning awareness, stirs up inspiration and lends authenticity to writing.
wallpaper	Clichéd, overused or predictable description that does little to trigger the reader's imagination.
webbing*	The natural aptitude of humans to connect disparate things or ideas. Though crucial to intelligence and storyline-making, it can also create dull, clichéd thinking.
x-point	A curious or intriguing possible moment or situation which generates questions about what

might have happened before it to have caused it to have come about. X-points trigger the 'five w's and an h' questions used to create possible story excuses, a process which helps develop original and logical plot lines.

Yoda-speak

Creating a badly sequenced phrase or line of poetry which sounds foreign or unwieldy, often done in an attempt to fit language into a specific rhythm pattern or line length. It is sometimes caused by exposure to mainly older styles of poetry.

Author availability

for educational conferences,
in-service teacher training,
PGCE workshops,
school residencies, etc.

Although in great demand, the author is occasionally available to talk and run workshops at educational conferences and INSETS, or to train student teachers in teaching creative writing and related thinking skills.

Please email enquiries to:

tellingt@aol.com or colinianmacfarlane@googlemail.com